THE SEARCH FOR GOD

By

MARCHETTE CHUTE

NEW YORK

E. P. DUTTON & CO., INC.

TO
MOTHER
*to whom this book
belongs already*

THERE are two ways in which it is usual to interpret the Bible: the way of the theologian and the way of the scholar. Neither is wholly satisfactory. The theologian, whether Jewish or Christian, is handicapped by the fact that he must read his Scriptures by the light of a pre-conceived theory, so that anything in the text which is alien to his particular doctrine must be either omitted or forcibly re-interpreted. The scholar, on the other hand, is handicapped by the fact that he must read the Bible by no light at all. He has no exact selective principle to guide him through the mass of confused and frequently contradictory material that the book contains. He must select and reject according to the fragmentary historical evidence that is available to him, and the turn of an archaeologist's spade can at any time overturn the whole of his carefully constructed theory. Moreover, historical evidence, even at its most trustworthy, does not offer an adequate basis for an interpretation of the Bible. The history of Israel is primarily the history not of events, but of ideas.

The Bible at its highest is a book of the spirit, unfitted to be interpreted solely from the historical point of view. It is also a free book, and equally unfitted to be used as a series of texts in support of a theological proposition. It is the attempt of this interpretation to do neither, but to let the Bible illuminate itself.

The interpretation that is presented in the following

7

pages is not altogether new. The conception of the Bible as the record of a search for God, a search that culminated in Jesus, is one that has been expressed many times before and in a variety of ways. It was most perfectly expressed, perhaps, by the author of the *Letter to the Hebrews*, when he characterized the writers of the Old Testament as men "in search of a country of their own." (*Heb.* xi. 14)

The difference between *The Search for God* and all other interpretations of the Bible lies in the nature of this "country" for which the men of Israel were looking. On the evidence of the Bible itself, it seems to have consisted of something far greater than Jahwism, Judaism or Christianity. Authority for all three of these religions may be found in the text of the Bible, just as contradictions of all three may be found also. But none of the three is the final clue to the exact desire that drove the men of Israel for ten centuries until it finally reached fulfillment, the longing for a country of their own that did not cease until the country was ultimately found.

It is the continuity and passion of this desire that make it possible to present a single interpretation that will fit the Bible as a whole. It is true that the Bible is not a single book. It is a collection of a number of books, composed in a variety of literary forms over a period of many centuries by a great variety of men. Nevertheless, it is a collection so dominated by one idea that the individual differences of the men who wrote it no more affect the singleness of its purpose than do the cross-currents of a river affect the direction of its flow; and therefore the literature of Israel can be interpreted as a unit in a way that would be possible with the literature of no other nation in the history of the world.

The translation of the Bible which has been used

throughout *The Search for God* is the one made recently by the University of Chicago and called *The Bible: An American Translation.*

The familiar King James version of the Bible is more beautiful, but less easy to read intelligently. The poetry is written as prose and then divided into chapter and verse for convenient ecclesiastical reference, so that the essays, the dramas, the stories and the songs all degenerate into numbered texts and it is difficult for the average reader to read them intelligently or as a whole. Both the epic Hebrew of *Job* and the colloquial Greek of the *Gospels* are presented in the same stately seventeenth-century English diction, which is beautiful diction but fails to mirror the differences existing in the style of the original authors. Moreover, the familiar, echoing loveliness of the King James version is in itself almost a handicap to an understanding of the original. The reader is sometimes lulled to sleep by the beauty of the rhythms and forgets to look for the meaning in the music.

The translation made by the University of Chicago is not perfect; no masterpiece can be translated with whole success into an alien tongue. But it possesses the greater accuracy that the intervening years of Hebrew and Greek scholarship have made possible, and it puts the emphasis where it primarily belongs—on the meaning rather than on the sound of the words.

This translation has been used throughout *The Search for God,* with an occasional variant reading, but with only one important exception. In the twenty-second psalm, the translator seems to have altered the intention of the original poet by offering a paraphrase of the key line instead of making a literal translation from the Hebrew.

I am deeply grateful to the University of Chicago Press

for permission to quote from Smith and Goodspeed's *The Bible: An American Translation.* Acknowledgement is also due Richard Moulton for his comments in *The Modern Reader's Bible* on the literary structure of the *Book of Isaiah.*

M. C.

SINCE the line of argument in *The Search for God* is an unfamiliar one, a brief résumé of its general character is given in advance.

The book is divided into four parts:

> The Right to Search
> The Object of the Search
> The Search
> The Finding

The first part concerns the *Book of Job*, since *Job* is the clearest single statement in the whole of the Bible of the mental atmosphere in which the men of Israel moved. They were free men; and *Job* portrays the quality of that freedom, without which the search for God that the Bible records could never have come into existence.

The second part concerns the three opening chapters of the *Book of Genesis*, and the abrupt juxtaposition in these chapters of two conflicting interpretations of God. In this juxtaposition may be found an indication of the object of the search, as *Job* is an indication of its method.

The third part concerns the rest of the Old Testament, and the search itself.

The fourth part concerns the life of Jesus of Nazareth, and the end of the search.

CONTENTS

THE RIGHT TO SEARCH

CHAPTER I

> Strive for the truth unto death, and the Lord God
> shall fight for thee.
>
> *Ecclesiasticus* iv. 28

JOB was not a patient man.

The epic that bears his name could not be used as an introduction to the history of Israel, nor could it have any real claim to greatness, if Job were the kind of man that tradition has pictured him, an uncomplaining sufferer who sat down patiently on an ash heap to wait there until it might please the Lord to remove the intolerable burdens that had been heaped upon him.

On the contrary, the vitality and power of the *Book of Job* have their origin in the fact that its hero possessed neither meekness nor patience nor resignation. He refused to accept the idea that his suffering was a penalty visited upon him by God to lead him to repentance. He rejected the consolations of orthodoxy offered him by his three friends. Instead of submitting, he revolted. Instead of prostrating himself, he stood upright and cried out: "I desire to reason with God." (*Job* xiii. 3)

The story of the *Book of Job* is the story of the fierce and unorthodox *Why?* that its hero sent thundering against the very gates of heaven; and the philosophic value of the story lies in the fact that the gates of heaven opened to let his question in. Unlike Prometheus, Job was not punished for being a hero. "The Lord blessed the end of Job more than his beginning." (*Job* xlii. 12) The hero of the book is a great man at the beginning of the story, but he is a greater man at its end.

It is primarily this quality of intellectual freedom that

15

makes the *Book of Job* so important. It is true that its author was a poet, and a great one. Even in the most inadequate translation, the splendor of the original Hebrew shines like fine gold. Nevertheless, it is not its literary quality that gives the *Book of Job* its final distinction. It is its vindication of the right of mankind to free inquiry.

It is for this that the *Book of Job* makes a fitting introduction to the Bible as a whole. It was not the usual subjects for poetry that stirred the writers of Israel: nature, passion, the lives of men or the heights and depths of their own beings. It was, instead, the desire to find God. It is this intense and exalted preoccupation that binds together such otherwise dissimilar works of art as the *Book of Isaiah*, the *Psalms* and the *Gospel of John*, and that runs like a gleaming thread through the collection of dramas, histories, essays and poems that go to make up the book that is called, quite properly, "the holy Bible." Certainly, the literature of no other nation on earth can show a like wholeness.

The search for God that is recorded in the Bible was conducted by men who moved consistently in an atmosphere of intellectual freedom. With a few unworthy exceptions, the men who wrote the Bible were not cautious theologians. They were innovators; and so radical in their innovations that they seemed blasphemous to their contemporaries, as Job seemed to his shocked and orthodox friends.

The prophets of Israel let no blind reverence for tradition stand in their way. The name "Israel" does not mean "worshipper of God." It means "striver with God," and the men of Israel were worthy of their name.

The *Book of Job* is a vindication of this right to free inquiry, the right without which the Bible could not have been written. It is characteristic of Israel, also, that so great an idea should have been expressed in great poetry, for in Israel the poets were prophets and the prophets were poets.

The rhythm and beauty of language were never ends in themselves to the Hebrew writers. They made their literary art the servant of a definite purpose, and they were perhaps the only poets in the history of the world who ever did it successfully. For once, the Grecian urn of abstract beauty held within it a wine of such value that the contents of the cup became of more importance than the grace of its proportions. The cup is beautiful, but it is the wine that is immortal.

In reading the *Book of Job*, it is of the highest importance to remember that its author was both a poet and a dramatist. The book is a play, with a prologue and epilogue in prose, and it must be treated as such. To attempt to isolate single passages out of their context to support a pre-conceived theological position results in disaster. The author's meaning becomes as confused as Shakespeare's would be if *Hamlet* were first translated into German prose, then sub-divided into a series of numbered texts, and then treated as a series of quotations in which speakers as unlike as Hamlet and Polonius were given equal authority as interpreting the mind of the author. Under such treatment, *Hamlet* would become an impenetrable mystery; yet to clear the mystery, all that is necessary is to read the book as the author wrote it.

The prologue in the *Book of Job* is designed to introduce the cast of characters, set the stage, and present briefly the problem with which the poem itself is to deal.

The hero of the book is the chief patriarch of the Land of Uz, a man of great wealth and greater virtue. So outstanding is his righteousness, that his name is mentioned with approval in the courts of heaven, on a day when the heavenly beings come to present themselves before the Lord. Among them is the Adversary, who suggests that Job has been so sheltered and blessed that it is easy for him to praise God. He hints that if Job's wealth were taken away his godliness would disappear also, and is given the power to take away all the patriarch's possessions.

This calamity Job bears without complaint. Misfortune has touched only his sense of ownership rather than the man himself; he has not yet been brought to the point where

> For himself his flesh has pain,
> And for himself his soul mourns. (*Job* xiv. 22)

The Adversary suggests as much and is given power over Job's body, which he smites with an agonizing skin disease.

"The Adversary" may equally well be translated "the Satan," but the latter term is unfortunate since it immediately suggests the devil of both Jewish and Christian dogma. Whatever associations may later have gathered around the word, there is nothing in the *Book of Job* to suggest that the Adversary has anything diabolical about him. He appears among the heavenly beings to present himself before God, and there is nothing to indicate that he is out of place. Nor is there any malice in his suggestions, which seem to be a clear attempt to find out if there is any flaw in the jewel; and his remarks are received entirely without displeasure.

What the Adversary really is intended to represent is a more difficult question. Perhaps the closest parallel to his office is that of the Wrestler who strove with Jacob all one night. In each case, what appeared to be a great evil was striven with by a man until it appeared at last as a great good. If the Adversary had left Job alone to live his life in peace, cradled in wealth and security, Job

would have remained a worthy and conventional man,
honored and self-satisfied. But the action which the Adversary urged upon the Lord forced Job out of his safe
piety into a hunger for the truth so great that it dared
to demand satisfaction. It was the Adversary who did
Job the greatest service of his life, by changing him from
a believer into a seeker.

It is not to be supposed that this scene in heaven is to
be taken at its face value, coming as it does from a poet
whose major theme is the mystery of God. The poets of
the Old Testament wrote in pictures as Jesus spoke in
parables, and with no more thought of being taken literally. It is vitally necessary to the progress of the drama
that the reader shall understand that Job's sufferings are
undeserved and come through no fault of his own. Such
a conviction has to be firmly fixed in the mind of the
poet's audience, for a reason that will later be obvious;
and the scene in the court of heaven is the quickest and
most effective way in which such a conviction can be
secured.

The prologue ends with the introduction of three new
characters: Eliphaz, Bildad and Zophar. These three patriarchs, dignified and venerable, are friends of Job, and
they have travelled from their own lands to come and
comfort their stricken friend. Tragic emphasis is made
of the fact that when they arrive they do not recognize
him. It is not only the extent of his disfigurement, but
also that he, the greatest of all the people of the East,
should be crouching in poverty-stricken degradation
upon an ash-heap to be jeered at by any passer-by. With
rent mantles they sit beside him on the ground, remaining silent for seven days and nights out of respect for his
grief. It is Job who finally breaks silence, and with his
speech the prose turns to poetry and the drama begins.

Job begins with a curse. It is not against God, for he

never renounced God, but against the day of his own birth.

"Perish the day wherein I was born,
And the night which said, 'A man is conceived.' "
(*Job* iii. 3)

He heaps upon it every conceivable form of darkness, in a lyric elegy of such tragic passion that it is a very sword-thrust of despair. Let the stars of its twilight be darkened, its hours blotted out from the days of the year, and may it never see morning again. If Job had died in his mother's womb he might now be lying down among the kings of the earth, in the place where the slaves are free and the weary have rest. For why should life be given to

"Those who would rejoice exultingly,
And would be glad, if they could find the grave?"
(*Job* iii. 22)

Job's wild plea for extinction puts his three friends in a difficult position. They are sure they know why Job's misfortunes have come upon him. But the explanation is not an easy one to offer a man to his face, nor does Job seem to be in a sufficiently calm frame of mind to receive it. Nevertheless, it is a poor kind of friendship that will not brave a man's temporary displeasure when his spiritual welfare is at stake; and at last Eliphaz, who is probably the oldest, begins with an embarrassed apology.

"If one should venture a word with you, would you be grieved?
Yet who can refrain from speech?" (*Job* iv. 2)

The man who has comforted others in their misfortunes cannot endure it now that he himself is struck down. Yet why should a man be punished unless he is guilty? Eliphaz intimates tactfully that this fact is no reproach to

Job. No man can be wholly perfect in the sight of God, who charges even his angels with folly. But let Job submit to the chastening of the Almighty and he will be delivered from all his misfortunes. Even the beasts of the field will be at peace with him then, and he will go to his grave in a ripe old age, like a shock of corn in its season.

With great beauty and with the most courteous delicacy, Eliphaz has expressed the orthodox religious opinion that suffering is the result of sin. He avoids any direct accusation, but he makes it clear that he and his friends expect Job to confess the grave sin he must have committed to so have incurred God's wrath. Then they are prepared to comfort him with words of kindness and encouragement, and, after Job has repented, his misfortunes will pass away.

The one difficulty in this program is Job's own honesty. He flatly refuses to acknowledge his sins, since he knows perfectly well (as does the reader) that he has not committed any. And to Eliphaz, complete gentleman but very conventional thinker, his friend's reply must have come as a shock and a disappointment.

Instead of acknowledging his sins, Job turns on his three friends for forsaking him, comparing them bitterly to the little rivers along the caravan routes that dry up just when they are most needed. Job has not asked them for goods or money, but only for consolation; and all they can find to offer him is reproaches for words he himself knows to be wild. But let them show him, if they can, where he is wrong! Then Job turns in agony on God, and begs to be let alone. Is he the sea, or a dragon, that such a watch should be set over him? "I shall not live forever. Let me alone!" (*Job* vii. 16) And even if he has sinned, why not forgive him, since his life is so short?

"For soon I shall lie down in the dust;
And thou wilt search for me, but I shall not be."

(Job vii. 21)

The three friends are still loyal to Job and still trying to make every allowance for him; but this last speech is obviously sheer blasphemy, and Bildad's reproof is very grave. For Job's own sake he must be made to realize not only the righteousness of God's judgments but also his own personal iniquity.

"If you were but pure and straight,
Then, indeed, he would bestir himself in your behalf."

(Job viii. 6)

But if Job will make his humble prayer to God he can yet be restored, and his mouth will be filled with laughter and his ways with peace.

All Bildad's beautiful eloquence is equally in vain, for Job neatly removes the ground from beneath his feet.

"Of course, I know that it is so.
But how can a man be right with God?" *(Job* ix. 2)

Some power is destroying innocent and guilty alike. "If it is not he—who then is it?" *(Job* ix. 24) If God were a man like Job, some umpire might be placed between them to see that the argument was kept fair. Or if God would take away the physical torment, then might Job speak and not be afraid of him. But, as it is, God condemns without showing any reason for condemnation. Is it reasonable to him that he should persecute his own handiwork, and that he should search out a sin that does not exist while the man he has made stands helpless before him? And yet at the same time Job is aware that

"Life and love hast thou exercised with me,
And thy watch-care has preserved my spirit."

(Job x. 12)

Job is not trying to justify himself to his friends. He is talking out loud to himself in an agony of indecision. The others are safe and comfortable behind the sheltering walls of a religious orthodoxy that they see no reason to abandon, but Job's former beliefs have crashed about him in ruins. With the courage of an epic hero, he is willing to forsake his old religious views, now that they have crumbled under the first test applied to them, and is prepared to start all over again. Job has been thrust into a mental wilderness, with no chart or compass for guide, and at first his footsteps are wildly at random. Yet he continues to go forward, and if he fails to find a way out it is not for want of trying.

Job's desperate search for the truth is taking him farther and farther away from orthodox piety, and his three friends grow more and more troubled. Zophar, who has not spoken before, now takes a hand in attempting to recall the lost and wandering sheep to the fold. But, with unintentional precision, he attempts to rule out the one thing Job is striving for, the possibility of discovering something about God, and the gulf between the two points of view has by this time widened so far that it cannot be bridged. Job is a seeker; his three friends are believers.

Anger begins to rise between them, caused entirely by this mental estrangement. The three friends insist upon offering Job traditional arguments, and Job insists with equal determination that they are false. What the truth actually is he does not know, and does not pretend to know. Nevertheless, he stands firmly upon his right to look for it and to continue looking until he finds something that is satisfactory. "I desire to reason with God." (*Job* xiii. 3)

As a result of this desire for the truth, Job is already beginning to make discoveries. Growing within him is the conviction, later to become so overwhelming as to overshadow all Old Testament literature, that somewhere there was an end to the struggle, a meeting-place with God where everything would be explained. At first this is only the vaguest of hopes, born of sorrow that a man should go to extinction utterly when even a tree has the power to bud and grow green again after it has been cut down. Perhaps Sheol was not a place of complete annihilation and nothingness. Perhaps God was planning to use the land of departed spirits only as a hiding-place for the man he had made until the time came when the two of them would be reconciled to each other.

> "All the days of my service I would wait
> Until my turn should come;
> Thou wouldst call and I would answer thee;
> Thou wouldst yearn for the work of thy hands."
> (*Job* xiv. 14-15)

But this is the expression of only the shadow of a hope, and again Job sinks back into despair.

Meanwhile the argument continues in a blaze of mounting fury on both sides. Are you the first man to be born, demands the formerly gentle Eliphaz, that you should suddenly start to question the ways of God? God does not even consider the heavens pure, and should he hold a man like you guiltless? Any man who acts arrogantly towards God is as a plant whose green leaves are shriveled by fire and whose blossoms are torn off by the wind; and such a man is Job.

> "You destroy reverence,
> And you do away with meditation before God."
> (*Job* xv. 4)

Job's natural reaction is one of angry reproach. He is in mental and physical agony, and his friends insist on harping on an old theme. "I have heard many things like these. Troublesome comforters are you all!" (*Job* xvi. 2) But it is not before men Job is pleading his case. It is before God; and he is beginning to believe that he has found a witness, an intercessor, for himself in heaven. "My thoughts are my intercessors." (*Job* xvi. 20) With such an intercessor it might be "that one might plead for a man with God, even as with a man for one's friend." (*Job* xvi. 21) But his speech ends again on a note of discouragement and Bildad breaks in to take advantage of it, picturing in terrifying detail the doom "of him who knows not God." (*Job* xviii. 21)

Job answers with a characteristic flash of spirit that his own sins are not the affair of his friends in any case.

"Suppose, indeed, I have erred;
With myself my error dwells." (*Job* xix. 4)

But then the sense of his utter loneliness and desolation descends upon him with such overwhelming force that he can bear it no longer.

"Have pity on me, have pity on me, O you, my friends,
For the hand of God has struck me!
Wherefore do you pursue me like God,
And are not satisfied with my flesh?"

(*Job* xix. 21-22)

Physical pain he might have endured, but he cannot endure such mental torment.

At this moment there happens what happens so often in the *Psalms*. Out of the intensity of his desire and the blackness of his despair, Job suddenly feels himself lifted up to the serene heights of a moment of perfect assurance. So complete is the assurance that Job longs for a pen of iron and a scroll of rock that his conviction might be recorded forever.

> "I know, my Vindicator lives . . .
> And from my flesh, I shall see God;
> Whom I shall see on my side,
> And my eyes will see unestranged."
>
> (*Job* xix. 25-27)

Job cannot sustain this moment of exaltation, and falls back with a faint "My emotions are spent within me!" (*Job* xix. 27) Nevertheless, he has come a long way since the opening of the drama. Out of his doubts and protests, the product of his own furious honesty, there has come a conviction of absolute certainty: that somewhere there exists a perfect answer to the mystery of his relationship to God, and that ultimately it would be found. Job is no longer searching because he has been torn away from his old beliefs and there is nothing else for him to do. He is searching now because he knows that eventually the search will end in success.

His friends are aware of none of this. They still see in Job only a man refusing to acknowledge his own obvious sinfulness, and are as much shocked by this as they are by his unruly efforts to find God. Zophar makes another effort to frighten him into repentance. Does he not realize "that the triumph of the wicked is but short, and the mirth of the ungodly is but for a moment?" (*Job* xx. 5)

Even this time-honored theory Job is no longer able to accept, and he meets it with a frank, if worried, scepticism. For, in actual fact, the wicked are just as likely to enjoy prosperity as are the righteous.

> "They sing to the timbrel and harp,
> And they make merry to the sound of the flute.
> They complete their days in prosperity,
> And in a moment they go down to Sheol.

Yet they say to God, 'Depart from us;
We do not want to know thy ways.
What is the Almighty that we should serve him?
And what does it profit us that we pray to him?' "
                                        (*Job* xxi. 12-15)

Job does not say this in any dogmatic spirit. He is honestly puzzled, and thinking aloud. But Eliphaz is shocked
beyond all bearing at the boldness of such blasphemy,
and even goes so far as to make a specific list of all the
evil deeds that Job must have committed to have arrived
in his present position. Yet he makes one last plea with
his old and loved friend to put these things from him, to
acquaint himself with God and be at peace.

This is the one thing Job has been trying to do since
the drama began, but with scant encouragement from
his friends and little gain in peace. Eliphaz has been indulging in oratory. What he is really expressing under
his beautiful language is a desire that Job follow the
traditions of his forefathers patiently and blindly; and
this Job cannot do. Too clear before his eyes is the un-
fairness of men's lives, the poor who have no clothing to
protect them from the beating of the mountain rains and
who snatch a precarious living by gleaning the fields of
the fat and prosperous tyrants who have despoiled them.
Bildad attempts to explain this, but all he can offer is the
doubtful consolation of contemplating the infinite and
unbridgeable distance between God and "the son of man
that is a worm." (*Job* xxv. 6)

"How you have helped him that was powerless,"
(*Job* xxvi. 2) cries Job in ironic bitterness and repeats
his refusal to consider himself a hopeless sinner.

"Till I die I will not put my integrity from me.
I will hold on to my innocence and will not let it go."
                                        (*Job* xxvii. 5-6)

In all his world of shifting values, Job still knows that he has committed no sin. This may disrupt the whole religion of his forefathers, with its claim that only the guilty suffer; nevertheless, Job proposes to cling to the one fact of which he is sure until he is proven wrong.

Job's friends cannot prove that he is wrong; but they make one last effort, the moving and beautiful appeal which is usually attributed to Zophar and which contains the famous lyric on understanding. It is easy to mine precious jewels out of the earth. "Its stones are the source of sapphires, and it has dust of gold." (*Job* xxviii. 6) But no one has ever discovered where understanding can be mined, and all the gold of Ophir is not sufficient to buy it. The sea does not contain it, nor does the land. Only God knows where it may be found, and he has said to man: "To depart from evil is understanding." (*Job* xxviii. 28)

Again there has been a lapse from reason for the sake of oratorical effect. As Job says in his reply, he has spent his whole life departing from evil, and the only result has been that the man whom princes once delighted to honor has been cast on an ash-heap to be brother to jackals. He has waited for light, "but darkness came"; (*Job* xxx. 26) and yet he knows that he has not sinned.

The debate has now reached a complete deadlock. Job ends it, insofar as it can be ended, by rising and delivering a formal and deeply serious oath testifying to his innocence. He demands a much higher standard of righteousness in himself than his friends ever did, since he passes in review not only his deeds but his thoughts. If Job has ever looked with desire on his neighbor's wife, if he has ever been unjust to a servant, if he has ever loved gold, ever rejoiced in an enemy's downfall, ever hesitated to share what he possessed with those who needed it, or if he has ever failed to confess some secret

sın in public for fear of "the contempt of the clans,"
(*Job* xxxi. 34) then may he and his lands be forever
cursed. This is Job's formal oath of innocence, presented
"like a prince." (*Job* xxxi. 37) Further than this he
cannot go.

Throughout the long and intricate debate between Job
and his three friends, two points of view have been given
clear emphasis, and two contrasting themes have been
played upon with endless beauty and variation. One concerns the question of Job's guilt, which the three friends
insist upon since it is indispensable to their theory that
God in his righteousness punishes only the wicked. To
this Job makes answer:

> "I will hold on to my innocence and will not let it go.
> My conscience does not reproach any of my days."
> (Job xxvii. 6)

The second argument, growing out of the first, is the
question of Job's presumption in daring to try and find
God for himself instead of accepting the traditional theories about him. The conviction that this is blasphemy is
implicit in everything that the three friends say; and to
it Job can offer only the heartfelt cry,

> "I would speak to the Almighty,
> And I desire to reason with God." (*Job* xiii. 3)

The position of the three friends has been clear from
the beginning. They have travelled many miles to comfort an old friend in his afflictions. But when they arrive
they encounter, not the man of piety they remember, but
a stiff-necked heretic who shouts aloud his own righteousness and troubles the throne of God with his blasphemous
questions. Shaken in their hearts, they yet remain un-
shaken in their convictions; and, as Job's nearest friends,
they do everything in their power to turn Job back from

the path he has chosen for himself before it is too late.

These three were good men, but Job was a great man. His life had crashed into ruins, bearing his former philosophy with it. Instead of trying to salvage it, or of following his wife's bitter suggestion, "Curse God and die," (*Job* ii. 9) Job showed his greatness, the greatness of an epic hero, by standing up to his creator and demanding a reason for what had occurred. As happens to all men who dare to think for themselves, some of the limitations that conventional thinking had imposed upon his mentality began to dissolve. There is nothing more extraordinary in its way in all literature than the gradual shifting and brightening of Job's thought in contrast to the granite-like mental immobility of his three friends.

Of the four of them, it was Job who had the most profound humility. He asked to know God and God's intentions towards himself, but he never attempted to explain God's purposes with the bland assurance of his three friends. Yet even their pride in their wisdom pales before the arrogance of the next actor to appear in the drama. His name was Elihu, and he was very young.

Elihu was admitted to the council of his elders only as a listener, and the last thing expected of him was that he should take part in the debate. Yet the debate is over, and Job's three friends have apparently given up the attempt to convince him of the error of his ways. At last this becomes too much for Elihu to endure in silence, and he decides to carry on the debate himself. In the days of the patriarchs a youngster was not supposed to interfere with the meditations of his elders, and the new speaker is fully conscious of his temerity; but he is a very self-confident young man.

Elihu begins his speech with an apology, but one that has a sting in its tail. He is young, and they are very old. Naturally he has not dared to offer his own opinions to

them, since years are supposed to give a man wisdom. But
in listening to their speeches, Elihu can see for himself
that this is not invariably the case, and now the responsibility rests on him alone to tell Job the truth. Sometimes
a man trembling on the brink of the pit may be recalled
by "an angel, a mediator, one of a thousand" (*Job*
xxxiii. 23) and Elihu makes it quite clear that he considers this to be his function in the present case. Job may
find it difficult to present his case before God, but before
Elihu, who is a man like himself, he need have no fear.

> "Lo, dread of me will not overwhelm you."
> (*Job* xxxiii. 7)

From Elihu's colossal assurance it might be expected
that he intends to present some entirely new and con-
vincing doctrine that will completely satisfy Job's questioning spirit. Yet when his explanation commences it
bears a strong resemblance to that of the three friends,
somewhat less elderly and somewhat more assertive but
essentially the same doctrine.

Elihu even begins in the same manner, by classing Job
with the sinners.

> "He walks in company with doers of evil,
>   And goes with wicked men.
>   For he says, 'A man gains nothing
>   By being on good terms with God.' "
> (*Job* xxxiv. 8-9)

This is not in the least fair to Job, who never made any
such statement. In fact Job, unlike his adversaries, has
made few statements of any kind. Instead, he has asked
questions; and in spite of the lofty rhetoric to which he
has been subjected these questions are still unanswered.

Unlike the reader, Elihu was not present in the court
of heaven of the prologue, and he therefore cannot know

that Job is entirely sinless. Instead, he makes Job's guilt
his major premise, since it is Elihu's conviction that God
requites each man "according to his way." (*Job* xxxiv.
11) But Job has done worse than just to sin.

> "For he adds rebellion unto his sin.
> He clenches his fists at us,
> And he multiplies his charges against God."
>
> (*Job* xxxiv. 37)

It is this aspect of Job's conduct that disturbs Elihu the
most, as it disturbed the three patriarchs before him. His
speech is a determined effort to justify the ways of God
to Job, so that the sinner may be saved from the sin of
his own honest bewilderment.

God, says Elihu impressively, is entirely just in all
his ways, giving each man exactly what he deserves.
Would Job dare ascribe partiality to God, the great ruler
who has no respect even for princes? Job has said that
his virtue has done him no good with God, and has im-
plied that his wickedness has done him no harm either.
But here he is judging by human standards. Good and
evil affect only men like himself; they do not affect the
Lord. Yet because God is slow to wrath, Job considers
it safe to go on railing against him.

Elihu pauses here, probably to give Job time to answer; but Job says nothing. Elihu is a little disconcerted
by his silence, and hastens to add that "there are yet
things to be said in God's behalf" (*Job* xxxvi. 2) and
that "one who is perfect in knowledge is with you."
(*Job* xxxvi. 4) For one who is perfect in knowledge,
Elihu does not show much skill. In his next speech he
falls back on the old device of the three friends, delivering statements that have orthodoxy to support them but
no proof. He states flatly that God supports the righteous,
who "fulfill their days in prosperity and their years in

pleasure," (*Job* xxxvi. 11) but that the wicked pass away quickly into Sheol.

Elihu observes that his stubborn listener is still unconverted by what seems to him a self-evident fact, and he shifts ground a little. He begins to enlarge, as all the speakers before him have done, on the greatness of God. This is an entirely safe subject, one on which his listeners are already agreed; but to give force and reality to his discourse Elihu goes farther and begins to draw illustrations from what he can see going on about him.

A storm is coming up. The structure of the poem naturally does not include stage directions, and it is by this speech of Elihu's that its gradual approach is indicated. This is a dramatic device often used by Shakespeare and other dramatists, and in this case its use is particularly brilliant. The rising storm is linked with the rising terror of the young man until a sudden climax is reached that is nearly as overwhelming to the reader as it was to Job.

Elihu begins graphically, but impersonally. Great and mysterious are the works of God as he draws up drops of water from the earth, distills them into vapor, and sends the vapor back to earth again as rain. Great is the force of his lightning, charged to find its mark, and the shout of thunder that tells the uneasy cattle of the coming storm.

At this there is a loud crash of actual thunder, and Elihu's heart "leaps from its place." (*Job* xxxvii. 1) He is nevertheless intent on drawing a lesson from this for Job's benefit.

> "Listen closely to the roar of his voice,
>   And the rumbling that goes forth from his mouth.
> Beneath the whole heavens he lets it loose."
>   (*Job* xxxvii. 2-3)

Even the lightning is loosed to do God's bidding, and the fury of the pouring rain. The rising winds begin to find

an echo in Elihu's speech, the sudden heat, the glitter
of the lightning, and then, all at once, the curtain of the
dark.

Elihu can no longer see the man to whom he is speaking. In the darkness he cannot even order his own speech,
and he apparently is struck by a sudden doubt of his own
worthiness to explain so glibly the ways of God to man.

> "Shall it be told him that I am speaking?
> Or if a man talk will he be swallowed up?"
> *(Job* xxxvii. 20)

Almost as if in answer the wind clears away the clouds
and the light returns; but even more terrifying than the
former darkness is the golden supernatural radiance that
fills the north. Elihu gives one last cry.

> "We have not found the Almighty . . .
> He does not consider any that are wise of heart."
> *(Job* xxxvii. 23-24)

And with that comes a Voice out of the whirlwind, in as
perfectly prepared an entrance as any dramatist ever
conceived.

The Voice that has resolved itself out of the winds
and the storm ignores Elihu and speaks directly to Job.
It may be that the others did not even hear it. It is Job
who is the hero of the poem, and it is as a hero that he is
called upon to rise and give answer.

No adequate paraphrase can be given of what the
Voice of the Whirlwind thunders to the man who called
it forth. It comes in such a vast, driving sweep of sustained energy that it is no wonder it brought Job to his
knees, and it voices in one overwhelming, cumulative
shout of irresistible force the very heart of the mystery
of all natural things. The poetry of the Greeks surges
against far-off shores, but there its bounds are stayed.

The Hebrew poet imposed upon himself no such limits.
All creation was his province.

> "Where were you when I laid the foundations of the
> earth?" (*Job* xxxviii. 4)

Where were you when the seas broke forth, when morning was ordained, when snow was forged in the secret
treasuries of creation? What do you know of the secret
of light or the path of the east wind? When did you discover the father of rain and from what birth the dew
came forth?

> "Can you bind the chains of the Pleiades,
>   Or loosen the girdle of Orion?" (*Job* xxxviii. 31)

Can you give the stars their courses, or lead the storm in
the path it should take? Do you know the mysteries of
birth and the strange secret of its timing, the glorious
power and beauty of animals, the strength of birds?

"Behold," says Job, "I am insignificant; what can I
answer thee?" (*Job* xl. 4)

The Voice continues with two specific miracles of creation, the intricate structure and vast power of Behemoth
and Leviathan. But the mystery of one part of creation
is no greater than that of another, since a leaf is as strange
as a star; and the Voice begins to recede, leaving Job to
cry out:

> "I had heard of thee by the hearing of the ear;
>   But now my eye has seen thee.
>   Therefore I retract and repent,
>   In dust and ashes." (*Job* xlii. 5-6)

Job had always known theoretically that there was an
unfathomed mystery in the world, but as he heard the
Voice he was like a blind man whose eyes are suddenly
opened. For a moment, before familiarity again dulled

his vision, he saw the world with all its violence and its beauty and its strangeness undimmed. He could not sustain the vision, but it was enough to send him to his knees and satisfy him.

Throughout the whole drama, Job has been asking for one thing only: the right to stand face to face with God and contend with him in a reasonable manner. The drama ends when Job discovers that even one small aspect of reality, external nature, is too much for him to contend with; but it is left to the epilogue to prove that his request was nevertheless considered legitimate.

The epilogue opens with the Lord of the prologue rebuking Eliphaz, that noble but orthodox disputant. "My anger is hot against you and your two friends, because you have not spoken regarding me what is true, as my servant Job has." (*Job* xlii. 7) All their elaborate and conventional justifications of God have been incorrect, and Job is told to pray for them lest they be dealt with according to their folly. As for Job himself, he is given back more possessions than he lost and his end is more blessed than his beginning, since in the face of endless possibilities for evil he has spoken "what is true." Job was right, then, in seeking to know God, and his friends were wrong in trying to limit that search.

Job never found what he was looking for. He could not, because his creator, the author of the poem, did not know the answer himself, and had too much integrity to offer a weak compromise. His hero's cause was just, and he left it at that.

Part of the poem's greatness lies in the quality of this honesty, that it does not attempt to offer some comforting half-truth for the sake of the reader's ease. But greater still is the philosophic strength that can present in such beauty the central mystery of creation, the problem of how torment and death may be reconciled with the existence of a good God, and then can insist that there is really an answer to the question and that mankind has a right to search it out.

The author of *Job* was no churchman with a doctrine to prove. His heart was with the lonely men of God who went out to find reality for themselves, forsaking every intellectual belief and emotional comfort that might hold them back; and in writing the *Book of Job* he became himself not the least of these.

It is not known when the book itself was written, but it is fitting that its action should take place in the days of the patriarchs and that it should mirror the oldest civilization known to the Bible. According to all the available evidence, freedom was the birthright of the men of Israel from the beginning, and the great patriarch of the land of Uz serves as a worthy symbol both of the antiquity of the search for God and of its freedom.

He serves also as an emblem of its passion. The search for God was no casual intellectual exercise. It was born of a hunger and thirst so long-enduring that its origins are lost in antiquity, and so deep-rooted that nothing but fulfillment could satisfy it.

It was inconceivable to the men of Israel that this desire should go unfulfilled, that they could seek and not find, ask and not be answered. Like Job, they were convinced that somewhere the answer existed and that it could be found.

They were convinced also that this ultimate discovery of God would bring with it in some way a perfection that would fill the whole earth with its glory. This conviction finds its most beautiful and complete expression in the writings of the prophet Isaiah, although it did not originate with him. Where it did originate no one can say, but it finds its first expression in the Bible in the opening chapter of the *Book of Genesis*.

THE OBJECT OF THE SEARCH

CHAPTER II

> God created man for incorruption, and made him
> the image of his own eternity; but by the envy of
> the devil death entered into the world.
>
> *The Wisdom of Solomon* ii. 21

THE first three chapters of the *Book of Genesis* have been
discussed with more passion and fewer results than any
other part of the Old Testament. They have been proven
to be everything from God's express and final revelation
on the subject of his own creation to a re-working of the
old Babylonian legend of Marduk with elements from
the Sumerian thrown in. They have been compared with
each other and found contradictory; they have been
compared with scientific discoveries and found inaccu-
rate; and they have been the storm center of a series of
controversies that have ultimately proven nothing.

The weakness of all these explanations is that they
ignore the fundamental problem that the three chapters
present a problem which is obvious to the most casual
reader and yet one for which no satisfactory explanation
has ever been given.

The first three chapters of the *Book of Genesis* do not
tell of one creation of the world. They tell of two. In the
first chapter and continuing into the second, God creates
the world. Then, beginning with the fourth verse of the
second chapter, another God creates a different kind of
a world altogether.

This second creation is not an amplification or con-
tinuation of the first one. Everything has been "finished"
(*Gen.* ii. 1) in the first creation, including man, and
the work has been pronounced "good." (*Gen.* i. 31)
Whereupon a new creator with a different title appears

41

and makes man and the world all over again, by a different method and with different results.

These two creations stand side by side in the *Book of Genesis*, without connective and without explanation. Mankind is given two origins and two deities, and there is no suggestion in the text of how the two may be reconciled. They cannot, in fact, be reconciled. There is no point of contact between the two creators or between the two creations.

Theology, both Jewish and Christian, has concentrated itself upon the second creation, the familiar one of Adam and Eve, and has left the first almost unnoticed. Nevertheless, however much the problem is ignored, it still remains: there are two creations in the *Book of Genesis*, and they contradict each other.

Recent scholarship has offered a hopeful explanation of this phenomenon. *Genesis*, like the rest of the books of the *Pentateuch*, is now generally agreed to be a compilation of old documents rather than the work of a single man, the product of a long line of literary development rather than of a single creative act. It is the result of at least two major traditions about God, and the scholars have therefore concluded that the first creation is the product of one tradition and the second of another.

The objection to this theory lies in the amount of careful investigation that was necessary to construct it in the first place. It took many years of research and a microscopic scrutiny of the text to bring to light enough minor contradictions and repetitions to establish *Genesis* as the work of more than one man. Whoever the final editor of the book may have been, he did his work well. There is no surface evidence of the skillful cutting and joining that must have been necessary to give the book its present appearance of unity.

Under such circumstances, it is difficult to believe that

the final editor of *Genesis* was so absent-minded as to overlook the fact that his book began, not with one story of the origin of man, but with two, and that these two accounts of creation involved two mutually contradictory creators. Even the most careless of editors could see that this was an odd way to begin a book whose whole purpose was to record Israel's devotion to the idea of one God; and the man responsible for *Genesis* in its present form was not a careless editor. Nor would he have been obliged to omit one creation entirely in order to remove the contradiction that now exists. A little editorial work and a few excisions would have been sufficient to make the two accounts seem, on the surface at least, to be concerned with the same creation.

Nevertheless, the fact remains that someone who was both a skilled editor and obviously a monotheist placed at the beginning of the book two Gods and two creations, and allowed them to remain there to contradict each other. This cannot have been accidental. It must have been an act of conscious deliberation, done by the editor for what seemed to him a good and sufficient reason. It remains, therefore, to discover on the basis of the text itself what this reason was.

The mystery which surrounds the first three chapters of the *Book of Genesis* is not dissimilar to the mystery which surrounds the *Book of Job*. It is caused by an attempt to read the text in the light of a pre-conceived theological position. The second creation, the story of Adam and Eve, later became the foundation of the doctrine of fall and redemption upon which Judaism based itself, and, through Judaism, Christianity. The story has therefore become entangled in a series of religious propositions through which it becomes extremely difficult to see the actual text. Yet it is only by a careful reading of the text itself that it is possible to understand why two different creations and two different creators are included in the *Book of Genesis*.

The vast difference between these two creators can never become evident to anyone who feels obliged, for theological reasons, to maintain a reverence for the God who made Adam and Eve. Yet, on the basis of the actual text, this God is not entitled to reverence. He appears throughout the story as a tyrannical and inefficient Eastern overlord who has no control over the unruly creation that he has laboriously formed. He is a deity who can punish sin but is quite incapable of preventing it.

The reverse is true of the God of the first creation. He is an orderly God who brings into being an orderly world, a world of light and order and peace that is "very good." His is a creation of harmony and life. The creation of the God of Adam is one that results in confusion and death.

In spite of its brevity, the narrative of the first creation succeeds in giving a remarkable impression of effortless, accurate force. Its creator is no laborer, toiling to build a universe as a man would build a house. He creates by his word.

> God said, "Let there be light!" and there was light.
> (*Gen.* i. 3)

Characteristically, this creation of light has nothing to do with the sun; it is the fact of light that is created, brought into spontaneous being by the word of God.

The creation itself is divided into seven days, or periods. Seven was a holy number to the Hebrews, the symbol of completeness, and its use in this connection emphasizes a fact which is also explicitly stated by the text itself. "Thus the heavens and the earth were finished and . . . on the seventh day God brought his work to an end." (*Gen.* ii. 1-2) When this creation is finished, it is finished. Nothing can be added to it, and nothing taken away.

Further, this creation is characterized throughout by a reiterated refrain. After each single act of creation comes the phrase, repeated again and again, "God saw that it was good"; (*Gen.* i. 4, 10, 12, 18, 21, 25) and after the whole of creation has been finished the phrase is repeated and intensified.

> God saw that all that he had made was very good.
> (*Gen.* i. 31)

There is therefore no evil in this creation. The same quality of order and rightness that is praised in the sun and the stars is shared also by every other aspect of the universe, even to the birds of the air and the fishes of the sea. Nor does death exist in this creation, for no animal need kill to eat. "I give all the green plants for food." (*Gen. i.* 30)

On the sixth day of this creation man is made; and three times the narrator emphasizes the fact that this man is like the God who makes him.

> "Let us make man in our image, after our likeness,
>   and let him have dominion . . ."
> So God created man in his own image;
> In the image of God he created him. (*Gen.* i. 26-27)

And God "blessed" (*Gen.* i. 28) the man that he had made, for he saw "that all that he had made was very good." (*Gen.* i. 31)

In spite of the superficial familiarity of its catalog of birds and plants and stars, the creation that is recorded in the first chapter of *Genesis* is not a familiar one. It bears no resemblance to the world we know. It is a world of serenity and order, in which everything is "good" and there is no evil. It contains within itself nothing that is dying or accursed, and there is no opportunity given for anything alien to enter in.

This perfect and undying creation which is called forth by the word of God has no relation to our familiar cycle of birth and decay. Nor has it any relation to the rest of *Genesis*, with its unsparing historical account of adultery and murder and bitter warfare, and its patient, stumbling attempt to struggle with the problem of evil.

What the first creation does resemble, and very closely, is the perfect world which the prophets of Israel came to believe would become established on earth on what they called 'the day of the Lord.'

> Then the wolf will lodge with the lamb,
> And the leopard will lie down with the kid . . .
> The suckling child will play on the hole of the asp,
> And the weaned child will put his hand on the viper's
>   den.
> They will do no harm or destruction
>   On all my holy mountain;
> For the earth will have become full of the knowledge
>   of the Lord
> As the waters cover the sea. (*Isa.* xi. 6-9)

With Isaiah, as with all the major prophets, this perfect world from which death and destruction would somehow have vanished was dependent for its existence on "the knowledge of the Lord." There is no such idea in the opening of *Genesis*. A perfect creation is simply presented as a fact, as the way God made the world. The creation is in the likeness of its creator.

As has been previously suggested, it would have required only a little ingenuity for the editor of *Genesis* to have linked this creation with the subsequent fall of man and entrance of evil. He could have modified the reiteration of the word 'good,' and the emphasis on the fact that this is a "finished" creation; and he could have told how

the man God had made was nevertheless tempted by a
serpent to let death into the world. In so doing, he would
have destroyed the spirit of the story, and he would no
longer have had a perfect God. But at the same time he
would have had a practical introduction to the history of
his race, and he would have avoided the one great contradiction in the *Book of Genesis*.

Nevertheless, the editor left this story of the creation
untouched. He made no attempt to explain into the text
the phenomena of evil and death. A perfect God has made
a perfect world, and that is the end of it. The creation
bears no relation to history, and it bears no relationship
to any available fact. Nevertheless, God so made the
world, according to the first chapter of *Genesis*.

In the following chapters of *Genesis*, another God
makes another kind of a world. This creation is introduced with the statement: "The following are the origins
of the heavens and the earth in their creation" (*Gen.* ii.
4) and continues with a wholly new account of creation
made by a completely dissimilar creator.

It is this second creation which serves as an introduction to the ancient history with which the rest of the
Book of Genesis is concerned, and it is this story of creation that became the cornerstone of Judaism. A glow of
reverence surrounds it through the writings of great and
holy men, both Jewish and Christian, and this natural
reverence has made it impossible to recognize the fundamental difference between the second creation and the
first one.

In the first chapter of *Genesis*, a perfect creation is deduced from a perfect God. Given a creator in whom there
is no shadow of evil or failing, the world that is described
is exactly the kind of world that he would have made. In
the second account in *Genesis*, this process is reversed,
whether consciously or unconsciously, and an imperfect

God is deduced from an imperfect creation. Given an existence such as ours, lived under the constant shadow of sin and pain and with death always at the end of it, the kind of God who would make such a world is exactly the kind of God who appears in the story of the second creation.

The story of Adam and Eve and the Lord God is an extraordinary piece of work. It succeeds, in the space of a few short pages, in supplying an origin for every major evil that the world knows. It not only explains death, which is the primary purpose of the story, but it also explains mankind's whole way of life. It explains the phenomenon of a potentially good, potentially evil mind, forever at war with itself and imprisoned in a body of alien clay. It explains the labor this body must undergo to keep itself alive, since if it is not continually fed and clothed and sheltered it will die. It explains the lust that is necessary to originate another such body, and the danger and pain of childbirth. And finally it explains, as the unavoidable end of all this labor and torment, the return to the dust.

The basis of this explanation is not to be found either in Adam or in the serpent, but in the nature of the Lord God himself. As the narrative clearly shows, in what is possibly the most brilliant single piece of story-telling in the world, the conclusion of the story is inevitable once the premise is accepted. The premise of the story is a creator so inefficient that he has no control over his own creation; the conclusion is the coming of death.

This conclusion is of course foreordained. Death exists in the world; therefore the story must explain its coming. Both the structure of the plot and the nature of the characterization move towards a pre-determined end, and the Lord God obviously has to be the kind of creator who would make such an end inevitable.

Unless the nature of this compulsion is understood, the story of Adam and Eve and the Lord God becomes a tissue of absurdities. It tells of a creator who did not want his creation to sin and yet did everything in his power to help the situation along. Even Milton, with all the good-will of a conscientious Christian and all the ingenuities of logic he learned while defending the Commonwealth, could make no sense of such a plot. It is only if the story is seen as an attempt to explain the illogical and tyrannous world in which we live that the reason for the lack of logic and the tyranny of the Lord God becomes clear. This deity is exactly like the world he makes. He cannot be justified, but neither can the world from whose existence his nature is deduced.

The story of the second creation does not go into specific detail over the making of the universe. Its primary interest is the making of Adam, since it was through Adam that death entered the world. Brief mention is made of the fact that the Lord God made the earth and the heavens, but the first sign of actual life is the rising up of a mist. This mist is characteristic of the second creation. It is without jurisdiction, since no act of the Lord God's brought it forth, and it is without power, since a literal translation makes it clear that it cannot make the plants grow.

> Then the Lord God molded man out of the dust of the ground, and breathed into his nostrils the breath of life, so that man became a living being. (*Gen.* ii. 7)

This making of Adam, in which clay is shaped and breathed upon until the result is a man, is also characteristic of the second creation. The laborious re-working of old material into a new shape is not only in complete contrast to the first creation, called into spontaneous existence by the word of God, but the manner of creation is an integral part of the story of the coming of death. Just as in a well-made tragic drama the catastrophe that overtakes the hero is implicit in his own character, so in this tragedy is death implicit in Adam's own make-up. His body originated in the dust. It is therefore possible for him to die.

Up to this point the earth has been sterile, and the Lord God now plants a garden to the east, in Eden, and places therein the man that he has made. In this garden he places also the tree of life and the tree of the knowledge of good and evil.

> "From any tree in the garden you are free to eat; but from the tree of the knowledge of good and evil you must not eat; for the day that you eat of it you shall certainly die." (*Gen.* ii. 16-17)

These instructions are brief; but they expose the nature of the Lord God, the nature of Adam, and the whole structure of the plot.

The Lord God is not the lord of his creation. He can make laws, but he cannot enforce them. He can punish Adam's body but he cannot control Adam's mind, the mind he himself has made. He may attempt to exert authority by a system of threats and punishments; but his disorderly creation is not bound to obey him, and, according to the story, does not. This creator is a ruler who cannot rule. He may punish a sin, but he is helpless to prevent it.

Adam is equally helpless. He has been made out of the dust, and to this dust has been added a mentality which is potentially capable of a sin great enough to merit death. The symbol of this sin is the fruit of a tree placed where he cannot fail to see it, continually present and continually tempting, in a garden where he is obliged to remain. Add to this a serpent whose only purpose in having been created seems to be to draw Adam into the sin he is trying to avoid, and the end becomes inevitable.

The whole story is arranged to lead to the coming of death. No other ending is, of course, possible. The narrator is under a compulsion to bring the plot to its tragic and foreordained conclusion which is similar to that of his own characters. He has no choice. He must explain how death came into the world, and both Adam and the Lord God are part of the explanation. They naturally cannot prevent what they themselves are designed to produce.

The next factor in the plot is Adam's increasing loneliness. The Lord God makes an attempt to comfort him by making animals, also out of the dust, to be Adam's companions; but in this, as in so much else, he is unsuccessful. Adam wants someone who is "like him," (*Gen.* ii. 20) and the animals do not prove to be satisfactory. They do not share his doubtful gift of intellectual life.

Adam is therefore thrown into a deep sleep, and Eve is made, in the now-familiar secondhand manner, out of a part of his own flesh. The subsequent action makes it clear that she also has been given the same mentality as her husband's, the mentality that is prohibited from sinning and yet given the power to sin.

Next appears the serpent, who was created by the Lord God to be "the most clever of all the wild beasts." (*Gen.* iii. 1) The serpent is also under the general compulsion to bring the story to its inevitable conclusion, and he plays his part convincingly and well. There is about him a reasonableness and a capacity for special pleading that ought to convince anyone, and he succeeds in making the eating of the forbidden fruit not a sin but a delightful duty.

The serpent's conversational approach to Eve is really

brilliant, it has about it such an air of polite interest and
of an innocent desire to be informed.

> "And so God has said that you are not to eat from any
> tree in the garden?" (*Gen.* iii. 1)

Eve rises at once to the bait, and hastens to correct him.

> "From the fruit of the trees in the garden we may
> eat; it is only concerning the fruit of the tree which
> is in the middle of the garden that God has said,
> 'You may not eat any of it, nor touch it, lest you
> die.' " (*Gen.* iii. 2-3)

The serpent is surprised at such ignorance.

> "You would not die at all; for God knows that the
> very day you eat of it, your eyes will be opened, and
> you will be like gods who know good from evil."
> (*Gen.* iii. 4-5)

With one efficient sweep, the serpent removes the only
curb that the Lord God has been able to put upon his
creation: fear of punishment. He assures Eve that the
eating of the fruit will not bring death. On the contrary,
it will bring a wonderful reward, the "gift of wisdom."
(*Gen.* iii. 6) Naturally the Lord God does not want any
rivals, and it is for this reason alone that he has forbidden the fruit to Adam and Eve.

The argument is ingenious, and it convinces Eve. She
shares the fruit with Adam, they eat, and at once the
results of their new knowledge begin to appear. The first
result is guilt and the second, fear. Nakedness is used as
the symbol of the guilt, since the sensation of shame is
usually connected with sexual functions. But the fear is
more fundamental, being the universal and inevitable
fear of consequences, and in their terror Adam and Eve
try to hide themselves from their creator among the
trees of the garden.

This attempt at concealment is actual confession that the command has been broken, although the Lord God, who is by no means omniscient, is obliged to inquire pointblank if he has been disobeyed. Adam immediately uses his disastrous intellect in an attempt to avoid punishment, and undertakes to divide the blame equally between the Lord God and Eve.

> "The woman whom you set at my side, it was she who gave me fruit from the tree; so I ate it."
> (*Gen.* iii. 12)

Since the Lord God gave Adam the woman, and the woman gave Adam the fruit, Adam himself has clearly no reason to feel responsible for the unfortunate results. Asked for her version, Eve is rather more honest.

> "It was the serpent that misled me, and so I ate it."
> (*Gen.* iii. 13)

For this the serpent is cursed, although it was the Lord God who made him clever. Upon Eve is set the curse of childbirth, and upon Adam that of endless labor. Yet for all their suffering they will not be able to keep themselves alive.

> "For dust you are,
> And to dust you must return." (*Gen.* iii. 19).

The story closes with Adam and Eve being driven from the garden of Eden, the curse laid upon them forever. What follows in the history of their descendants is not really part of the same story. The allegory of the coming of death is finished; the rest of *Genesis* is to tell the story of man's experiences in the world that resulted.

The story of Adam and Eve has done exactly what it set out to do. It has given an origin not only for death, but for guilt, for fear, for lust and for pain. All this is not explained by the actual Fall, since the seeds of it lay in the manner of Adam's creating. What does explain the whole of it is the character of the Lord God himself.

This God, tyrannical, arbitrary and inefficient, is the obvious creator to have made the world as we know it. From the existence of good and evil can be deduced his knowledge of them both, from the existence of death his power to destroy, from the existence of sin his inefficiency, from the existence of pain his tyranny. He is the God who gives man the capacity to sin, and then punishes him for his own evil gift. He is the God who can be placated only by the prayers of his helpless creation, and whom the magnitude of a sacrifice may perhaps move to pity.

He is, in fact, the natural result of mankind's attempt to explain the agony, the disorder and the terror of the world in terms of some kind of creator, even though the result is a being less to be admired than his own Adam. He is the obvious God.

The history of the Bible is the history of the long, slow, steady repudiation of this God. The men of Israel did not want an obvious God. They wanted the truth.

Little by little, and each according to his capacity, the men of Israel rejected the various attributes of the creator of Adam. They came to believe that these attributes did not belong to God, but only to their own ignorance concerning him. They began to dream of a 'day of the Lord' on which God would become fully known; and on this day they believed that death and destruction would disappear, never to return.

> And he will destroy on this mountain
> The veil that veils all the peoples,
> And the web that is woven over all the nations—
> He will destroy death forever. (*Isa.* xxv. 7-8)

The man who set the two stories of creation side by side was expressing in his own way this same conviction of a holy world. He may not have originated either story. But what he did do was to set the two stories side by side, and in so doing cancelled out one of them.

No man can believe in two Gods, and it is obviously the God of the first creation whom the editor of *Genesis* honored. He would never have included the account of the first creation if he had not believed in the God who made it. From the literary point of view, its inclusion mars the text. It is the story of Adam and Eve that makes the proper introduction to the rest of *Genesis*. The story of the first creation is contradictory and alien, damaging the unity of the book, and from the technical point of view it would have been much better to have omitted it entirely.

Nevertheless, the editor of *Genesis* could not omit it. He could not begin the history of his people with a God in whom he did not believe. His God was the God of the first creation and not a being inferior to himself.

How this conviction of the existence of a perfect God might be reconciled with a world of sin and death, the man responsible for the inclusion of the two creations in *Genesis* did not know. Like the author of *Job*, he possessed no explanation and therefore he gave none. At the same time, he clung to his vision of a perfect God and would not let it go. He could see a perfection that bore no relation to the visible world in which Adam, the man of clay, labors under permanent sentence of death; and it is with this vision that the Bible opens. It is a re-statement in fuller language of Job's sudden conviction:

> "From my flesh, I shall see God;
> Whom I shall see on my side,
> And my eyes will see unestranged."
>
> (*Job* xix. 26-27)

Somewhere there existed a perfect relationship between God and man, and it was capable of being found.

Out of this conviction came Israel's search for God, the search that was the most stubborn, the most magnificent, and the most perfectly rewarded in the mental history of any people on earth.

It was not, of course, a unanimous search, conducted spontaneously by the whole race. The Hebrews, like any other collection of ordinary people, were content enough with a state religion and a tribal god. But the spirit of Israel, working within them like an irresistible leaven, was not content. It was never satisfied, and it did not rest, until it reached fulfillment.

This spirit of desire, of the "striver with God," endowed a small Eastern tribe of Semitic origin with enduring life. The glories of Egypt and Assyria are now dust, with only a few chips of stone to bear witness to civilizations that were probably the equal of our own. But Israel raised for herself a living monument; and while the great empires that surrounded her rose and fell, Israel remained.

As the last and greatest of her prophets bore witness:

It is the spirit that gives life. (*John* vi. 63)

THE SEARCH

CHAPTER III

Listen, my son, and be wise,
And keep straight on the way.
The Book of Proverbs xxiii. 19

THE early stories in the *Book of Genesis* are half history, half legend, and of them not much can be definitely said. What great, shadowy names like those of Enoch and Noah stood for in the memories of the Hebrew race may have been clear three thousand years ago, but the knowledge is lost today.

One thing, however, is sure. The Hebrews honored such men as the ancestral heroes of their race, not because they were kings or warriors or conquerors, but because they were men who knew God. The Hebrews were the one race on earth who held a man in reverence for the greatness of his ideas rather than for the length of his sword.

At the beginning, there is no attempt to be historical. Centuries are passed over as though they were years, and the growth of a people as though it were of a single man. By the time Adam's two sons, theoretically the first on the earth, make their appearance, the earth is already populated. The slow division of Eastern mankind into farmers and shepherds has already taken place, and there are women for Cain, and later for Seth, to marry.

These chapters are obviously not historical. They are rather an attempt to record the persistent survival of the knowledge of good, of a race that knew righteousness, in the face of great odds.

The first threat to this survival is Cain, who stands for the knowledge of evil as Abel stands for the knowledge of good. Cain is so well acquainted with evil that he can use it for his own ends, and he tries to rid himself of good by killing his brother. He is unsuccessful. The knowledge of good reappears in Seth, the third of Adam's sons; and when a son was born to Seth, says the narrator, "it was then that men began to call upon the name of the Lord." (*Gen.* iv. 26)

The righteousness of the descendants of Seth is threatened by no outside force. Of their own will they adulterate and nearly lose it. The hero who saves the heritage of Seth from disaster is Noah, and Noah's eldest son, Shem, is "the ancestor of all the Hebrews." (*Gen.* x. 21) It is of this line of Shem that Abraham was born.

Abraham is the first man to emerge out of these vague legends as a recognizable human being. Whatever temptation his historian may have felt to glorify the founder of a great race, he had too much respect for the truth to alter or suppress any of the material at his disposal. As a result, Abraham emerges a greater man for the honesty of his historian, and it is possible to believe in the essential truth of the narrative.

Abraham was a lord of the East like the patriarch Job, rich in cattle and silver and gold. But, unlike Job, he did not need to lose his position and his wealth in order to be filled with a desire for the truth. Successful, powerful, wealthy and at peace with the world, he was nevertheless possessed of a driving spiritual curiosity that forced him out of his country, away from his friends, and into a new land. Abraham was convinced that in Canaan he would become the founder of a race that would know God, and that through this race all the families of the earth would be blessed.

Abraham's unswerving faith in this conviction was the one great force of his life. The God he worshipped was "God Almighty" (*Gen.* xvii. 1). Whatever might seem to stand in the way, his God was all-powerful and nothing could prevent the fulfillment of his promise.

Abraham believed this with the full force of his powerful, inquiring mentality. It was on this account that he refused the offer of a king.

"I have sworn by uplifted hand to the Lord, God Most High, the creator of the heavens and the earth, that I would not take anything that belongs to you, not even so much as a thread or a sandal-lace, lest you should say, 'It was I who made Abram rich.' "

(*Gen.* xiv. 22-23)

God had called him forth; God was able to provide for him.

Abraham had need of all his faith; for the fulfillment of the promise depended on an heir and Sarah, his wife, had given him no sons. Sarah was a practical woman and suggested a practical way out of the difficulty, giving one of her handmaidens to Abraham so that a child might be conceived of the union and born of his line. But the plan failed, because of that lamentable quality called human nature rather than because of any dearth of good intentions; and Abraham, grown older, was still without an heir.

Abraham's attitude towards God remained consistent. The birth of a son might seem to be an impossibility, but nothing was so impossible as that God should forget his promise or be unable to fulfill it. It was true that Sarah was too old to bear a child, but, "Is anything too wonderful for the Lord?" (*Gen.* xviii. 14) To Abraham there was nothing, and in the end the promise was fulfilled. Abraham had a son.

Many things about Abraham have been misunderstood, largely because it is the consistent practice of the narrator to externalize what obviously took place in his hero's own consciousness and picture it either as a mes-

senger of God or as God himself. But nothing has been
more thoroughly misunderstood than the motive which
led Abraham to sacrifice the son of his old age upon an
altar in the hills.

Abraham loved God. As proof of this love he was prepared to offer up the most precious possession he had, the
one gift that was wholly worthy to be received by the
great author of heaven and earth. He did not feel that
the sacrifice of Isaac was murder, any more than a man
of today feels it is murder to give up his son to his country. Delivering a son up to possible death because of a
patriotic ideal is felt to be an act of great righteousness;
in Abraham's day delivering a son up to death because
of a religious ideal was also felt to be an act of great
righteousness.

In Abraham's day, a father had much greater control
over the body of his son; but the idea behind the two
points of view is much the same. Both depend on the emotions rather than on the reason, and in both the magnitude of the sacrifice is in some way connected with its
righteousness. In the case of Abraham, according to the
religious convention of the day, the righteousness he was
showing was particularly great. He was sacrificing not
only the body of his son but all those unborn generations
that were to have been the heirs of his treasured promise.

Any man of Abraham's day would have agreed that
the sacrifice of Isaac constituted Abraham's final proof,
to himself and to the world, that he loved God more than
he loved anything else in existence. It is to Abraham's
everlasting glory that he discovered the act to be nothing of the sort, and gave that knowledge to his descendants.

Abraham had deliberately and stoically prepared himself to offer up his son and the immortality of his race on
the altar of his religious idealism. The wood was ready,

the boy was bound, and his own hand was reaching for the knife. But at that moment, when any other man would have lashed himself into such a frenzy of blind religious zeal that anything like the exercise of reason would have been impossible, Abraham still remained an independent thinker.

There was no wavering in his love of God. What he suddenly questioned was the method he had taken to prove it. The method had the sanction of all antiquity behind it, but that did not in itself mean that it was the truth.

Abraham had never been a good believer. He was a searcher from the moment he set out for Canaan, and his search was leading him directly away from that conception of a tyrant God so perfectly pictured in the story of the second creation. Since God had given him Isaac, it was no profit to God to have the boy handed back again, his purpose unfulfilled. Religion might say that it was, but in this religion was mistaken. Abraham's own reason was more to be trusted than any orthodox rule the code of his fathers might dictate. As in the case of Job, his own stubborn independence of thought triumphed over his inherited beliefs; and he laid aside the knife.

The narrator of the story does not share his hero's suddenly enlarged conception. He takes the position throughout that God arranged the whole thing to see if Abraham loved him, and then stopped him from killing his son at the last moment for some reason that is unexplained. But this interpretation is at variance with the subsequent history of Abraham's descendants. Every nation but the Hebrew conducted, and continued to conduct, human sacrifice as a matter of course. It was only the sons of Abraham who never countenanced it again. In the exceptional cases when it was practiced it was not held up as a proof of love of God, but only as a sign that the Hebrew religion had been hideously defiled.

When Abraham died, Isaac was left to carry on the search for God his father had begun, and this he was not fully equipped to do. Isaac had a peaceable, easily satisfied disposition, and it is not such men who make discoveries. If the Philistine herdsmen filled up the wells his father had dug, Isaac cleared them out again without argument. If the herdsmen claimed them, he dug others and still others with unruffled good nature; and steadily he added to the already large fortune that his father had left him. But the greater, the spiritual heritage, he was not capable of grasping. He had faith in the God of Abraham and he knew that he had received a great promise; but he believed that he held it only in trust, in the vessel of his body rather than of his mind. God would fulfill his promise for the sake of "your father Abraham," (*Gen* xxvi. 24) not for anything that Isaac himself might do.

It was Isaac's son Jacob who made the heritage his own and carried on the search that Abraham had begun. Unlike his father, Jacob was not at all a righteous man, being neither honest nor even moderately brave. Moreover he was entirely without scruples, and quite capable of putting Jacob and Jacob's welfare above every other consideration. Yet he had sufficient spiritual insight to discover something more important than his own welfare, and once he discovered it he never let it go.

All the intensity which Jacob first used to make himself rich he ended by throwing into the struggle to find the truth; and in so doing he earned for himself a new name and a great one. It was Jacob who was given the title of Israel, the "striver with God"; and he deserved it.

The first quality which is evident in Jacob is that of ambition. His brother Esau was the first-born, and to him belonged all the rights and privileges of the older son; but to Jacob this was unendurable, especially since Esau himself placed no great value upon his birthright. Jacob's moral code was a highly elastic one, and he apparently felt that the birthright ought to belong to someone who could appreciate it. At any rate, he succeeded in bribing it away from Esau, who felt that food and drink were of more immediate importance than any vague abstraction.

Jacob's theft of his father's blessing was an even more serious matter. The blessing was the most precious gift a father could bestow upon his eldest son, and in order to get it Jacob had to practice a deliberate deception. Isaac's eyes were dim with age, and it was no difficult matter for Jacob to be disguised as his brother, who happened to be out hunting game at his father's request. It was Rebekah, full of ambition for her favorite son, who helped to disguise him and who gave him meat as substitute for the game that Esau was supposed to be bringing.

Jacob got his blessing, but at the price of a lie that is worth noticing. His father, believing him to be Esau, could not understand how he could be so prompt with the game. "However did you come to find it so quickly, my son?" (*Gen.* xxvii. 20) Jacob knew that his father was a deeply religious man, and, being a liar of much ingenuity, he turned that fact to account. "Because the Lord your God brought it in my path." (*Gen.* xxvii. 20) Jacob knew that an explanation which involved an effect of holiness would be sure to please his father, and he felt no compunction in using his father's God to explain the speedy appearance of the meat. It is clear that he did not believe in Isaac's God, after the usual manner of sons, or he would not have dared risk such a blasphemy. It was the "Lord your God" he spoke of, not his own.

Jacob's second offense against Esau was too heavy to be endured, and in his simple and whole-hearted fashion

Esau made up his mind to kill his brother. Jacob was forced to run away, although his mother's ingenuity made it appear that he was merely travelling back to the country of his ancestors to get himself a wife.

On this journey, an event occurred which changed the whole course of Jacob's life. It came to him as a vision, but if its origins had not been in his own nature he would never have seen the vision or accepted its implications.

It was night, and Jacob had settled down to wait for day before continuing his journey. Putting a stone under his head, he went to sleep; and there he dreamed. He saw a "ladder set up on the earth, with its top reaching the sky," (*Gen.* xxviii. 12) and this obvious symbol of the meeting of earth and heaven was followed by a voice.

> "I am the Lord, the God of your father Abraham and of Isaac . . . All races in the earth will invoke blessings on one another through you and your descendants. I will be with you, and guard you wherever you go, until I bring you back to this land; for I will never forsake you." (*Gen.* xxviii. 13-15)

This was Abraham's vision, and that night it descended upon Jacob as the one man capable of receiving it. Jacob had stolen the birthright and the blessing, but this greater heritage from his fathers was something that could not be got by stealing. The knowledge of a God who was a shield, and of a race that would bless the whole earth through knowledge of him, could only become the possession of the man capable of receiving it; and Jacob possessed such a faculty, as he found out that night.

Whatever latent force the vision may have released in Jacob, it did not alter his nature. His first reaction was profound astonishment that the God whom Isaac worshipped should be able to appear in a place so far from home. "The Lord must surely be in this place—and I did not know it!" (*Gen.* xxviii. 16) Apparently the Lord was more universal than he had thought. The idea struck him with an unfamiliar sense of reverence, so that he was afraid and said, "How awesome is this place!" (*Gen.* xxviii. 17)

Jacob's awe did not remain with him long. To replace it came his deep-rooted instinct for a bargain, and, of more importance, his eager desire to put his dream to the test.

> "If God will go with me, and watch over me on this journey that I am making . . . so that I come home safely to my father's house, then the Lord shall be my God." (*Gen.* xxviii. 20-21)

Jacob did not have his father's capacity for unquestioning belief. He was satisfied with nothing until he had tested it; and, if the test he offered was characteristic of him, it was nevertheless in its essentials an honest one.

It did not occur to Jacob to trifle with his vision, but in other respects he remained the trickster he had been before. He was travelling to his uncle Laban's to find himself a wife, and his uncle Laban belonged to the same breed as himself. Laban cheated his sister's son with a skill and enthusiasm that were surpassed only by the skill and enthusiasm with which Jacob cheated his mother's brother.

Since the women of the household were on Jacob's side he won the contest, and succeeded in going off in the most correct manner with the larger part of Laban's possessions while his uncle was out shearing sheep. Laban went after him in hot pursuit and there is the delightful scene of their subsequent meeting, Jacob all wide-eyed innocence and Laban sunk in philosophical resignation. He knew quite well that the camels, the flocks and even the women and children belonged to him, just as he knew that somewhere in the encampment his household gods were hidden. But he also knew that there was nothing he could do about it, and he took his leave of Jacob in what must have been profound relief.

Jacob's chief worry, now that Laban was safely departed, was the question of Esau and his smouldering anger. To avoid unpleasantness, he sent messengers with many soft words to "my lord Esau" (*Gen.* xxxii. 4) from "his servant Jacob," and the messengers brought back the unsettling report that Esau was coming out to meet him with four hundred men. Esau was "a skillful hunter, a man of the open country" (*Gen.* xxv. 27) and the thought of his prompt and vengeful arrival in the company of four hundred men was too much for his brother.

Jacob was not a fighter, and never had been. His first idea was to divide his company into two parts, so that if one division were attacked the other might escape. But his second idea was worthy of Abraham, and shows clearly what had been occupying his mind in the long years since the vision.

> "O Lord, God of my father Abraham and my father Isaac. . . . I do not deserve all the acts of kindness and fidelity that thou hast shown thy servant . . . Save me, I beseech thee, from the power of my brother Esau; for I am afraid that he will come and slay me, as well as the mothers and children."
>
> (*Gen.* xxxii. 9-11)

In his terror Jacob turned almost instinctively to the highest thing he knew; but, being Jacob, he did not do it unreservedly as Abraham had done. He took the added precaution of sending out some cattle as a present to his brother, hoping that by the time Esau had made his way through the droves of camels and goats and bulls he might be more favorably disposed towards their giver.

That night Jacob sent his people across the river and remained alone in the deserted camp. There he wrestled, in his fear and his torment and his desire for the truth, with "a man." (*Gen.* xxxii. 24) For a whole night, with all the fury and passion and persistence of his tempestuous nature, he fought and would not let go, although the struggle brought him only agony. At daybreak his antagonist said, "Let me go," (*Gen.* xxxii. 26) and Jacob, who had grown out of all recognition in the long warfare, replied, "I will not let you go, unless you bless me." (*Gen.* xxxii. 26)

Jacob had left off his prayers and his bargainings. Neither weariness nor fear could persuade him to loose his hold on his antagonist. He fought; and he proposed to keep on fighting until he had wrested a blessing out of his travail. He was no longer the man who glibly promised to serve God if God would serve him. He was the man who demanded the reward of truth from the search for truth, and who intended to continue the struggle until he got what he wanted or died trying.

> "What is your name?" he said to him.
> "Jacob," he replied.
> Then he said, "Your name shall no longer be Jacob, but Israel [wrestler with God], because you have wrestled with God and man, and have been the victor." (*Gen.* xxxii. 27-28)

So Jacob won, and knew the fight had been worth everything it cost. The next morning he went out to meet Esau, and Esau ran to embrace his brother with tears in his eyes.

The warfare that Jacob began that night was continued by the sons of his race. As 'Israel,' the striver with God, Jacob was the founder of a nation that fought throughout its whole history to find God and did not let go until he was found.

This desire for the truth was the one great heritage of the house of Israel. It did not belong to the oldest son or even to the direct line. It passed to the man most capable of receiving it, as Jacob had discovered for himself. It was perhaps because of his knowledge that the inheritance was not physical that Jacob deliberately reversed the customary procedure when Joseph brought his own two sons to their grandfather to be blessed. Jacob gave the younger son the blessing that should have gone to the elder, and when Joseph tried to point out to him what he was doing, he replied serenely, "I know, my son, I know," (*Gen.* xlviii. 19) and did not attempt any further explanation.

Joseph, the product of Jacob's old age and the great love he bore Rachel, was a man very unlike his father. Temperamentally he was more like Abraham in his attitude towards God, although he arrived at it in a different way. Abraham had a strongly original and inquiring mentality, and through it came faith. Joseph had an untroubled, almost unquestioning trust in the power of God, and through that also came faith. Unlike Jacob, he always trusted God before he trusted himself, and as a result he avoided the repentances and arguments with himself that his father had undergone.

There was a definite innocence about Joseph. He was skillful in interpreting dreams, and it did not occur to him that the correct interpretation might not always be a pleasant one to hear. A fact was a fact to Joseph, to be treated as such; and the greatest fact of all was that everything belonged to God, and nothing to himself.

His brothers envied Joseph, and with good reason. Their first impulse was to kill "the dreamer" (*Gen.* xxxvii. 19) while they were out in the fields together with the flocks. Fortunately for Joseph, their hatred of him did not carry them quite to this point, and they sold him instead to some merchants who were passing through on their way to Egypt. There he was sold as a slave, and entered into the household of the Pharaoh's head steward.

This complete upheaval of his quiet country life left Joseph with his calm sense of God's friendliness towards him entirely undisturbed. He conducted himself with his usual imperturbable assurance in the house of the Egyptian and was eventually appointed superintendent of the estates, which prospered greatly under his management. His integrity pleased the Egyptian, but it was Joseph's good looks that pleased his wife. Not being a woman of much imagination, she tried to seduce him, although she should have known that Joseph was the last man to betray a trust.

> "My master . . . has committed all his property to my charge; there is no one in this house greater than I; he has kept nothing from me except yourself, and that because you are his wife. How then can I commit this great crime, and sin against God?"
>
> (*Gen.* xxxix. 8-9)

Such an answer naturally infuriated the steward's wife, and she had him thrown into prison.

In prison Joseph conducted himself in his usual manner, since, whatever harm the Egyptians might try to do him, there was a power stronger than Egyptians. His natural intelligence so endeared him to the warden that gradually all the details of prison management were left to his care, and in the end Joseph found himself in charge of the royal butler and the royal baker, two officials who had been unlucky enough to offend the ruling Pharaoh. When they dreamed, Joseph interpreted their dreams for them, with little concern for their feelings but with much accuracy. The baker was to be hanged, the butler pardoned. Two years later, when Pharaoh himself had a disturbing dream, the butler remembered the young interpreter and Joseph was ordered into the royal presence.

Joseph faced the ruler of Egypt with his accustomed calm. He was a prisoner in a land of many and powerful gods, brought out to undergo a test before which all the wise men in the kingdom had quailed; but he was not disturbed. He had never before trusted to his own talents, and he did not intend to trust to them now. "Does not dream interpretation belong to God?" (*Gen.* xl. 8) It was God, not Joseph, who would give the king his answer.

Such really splendid assurance was in the direct line of Abraham. It even overwhelmed the Pharaoh, who called Joseph the "man with the spirit of God in him," (*Gen.* xli. 38) worthy to be his deputy. It was Joseph who ruled over Egypt's supply of grain and apportioned it during the years of famine that his interpretation of the dream had foretold.

The story of Joseph's meeting with his brothers, beautifully told and worthily familiar, is characteristic of him. Forgetting the large simplicity of his point of view, his brothers expected him to take advantage of his exalted position to avenge himself. But Joseph believed that neither rank nor anything else gave one man the right to sit in judgment on another. "Can I take God's place?" (*Gen.* l. 19)

In this perfect consistency of his, Joseph was in shining contrast to his father Jacob; yet he was in no way so remarkable a man. Joseph had a conviction of the nearness and availability of God that satisfied him completely, and he felt no desire to explore the mountain tops that stretched out beyond.

Like his grandfather Isaac, Joseph was more the saint than the seeker. The weaknesses of Jacob were wholly foreign to him, but so was the strength of Jacob, the fierce desire to fight, even with God if need be, if from the struggle could be wrested truth.

It is to the credit of the narrator that he makes no attempt to conceal the faults either of Jacob or of Abraham. They were men before they were heroes, and it is as men that the stories present them. Everything that was remembered about them, evil as well as good, is presented with impartial candor. The admirable narrative style takes in its easy stride everything from Jacob's lyric love for Rachel and the agonized figure of Abraham among the hills, to the squabbles of the women in the tents and the very human cowardice of the two patriarchs on at least four different occasions.

If the narrator of the stories does not always share the spiritual illumination of his heroes, he does share their honesty. He presents them as they were, ordinary human beings who were following an extraordinary vision, and he does not try to apologize for their humanity.

As a result, the founder of the house of Israel becomes a greater man through the honesty of his historian. In view of the qualities that Jacob had to combat in his own nature—his trickery, his cowardice and his greed—the night-long battle at Peniel takes on a quality for the reader that is almost epic in its magnificence.

Jacob and Abraham, Isaac and Joseph had only one quality in common: their love of God. It was for this that the Hebrew nation gave them reverence and considered their stories worthy to be told at such length. Yet the two men to whom the nation habitually gave the greatest honor were not Isaac and Joseph, who accepted God unquestioningly, but Abraham and Jacob, who doubted and who searched. It was of the spirit of inquiry that the major heroes of Israel were made.

CHAPTER IV

I proclaim the name of the Lord.
Deuteronomy xxxii. 3

THE third great hero of the Hebrew race, and one of the greatest men in the history of the world, is honored universally as a law-giver and teacher; and to the Hebrews he was a great deliverer. But his greatest achievement was deeper and more far-reaching than these.

The whole of Moses' achievement cannot be judged only by the four books of the Bible that concern him, or by the multitude of laws that bear his name. His chief influence was a deeper and more silent one, a discovery which gave the search for God a firmer foundation than it had had before and which made a love of God and a love of truth mean the same thing to the men that followed him. It was this discovery that gaves Moses his real greatness; the rest of his career, important as it is, is secondary.

When Moses was born in Egypt, the influence of Joseph had long since been forgotten, and the rapidly increasing Hebrew population had become only a source of annoyance to the Egyptians. Even after the Hebrews were enslaved they continued to worry the ruling Pharaoh, and with one of the sweeping gestures characteristic of ancient royalty he decreed the death of all their newborn male children. It was at this time that Moses was born; and if his mother had been of a more law-abiding nature the great law-giver would not have lived to grow up. Instead, as the familiar story tells, she hid him in a cradle of reeds on the banks of the Nile, and the king's daughter who found him there adopted him as her son.

Moses was brought up as an Egyptian princeling, but at heart he remained a Hebrew. He was deeply troubled by the condition of his enslaved and laboring people, and one day, when he saw an Egyptian kill a Hebrew, he killed the Egyptian. He buried his victim in the sand and hoped that would end the matter; but the next day his sense of responsibility towards his countrymen again led him to dangerous lengths, and he interfered in a quarrel between two Hebrews. It was not in the nature of an independent Hebrew to submit to the reproof of an Egyptian princeling, however well-meant, and the man who had started the quarrel retorted hotly, "Who made you ruler and judge over us? Are you thinking of murdering me as you did the Egyptian?" (*Exod.* ii. 14) Moses, who thought the incident had gone unobserved, became thoroughly frightened; and when he heard that the royal order had gone out for his execution, he fled the country.

He went to Midian, where he was of some service to Jethro, its priest. The two men took a liking to each other, and Jethro gave the young foreigner one of his daughters in marriage, while Moses took over the care of his father-in-law's flocks. He remained in Midian a long time, outwardly quiet; but inwardly he must have been in great travail. How great the labor was can be judged by the greatness of the result. The narrative is silent on the years between, but concerning the discovery itself it is explicit.

To understand the full force of Moses' discovery on Mount Horeb, the history of his past life must be taken into consideration. Moses had been brought up in the old and wise land of Egypt, not as a commoner but as a prince; and, as such, he had been initiated into the religious mysteries that were open to the princes, since the king was the head of the priesthood. A man of his curiosity and intellectual brilliance must have learned everything that the priests were capable of teaching him, which was a great deal. At that time, and for centuries afterwards, Egypt was a storehouse of what was called 'magic' and which largely consisted, judging by the results, of the form of mental manipulation that was rediscovered in the nineteenth century and called hypnotism. Aided by the faith of the people, the priests were able to produce extraordinary phenomena; and it is almost certain that Moses must have been thoroughly acquainted with all the possibilities of mental domination, of one mind over another.

In view of his subsequent history, it is clear that this mental lore of the Egyptians gave Moses no satisfaction. To a man of his fundamental honesty, the complex priestly system of half-truths must have seemed a mental jungle in which the strong preyed upon the weak for power and profit. Since Moses had once risked his life in a rebellion against physical domination, he must have disliked even more the great Egyptian hierarchy of mental control.

If Moses had been a rebel and nothing more, he might have spent the rest of his life tending sheep in Midian. But Moses was also a son of Israel, born of the line that had set out to find God, and it was not sufficient for him merely to discover the untruth of an ancient and powerful religious system.

Moses apparently became convinced that behind the art of manipulating facts in which he had been educated there was a Fact that was incapable of manipulation, a power which could not be controlled but was itself Control. It was this conviction, whatever its origins, that came to him in full and sudden force on Horeb, the "mountain of God." (*Exod.* iii. 1)

Not until the prophet Elijah was there a man who understood Moses' discovery, the implication of the new name he had found for God. But the impact of the discovery itself was intense. There was never any doubt among the Hebrews that it was Moses who had found this new name for God, and that it was his correct name. The name was "I AM," (*Exod.* iii. 14) Existence conscious of Itself. Such a name could never stand for a man-like tribal deity, depending for respect on the power of his priestcraft. Such a name permitted the acknowledging of no other power whatever.

This was the fact that Moses succeeded in driving so deep into the Hebrew consciousness that in spite of their best efforts the people were never able to escape from it. Through Moses, they became the one people on earth with a completely monotheistic religion.

This is not to say that the Hebrews understood the name for God that Moses had given them. In its Hebrew form, Yahweh, it was used to cover many varying conceptions of God, as any other name would be so used. Nevertheless, the actual, literal force of the name remained. All Hebrews knew in a vague way that it was holy, although they might not know exactly why, and they also knew that it had originated with Moses. The patriarchs had known that God was all-powerful, but, as the narrator of *Exodus* makes clear, they had not known that he was I AM.

> "I am the Lord; I appeared to Abraham, Isaac, and Jacob as God Almighty, but did not make myself known to them by my name Yahweh." (*Exod.* vi. 3)

Moses decided that he could not teach this discovery of his to his people as long as they remained in Egypt. They needed a land of their own, the land of Canaan where the founders of the line of Israel had been born.

There they could form a nation that would stand as a living witness to the truth he had discovered, and that would learn to know the God whose existence he had established as I AM.

This was Moses' dream. The first step towards making it a reality was to deliver his people from the bondage of Egypt and persuade them to make their way into the hostile land of Canaan. Left to himself he could have done nothing, he mistrusted so profoundly his own powers as an orator. But he had within him the safety of the conviction: "Who gives man a mouth? . . . Is it not I, the Lord?" (*Exod.* iv. 11) Upheld by this confidence in something stronger than himself, Moses went back to Egypt.

The Egyptian Pharaoh was willing to grant an audience to Moses and his brother Aaron, but his refusal of their request was prompt and decisive. "Who is the Lord that I should heed his plea to let Israel go? I know nothing about the Lord, and besides, I will not let Israel go." (*Exod.* v. 2) Moses' request was obviously nothing more than an attempt to distract the men from their work, and Pharaoh gave orders to have the work made more difficult so that the Hebrews would have less time to listen to revolutionary speeches.

The Israelites were equally displeased with Moses, who seemed to have gone out of his way to get them into trouble. As for his doctrine of a new God, there was nothing so remarkable about that. Egypt was full of gods of all kinds, and one extra could make little difference. The test of any deity was the amount of power he could wield; and all that the God of Moses had accomplished was to put the Hebrews in the position of being obliged to make bricks without straw. And so "they would not listen to Moses." (*Exod.* vi. 9)

Moses was now in the position of being obliged to

prove that his God was stronger than any other power
in the world. His people had neither the willingness nor
the ability, as yet, to follow an abstract principle. They
were prepared to follow the God of Moses only if he
could produce better and more terrifying miracles than
the temple priests.

It was for this reason that Moses' proof took the form
of the old magic he had learned in Egypt. Neither the
Hebrews nor the Egyptians would have understood anything else. But he now possessed something stronger than
the old system of the priests, so that he was able to take
their magic and turn it back on them. At first the court
magicians were able to keep pace with Moses, doing
everything he did; but eventually they felt themselves
outdistanced by a force unknown to them and in a panic
gave up the contest. So complete and overwhelming was
Moses' victory that the king's one idea was to get so dangerous a magician out of the country as soon as possible.

The Israelites followed Moses out of Egypt because
he had beaten the magicians, not because they understood or wanted to understand his God. If the contrary
had been true, they might have gone direct to Canaan.
But as it was, Moses did not dare lead them into a land
full of ancient gods that could make them forget their
own. They must be kept separate from all other nations
until he had taught them his discovery. The nature worship of Canaan would not influence them once they
understood the nature of the God who was I AM, and
for forty years Moses strove to make his conception of
God as real to his people as it was to him. He tried to
give the people his own loyalty, his steadfastness, and his
desire for the truth, and even at the end of forty years
he did not know if he had succeeded. They had betrayed
him so often: they might so easily betray him again.

Moses had few illusions about his people. In leaving

Egypt, the shortest line of march would have been towards the land of the Philistines, but Moses dared not
put his faint-hearted followers to the task of fighting
their way through a hostile country. Instead, he turned
towards the desert and the Red Sea, and Pharaoh
thought he saw an excellent chance of trapping Moses
and recovering all his lost workmen. He sent after them
the best of his cavalry, and over the level sand the terrified Israelites could see the chariots of the Egyptians.
Caught between the horsemen and the sea, they set up
the wail that was to become so familiar to Moses: "Was
it because there were no graves in Egypt that you have
taken us away to die in the desert? . . . It is better for us
to serve the Egyptians than to die in the desert." (*Exod.*
xiv. 11-12)

Moses answered the frightened Israelites out of the
steadiness of his own conviction that the truth could never
be lost. "Do not be afraid. . . . The Lord will fight for you,
while you have only to keep still." (*Exod.* xiv. 13-14)
The parting of the waters of the Red Sea is attributed by
the narrator to winds, or more possibly, considering the
terrain, it was volcanic in origin. Whatever happened,
Moses was correct, and the Israelites escaped from the
Egyptians.

The song of triumph that follows is similar to Deborah's great song of victory when the Canaanites were
defeated at the river Kishon, except that the central
theme of the "Song of Moses" is not triumph, but praise.
The Lord has rescued his people unaided, and for one
reason alone: that his people might be established in the
dwelling place of the Lord.

> The place of thy abode which thou, O Lord, hast made,
> The sanctuary, O Lord, which thy hands have estab-
>   lished. (*Exod.* xv. 17)

It was for this that the Egyptians were vanquished. They had tried to prevent the founding of a nation that should find its sanctuary in God alone.

Moses soon found that the chariots of the Egyptians were not the only threat to the fulfillment of his dream, or even the major one. It was endangered primarily by the temperament of the Israelites themselves, by their lack of understanding and their very evident unwillingness to take any but the easiest road.

From the first, the followers of Moses rebelled against the discomforts of the journey. The march led through barren places, and when the Hebrews saw that they were being led away from the fish and melons of the fruitful Nile they set up a great outcry. "You have brought us into this desert, to make this whole crowd die of famine." (*Exod.* xvi. 3) Moses did not feel himself to be their leader, neither he nor Aaron. God was their leader, and it was against God they were complaining. "What are we? Your complaining has really not been against us, but against the Lord." (*Exod.* xvi. 8)

Such complaints meant that the people did not understand the reason for the journey they were making, and might as well not be making it. Moses had to establish in their mind the elementary fact that the God who had led them forth was capable of providing for them, before he could make them understand his own conviction: "It is not on bread alone that man lives." (*Deut.* viii. 3) His was a faith in God more complete even than Abraham's, and it proved to be sufficient. Every morning something appeared on the ground, fine as hoar-frost and impossible to hoard. The Hebrews had no idea what this food should be called, and they named it 'manna,' or "What is it?" (*Exod.* xvi. 15)

Among Moses' other responsibilities was that of keeping the tribes in some kind of order. At first, all matters under dispute were referred to him, and later, as the population increased, to a system of judges operating under his jurisdiction; but, to Moses, this seemed a makeshift system at best. What the people needed was not individual arbitration, but a law. If every man followed a moral code that was unchanging and the same for all, there would be no need of a series of confusing personal decisions to hold the people to the narrow path of social responsibility. It was on Mount Sinai that this conviction descended on Moses, and the result was the Ten Commandments.

Not in all the world's history is there another code as brief or as comprehensive as these ten laws of Moses. They were designed to meet a specific set of local conditions, and yet they cover with so comprehensive a sweep the whole field of human behavior that they are equally living and effective after three thousand years of change. If in some manner the last five commandments could be universally and strictly enforced, there would be no need for any other laws on the statute books. Nearly every crime against society has for its basis a transgression of one of these five: "You must not murder. You must not commit adultery. You must not steal. You must not bring a false charge against your fellow. You must not covet your neighbor's home." (*Exod.* xx. 13-17)

One of the commandments goes deeper, however, and Moses put it first. The last commandments concern a man's relationship to the world; but the first and greatest commandment concerns a man's relationship to himself, and enables him to go exactly as far as his conception of God will let him.

"I, the Lord, am your God. . . . You must have no other gods beside me." (*Exod.* xx. 2-3)

It is certain that the Ten Commandments originated with Moses, but it is much less likely that the vast body of tribal, legal, social and religious ordinances which are attributed to him by the narrator are also his work. It is obvious that most of them belong to a later order of civilization, and in any case it is improbable that Moses should have cared to institute so arbitrary and minute a set of rules. It is difficult to believe, for instance, that he decided on Mount Sinai that if an ox gores to death a female slave the master of the ox must pay thirty shekels in silver and destroy the ox. Laws like this obviously developed later, and after they had received the slow sanctification of time they were naturally attributed to the one great Hebrew law-maker.

The intricate code of priestcraft contained in the *Book of Leviticus* is also very unlike Moses. A man so quick to strike to the root of things would not have concerned himself whether a sacrificial lamb were slain to the north or the west of the altar or have expounded at such length the exact value of a dove as a peace-offering. Moses was not interested in that sort of thing. It is the priesthood whose official life depends on the theory that if an act is performed in a certain manner once it must be performed in the same manner ever after, because it is Ritual and therefore sacred.

One of the greatest of Israel's prophets, Jeremiah, firmly refused to believe that the intricate religious forms and ceremonies of *Leviticus* dated from the days of Moses.

> Thus says the Lord . . . "On the day that I brought your fathers out of the land of Egypt, I did not speak to them, nor give them any command, regarding burnt-offering or sacrifice; but this one command I gave them, 'Listen to my voice, and I will be your God, and you shall be my people.' " (*Jer.* vii. 21-23)

This is almost an echo of Moses' own voice; the *Book of Leviticus* is not.

The portable tabernacle, or ark, is more likely to have dated from the days of Moses. Its building is an integral part of the narrative, and the ark itself appears so soon afterwards in the history of Israel that it must have been built at about this time. The idea of some visible symbol for the presence of God in the midst of the camp may very well have originated with Moses, although the intricate woodwork, the pedestals of bronze, the veil of purple and fine linen and all the rest of the splendor described in *Exodus* must have come later. Such an aura of holiness grew to surround the symbol of the ark that into its innermost sanctuary only the high priest could penetrate, and that only on the yearly Day of Atonement. Since the word 'atonement' in its literal rather than its derived sense means 'at-one-ment,' the ark must have served very well as a symbol of the truth Moses was trying to teach, and it was not his fault that his symbol eventually stiffened into a formula of prescribed ritual.

Nor, for that matter, was it entirely the fault of the Hebrew priestcraft. The blame can properly be put largely on the laziness of human nature, which would much rather avoid labor and responsibility by bringing a vicarious sacrifice which can be laid on an altar than follow Moses' great commandment:

"Listen, O Israel; the Lord is our God, the Lord alone;
so you must love the Lord your God with all your
mind and all your heart and all your strength."
                                        (*Deut.* vi. 4-5)

It naturally proved to be much easier to follow a set of rules and pay a priest than to accept the great freedom of Moses' command, and with it the great responsibility.

However far Moses himself had been advancing in his

conception of God, the children of Israel were still very much as they had been when they left Egypt. The Lord was unquestionably a powerful God, and in his name their leader was able to perform many wonders; but so heavy were the demands of this God that it was proving very difficult to live up to them. They really preferred older and more comfortable deities, and as soon as Moses had gone up Mount Sinai on their unworthy behalf they hurried to his brother Aaron to demand a more visible form of worship. "Come, make us a god." (*Exod.* xxxii. 1)

With a sort of weary cynicism Aaron agreed, and made a molten bull out of their women's gold ornaments for them to worship. When Moses, in a fury, demanded an explanation, Aaron had an explanation ready that neatly absolved him of all blame. "Let not my lord's anger blaze; you know yourself how bad the people are." (*Exod.* xxxii. 22) As for the golden image itself, that was apparently quite unexpected to Aaron; he threw all the ornaments into the fire "and out came this bull!" (*Exod.* xxxii. 24) Aaron did not really care what the people chose to believe, but Moses did. If they could not understand plain speech, he would use another, and sharper, method that they could understand. He used the sword; and there was a strenuous battle in the camp before the people finally capitulated.

Although it was on Moses that the whole responsibility of the journey rested, the last thing he desired was that the people should glorify him as their leader. Joshua, his lieutenant, was greatly annoyed that some unaccredited men were prophesying in the camp, and begged Moses to put a stop to such insubordination. But Moses replied only, "Are you jealous on my account? O that all the Lord's people were prophets!" (*Num.* xi. 29)

It was through no wish of his own that Moses stood alone in his greatness, or, as the narrator puts it, that he could speak with God face to face on Mount Sinai while the people could not endure even to gaze at the brightness of his countenance afterwards. Only once did Moses glorify himself rather than God, and he counted that single slip as the greatest sin of his life. His people had come as far as Kadesh, and, finding themselves short of water, they had turned on him in their customary manner. "Why have you brought us up out of Egypt, to bring us to this wretched place, since it is no place for grain, or figs, or vines, or pomegranates, nor is there any water to drink?" (*Num.* xx. 5) At this Moses lost his temper and cried out, "Listen, you rebels; is it from this rock that we have to produce water for you?" (*Num.* xx. 10) The water came; but Moses had for one moment linked himself with God as an indispensable equal. Because of that momentary betrayal of the highest he knew, he believed that he would never reach Canaan, that he would die within sight of his Promised Land and never enter in.

When his people finally reached its borders, Moses stopped them there. He could do nothing more for them. He had offered them a great heritage, but it was not theirs unless they were willing to accept it. It was their own choice whether they would continue to regard his I AM as a tribal god whom they could leave and return to at will, or whether they understood that their God was Reality itself, and that they could betray him only at the price of their own destruction.

Moses had tried to weld his people into a nation that would hold fast to his vision, and thus be set apart for a greater destiny than any other nation had ever known. Whether they would remain so consecrated he did not know; he seems to have underestimated his own work and believed that he had failed. All he could do for them now was to give them a final reminder of his reason for having brought them out of Egypt, the oration that con-

stitutes the *Book of Deuteronomy* and is one of the greatest and saddest of farewells.

The oration in its present form is not, of course, in the
words Moses himself used. What he said was carried
many generations in the memory of the people before it
was finally put on record, and even the very well trained
Eastern memory is not infallible. But in its matchless
picture of Moses' terror for his people and his entire
loneliness, the *Book of Deuteronomy* is too close to the
probabilities to be entirely the work of another man.
Additional material was added later; but it would have required more historical imagination than the later Hebrews ever showed to have invented the whole speech of
Moses, given as he gazed over an assembly in which there
was no one to whom he could speak as an equal. They
were only children, his children; and he was reduced
to bribing them with promises of reward if they would
stay on the path he had opened before them, and to
threatening them with disaster if they failed.

Moses began his farewell with a backward look over
the past, to remind the children of Israel how consistently they had been protected in their forty years of
wandering through the wilderness. He reminded them
also how they had been dedicated and set apart from the
rest of the world; "for what great nation is there that has
a god so near as is the Lord our God whenever we call
on him?" (*Deut.* iv. 7) They had also a code of laws
unlike the rest of the world; "for what great nation is
there that has statutes and ordinances so just as all this
code that I am putting before you today?" (*Deut.* iv. 8)
This code was a kind of covenant they had made with
God as a sign of their faithfulness to him, and unless
they obeyed it they would not be worthy to inhabit the
land that the Lord had given them.

The root of this covenant was not social morality. It

was something much more fundamental to Moses, and much more difficult to obtain.

> "Listen, O Israel; the Lord is our God, the Lord alone; so you must love the Lord your God with all your mind and all your heart and all your strength."
> (*Deut.* vi. 4-5)

This command is the beginning and the middle and the end of Moses' discourse, and every word of his oration is designed primarily to drive this fact home into the minds of his audience.

In order to reinforce his command, Moses was willing to appeal even to the childish weaknesses of the people before him. As long as he had known them, they had tried to travel the path of least resistance. They liked comfort, and it was their permanent grievance against Moses that he had taken them out of the rich land of Egypt into a barren wilderness. Moses was orator enough to make capital of this failing. The Lord had now brought them to a land richer even than Egypt, where no irrigation was necessary to produce corn and olives and grapes in abundance. If they were faithful to God the land would remain fruitful; but if they went what might seem to be the easier way and worshipped the fertility gods of Canaan, the land would become barren, and the easier way would be the harder way in the end.

> "I am putting before you today a blessing and a curse · a blessing, if you heed the commands of the Lord your God . . . and a curse if you do not heed the commands of the Lord your God, but swerve from the way I am appointing you today, by running after alien gods." (*Deut.* xi. 26-28)

At this point in the discourse there is inserted a series of extremely humane and reasonable laws. Every seven years all debts shall be forgiven; after seven years the

Hebrew slave shall go free, with a reward for his services; judges shall administer real justice and not take bribes; there shall be no accumulation of wealth in the royal treasury; the property rights of others shall be respected; no servant shall be oppressed, especially if he lacks means of redress; the accidental killing of a man shall not be punished as though it were intentional; no man shall suffer for other than his own sins; and so on. This part of the discourse closes with the formula for the ritual that was used to curse the more deadly of the sins, with the people joining in the responses.

As Moses said, he had put before his people a blessing and a curse, life and death. It was their own choice which they would follow. If they obeyed the laws and remembered that their God was One, they would become a great nation; if they did not, they would be destroyed. It was no strange mystery that Moses was enjoining his people to follow.

> "For this charge which I am enjoining on you today is not beyond your power, nor is it out of reach; it is not in the heavens, that you should say, 'O that someone would ascend to the heavens for us, and get to know it for us, and then communicate it to us, so that we may observe it!' . . . No, the matter is very near you, on your mouth and in your mind, for you to observe." (*Deut.* xxx 11-14)

All that was required was a willingness to obey the first commandment, and it was this willingness that Moses had done his best to instill.

From the first moment of his revelation on Mount Horeb, Moses had labored with his people to make them a fit instrument to carry on his vision. Yet he was afraid that all his work had not been sufficient, that when temptation came his people would run after alien gods and forget all he had taught them. They had not been faithful while he lived, and he had no reason to believe **that** they would be faithful after he was dead.

Moses was obliged to leave his people now, and to leave the truth he had discovered to take care of itself. He could do nothing more to make it as precious to his people as it had been to him. He had delivered them from Egypt, he had taught them a code of laws, he had led them safely through the wilderness; but they were still not ready to learn what he was prepared to teach. He was forced to leave them now, to go out of their sight forever; but in the same way that a Hebrew father always gave his sons a blessing when he was about to die, Moses gave each of the tribes a blessing as though they were indeed his children.

Each of Israel's sons he blessed, and then to all of them together he gave a reminder and a promise.

The eternal God is a refuge,
And underneath are the everlasting arms.

(*Deut.* xxxiii. 27)

Then he went up into the mountain and left them alone, to follow the truth if they could.

CHAPTER V

"Give us a king!"
The *First Book of Samuel* viii. 6

MOSES left the Hebrews no specific form of government. His were an ordained people, dedicated to one God, and they needed no kings and ministers to tell them what to do. The symbol of Israel was the vine, and a vine can climb higher only as it clings to one object. Moses intended this one support to be God, and it was his desire that the people should trust to their highest conception of truth rather than to a hereditary throne.

There is none like the God of Jeshurun,
Throned in the heavens as your help. (*Deut.* xxxiii. 26)

It was this power he wanted them to trust, and he deliberately supplied them with no other.

It is true that Moses gave his people judges, and that some of these judges developed into powerful leaders. But the judges had no innate authority, and their position was not hereditary. The judges came from the people and returned to the people, and the power of each man extended only through his own lifetime.

Moreover, the authority of the judges, in theory at least, was based on the same conception of authority that sent Moses, fully conscious of his own personal deficiencies, to free the Israelites. "Who gives man a mouth? Is it not I, the Lord?" (*Exod.* iv. 11) If a judge received from God his courage or his wisdom, his military ability or his capacity for leadership, then the people were following what was God-given, rather than a man named Gideon or a woman named Deborah.

The Israelites were, as nearly as can be discovered, the most democratic people of ancient times, and the institution of the judges was peculiarly well suited to their temperament. The usual Oriental conception of a ruler as an all-powerful despot, wielding unchecked the power of life and death and responsible to no man, was entirely foreign to the Hebrew point of view. Each man was an individual with the full rights of an individual, and no other man was to be allowed to take them away from him.

It was a long time before the influence of the outside world succeeded in making any impression on the Hebrew conception of government; and even after a monarchy was finally established, more than one king was to learn that absolutism might be the correct form of government everywhere else but that it was not popular in Israel.

This conception of the rights and importance of the individual did not find its clearest expression in Hebrew literature until it became seriously threatened under the later developments of the monarchial system, and the great prophets and poets arose to be the spokesmen of the common people. But the doctrine taught by Moses, that a man was responsible to his God and his own highest sense of right rather than to an overlord, ran like a deep, silent river through the intervening centuries, darkened and underground for the most part but rising to the surface in stories like that of the *Book of Ruth*.

The idyll of *Ruth* is founded entirely on this sense of the worth and importance of the individual. It makes no mention of those subjects so generally beloved by the historian: the pride of rulers and the wealth of empires, the catalog of victorious generals, "the thunder of the captains and the shouting." (*Job* xxxix. 25) It was not because she was the ancestress of the great king David that Ruth is given so many pages of lovely prose; it was because she was a woman who loved another woman so dearly that the idyll of their life together is worth recording. It was not because the baby was to beget kings that his birth was important; it was because he was a living little son, and the women wanted him.

It is not often that a nation holds its common people in such esteem that it can evoke such an echo as *Ruth* from the breathing past, and bring back the voices of those long dead with such unsurpassed simplicity and precision. Regardless of when the actual story was put into writing, it is fitting that its events should have occurred in the days when the judges judged and every man did what was right in his own eyes.

It is obvious that this individualism could degenerate into complete social irresponsibility unless each individual had an equally high standard of personal righteousness. Moses intended to supply this standard when he gave the law. But this law depended in its turn upon the conception of a lawful God who was One, so that both the basis of the individual's conduct and the unity of the nation as a whole rested upon allegiance to one God.

This allegiance, human nature being what it is, was extremely difficult for the nation to maintain. It is not surprising that the Hebrews should have spent much of their time worshipping the local fertility gods of Canaan, or that it was even their custom to confuse the local Baals with their own God and to worship both impartially and even sometimes under the same name. They were farmers, heavily in bondage to the caprices of sun and rain; and nothing was more natural than that they should try to placate the natural forces that pressed in upon them so closely, rather than try to live up to the difficult demands of a God who may have seemed near to Moses but who inevitably seemed far-off and unapproachable to them.

The remarkable thing, rather, is that the nation of Israel was able to produce a series of men who grasped Moses' discovery and made it their own. The usual course of any religious discovery is that of a steady decline from the ideals of its founder, until it is either crushed out of real existence by the weight of ritual that is superimposed upon it, or becomes so hopelessly entangled in local superstitions that it ends by being a superstition itself. The reverse happened in Israel. The great men of the nation did not accept the God of Moses as a holy name to be blindly worshipped by rote. The God of Israel became instead the object of the most intense spiritual curiosity, not a deity to be accepted by faith, but a truth to be explored, each man for himself, until it was fully understood. It is the history of this exploration which is the real history of Israel. Moses' discovery was not the end of the search. It was the beginning.

It cannot be said of the judges, either as a class or as individuals, that they possessed to any great degree this spirit of inquiry. They did have, however, a very strong sense that Israel's unity and safety lay in the worship of one God, and they made it their business to see that the people never forgot this fact. It was their conviction that only in God lay safety that enabled the judges to become great military leaders. They welded the Hebrews into a fighting unit so animated by one idea that it was irresistible.

A characteristic example of this is the exploit of one of the greatest of the judges, a woman named Deborah. The tribes of Israel had been conquered by one of the kings of Canaan and were in slavery for twenty years before Deborah came and roused them. Under the public leadership of her lieutenant, Barak, who operated entirely under her orders, she organized a successful revolt against odds that anyone else would have considered hopeless and succeeded in giving her people freedom.

From the gorgeous song of war that bears Deborah's name, some idea may be gained of the faith and fury that animated the scattered and enslaved Israelites once they found something worth fighting for. In their twenty years of bondage they had been consistently and completely disarmed,

> Armorers had they none . . .
> Was shield to be seen or lance,
> Among forty thousand in Israel? (*Judges* v. 8)

while Sisera had nine hundred chariots of iron. Yet it was the rooted conviction of the children of Israel, fanned into a blaze of courage by Deborah, that even though they themselves were weak, the very stars in their courses would fight against Sisera. As the Elizabethans thanked God for the storm that routed the Armada, so the Hebrews thanked God for the storm that routed Sisera and swept away his chariots in the mighty waters of the river Kishon.

The strength of the judges lay in the fact that both they and the people were sure they had been sent of God. They might have been chosen for leaders because of their personal ability, but since it was God who had given them their ability, God was still the one ruler of Israel. Wealth or high position had nothing to do with the choosing of a judge. Gideon, for instance, was an unimportant member of the lowliest of all the tribes; yet he was so great a judge that the people begged him to become their king, so that he might continue to do good through his descendants. Gideon's answer was a characteristic and exact expression of the spirit of ancient Israel.

> "I will not rule over you, nor shall my son rule over you, since the Lord rules over you." (*Judges* viii. 23)

All the judges did not have Gideon's wisdom. There was Jephthah, who slew his own daughter to placate his conception of the Lord, and Samson, the pitiful child-giant who lived woefully but died like a hero. But not to the worst of the judges did it occur to set himself up as a king. It was the people, with their extremely human desire to imitate their rich and powerful neighbors, who decided they must have a king; and it was Samuel, last and greatest of the judges, who reluctantly gave in to them.

It was not the authority of a king that Samuel so distrusted, as Gideon had distrusted it before him. Many of the judges wielded as much power as any king. It was the fact of the royal succession he distrusted, the right of a man to inherit power from his father instead of receiving it direct from God. Royal authority is innate, and must pass from father to son instead of to the man most capable of receiving it. Yet against the old Hebrew theory of leadership the tide of popular opinion was running. Samuel was old, no worthy successor to him had been found, and the people were weary of being so unlike their neighbors. "There shall be a king over us, that we also may be like all the nations." (1 *Sam.* viii. 19-20)

Samuel did his vigorous best to change the mind of the people. He painted a vivid picture of the disadvantages of a despotic king, how he would use their sons for armorers and their daughters for cooks, how he would seize their asses and tax their vineyards, and how he would treat themselves as slaves. There could be no worse threat to independent Israel, but Samuel's eloquence was of no avail. At last he chose for them the best king he could find, a man named Saul, of the tribe of Benjamin.

Saul made a brilliant if somewhat erratic king, but Samuel's heart was sore over what he had been forced to do, and he and Saul were never happy in each other's company. The last of the judges always believed that Israel had betrayed the force that made her a unit when she decided to have a series of kings instead of acknowledging only One; and the subsequent history of Israel as a monarchy proves that Samuel was entirely right.

Saul himself had reason to regret the new monarchial system. If he had been a judge instead of a king, with a power that lasted only for his own lifetime, he could have rejoiced when a greater man than he appeared in Israel. But Saul was a king, obliged to protect the succession for his own son, Jonathan, and he was therefore obliged to hunt down David, the son of Jesse, as an enemy to the throne. It was through no wish of Saul's that this was so. It was the inevitable result of the principle of kingship against which Samuel fought in vain.

Yet in spite of all Saul's efforts, it was David who became the next king of Israel, and in all her history Israel never had a better king. He was the most successful general she ever had, the most brilliant statesman, the most honorable and humane monarch, and the best-loved human being. He was a great poet, a great musician, and a great hero. He found Israel a group of scattered tribes, and he left her a secure and prosperous nation. Yet he regarded all these achievements with so casual an air of detachment that they might have been the work of a stranger for all the credit he took to himself. David was like the judges. He believed that all power, all authority, and all honor belonged only to God.

David's first appearance at the court of Saul was at a time when the armed might of the Philistines was threatening the security of the Hebrews. The country boy was not in the least afraid of Goliath, the champion the Philistine armies had chosen. "Who is this uncircumcised Philistine, that he should taunt the battle-lines of the living God?" (1 *Sam.* xvii. 26) To David it was a self-evident fact that, "Not with sword and spear does the Lord deliver." (1 *Sam.* xvii. 47) He went out against the heavily armed giant with five pebbles and a slingshot, and won a victory for which he claimed no credit at all. Nor did he consider himself worthy to be the king's son-in-law, and was both surprised and embarrassed when Saul gave him his daughter in marriage.

Jonathan, the heir to the throne, loved David at first sight, and the story of their unfaltering friendship is one of the most beautiful in literature. But Saul listened while the women in the streets sang the young warrior's praises, and as he listened he grew rigid with fear. He, too, loved David, but his first thought had to be for the succession of his own line. The more the common people praised David, the more Saul "stood in dread of him." (1 *Sam.* xviii. 15)

At last, and in spite of all that Jonathan could do, Saul turned on his son's friend in open enmity. David was forced to escape into the hills, where his military genius at once asserted itself. He collected the nucleus of a small army from his own clan and from "everyone that was in distress, and everyone that was in debt, and everyone who was embittered." (1 *Sam.* xxii. 2) Saul pursued David and his band of outlaws with the intensity of a thoroughly frightened man, but David always managed to keep just beyond the king's reach. Twice he succeeded

in getting Saul into his own power; but where the king
would have killed David, David let the king go free,
leaving the latter to inquire in deep astonishment, "When
a man finds his enemy, does he send him away safely?"
(1 *Sam.* xxiv. 19)

David was a good lover but a very poor hater, an
aspect of his character that was later a source of much
exasperation to his own officers. He never could understand that it is deemed both proper and necessary to return evil for evil. In this case, David's courtesy had its
own reward. He heard Saul call him "my son." (1 *Sam.*
xxiv. 16) Nevertheless, David was too wise to trust himself to the king's very uncertain generosity. Saul might
fall on his neck in tears one day, but that did not mean
he would not do his best to murder his son-in-law the
following morning.

After several years of alternate dodging and headlong
flight, David finally found refuge in Gath, one of the
smaller of the Philistine cities. The king of Gath was
glad to make so excellent a fighter one of his own officers,
but David was fortunately spared through the jealousy
of the other Philistine lords from taking part in the
slaughter on Mount Gilboa, the battle between the Hebrews and the Philistines at which Saul and Jonathan
were slain.

Saul died while "the chariotry and the leaders of the
horsemen were sweeping towards him" (2 *Sam.* i. 6),
and the Amalekite who slew him brought his crown to
David, apparently expecting a reward. But David was
appalled. Political advantage meant nothing to him beside the horror of such news, and he struck out blindly
at the man who had been responsible for Saul's death.
"When one told me, 'Behold, Saul is dead,' considering
himself a messenger of good tidings, I arrested him and
executed him in Ziklag, to give him a reward for his tid-

ings." (2 *Sam.* iv. 10) He served in the same way the men who murdered Saul's one surviving son, being wholly unable to condone an act of cruelty because it led to his own advantage.

David gave the two fallen warriors, Saul and Jonathan, one of the most beautiful memorials ever written, the lovely, mournful elegy of his love and grief that is called "David's Lament." Upon the hills all the beauty of Israel has been slain. The greatest of all her heroes have fallen. May the rain never fall again upon those fields of death where the warrior's shield is forever thrown aside. For Saul and Jonathan were swifter than eagles and stronger than lions. All their lives they were beloved and lovely, and in their deaths they were not divided.

In Saul, David mourns the great king who was his father and once his friend; but in Jonathan he mourns his own lover, the man who meant more to him than any woman and who was dearer than life itself. The poem ends on a deep note of personal agony before it reverts to the slow elegiac refrain,

How are the mighty fallen! (2 *Sam.* i. 27)

There is no evidence that David sought Saul's throne for himself; but he had already been offered the kingship of the tribe of Judah, and the logic of events ultimately made him ruler over the other tribes as well. He did not seize the throne. Instead, he made a covenant with representatives of the people at Hebron, and became perhaps the first constitutional monarch in the history of the world.

David's first work as king of Israel was to weld his scattered tribes into a real nation. This task was not finished until he ultimately succeeded in forcing out of the country the Philistines, the powerful overlords of the district; but his most successful single stroke was his cap-

ture of the almost impregnable fortress of the Jebusites
that was called Jerusalem.

Capturing the town of Jerusalem was a brilliant military achievement, but it was sheer genius that prompted
David to declare it his capital city. By that one act he got
under his control the best pass into the hill country of
Palestine, he destroyed forever what hopes the Philistines
may have had of consolidating an empire of their own,
and, most important of all, he united the northern kingdom of Israel and the southern kingdom of Judah by
giving them a holy city on neutral ground where they
could worship God together. David made Jerusalem holy
by placing within its walls the ark of the covenant, and
it was the dream of his life to build a great temple in the
city also.

David's brilliance as a statesman did not make him
equally wise in the conduct of his personal affairs. One
evening at twilight when he was pacing restlessly on the
roof of his palace, he saw a woman named Bathsheba
and fell violently in love with her. It was spring and she
was very beautiful. She was also, unfortunately, a married woman, and the king was obliged to arrange for her
husband's murder in battle before he should find out
about the affair.

From the modern point of view, there can be no excuse offered for David's conduct; but the extraordinary
thing about the story, aside from the deeply human and
subtle manner of its telling, is that David and his people
also thought he had acted inexcusably. In any other
Eastern country a king might do what he pleased with
the wives of his subjects, and no one could interfere. But
in Israel the king was under the same moral law as his
most humble subject. The prophet Nathan's unsparing
condemnation of the act and David's own instant and
bitter repentance show how well aware were both king

and commoner of an ethical principle that had no parallel anywhere else in the world. The story itself remains a narrative masterpiece, from the king's restlessness the spring night when he first saw Bathsheba, to his final eager blundering into the trap Nathan laid for him and baited with the king's own generosity.

While David was quick to acknowledge his own sins, he was slow and reluctant to acknowledge the sins of others. If the king could have brought himself a little sooner to acknowledge that his handsome, unscrupulous son Absalom was capable of plotting against him, then Absalom's plot to seize the throne need not have had even a temporary success. As it was, David was forced to flee the country. He tried to dissuade the men of Gath from following him, since he had no claim whatever upon their loyalty; and from the men of Gath he received the answer he must have heard many times in the course of his life. "As the Lord lives and as my lord the king lives, wherever my lord the king shall be—whether for death or for life—there will your servant be." (2 *Sam.* xv. 21)

While David could find many excuses for his son's conduct, he had so little sense of the righteousness and worth of his own actions that he was able to accept any man's reproof without anger. As the fugitive king rode through the countryside, a relative of the long-dead Saul sprang up and let loose on David a shower of stones and curses. One of the king's retinue wanted to avenge the insult with death, and it was to this man that David gave his only reproof, if such it could be called. "What have I in common with you? . . . Let him alone." (2 *Sam.* xvi. 10-11) David would no more have thought of killing Saul's friend for his insults than Nathan for his censure.

David was a great lover; yet all his loves betrayed him. He loved Saul, and Saul became his implacable enemy. He loved Jonathan, and Jonathan died at the hands of

David's own allies. He loved Bathsheba, and for her sake he committed a sin of black treachery that was wholly foreign to his own nature. He loved Absalom, and Absalom died the death of a traitor even while David was fighting to prevent him from being killed.

There was only one love that did not play the traitor to David during the course of his troubled, magnificent career, that brought him instead such happiness that he said its presence had been to his life,

> As the light of the morning, when the sun rises,
>   A morning without clouds,
> When the tender grass springs out of the earth,
>   Through clear shining after rain.
>
> (2 Sam. xxiii. 4)

This was his love of God.

David belonged to the race of searchers that was the chief glory of Israel. He desired a knowledge of God above all things in the world. His poems show how joyful such a desire could be, and how great a reward waited for any man who could obey the commandment of Moses and love God with all his mind, all his heart and all his strength. It was because David's acceptance of this commandment was so unforced and spontaneous that he obeyed also the further command of Moses: "You must love your neighbor as yourself." (*Lev.* xix. 18)

Into his desire for God, David threw all the passion and brilliance and intensity that had made him a great poet, a great warrior and a great lover; but because it was the only love of his life that was really worthy of him, it was the only love that brought him peace.

What David did, he did with his whole soul, without caution and with no mental reservations. Since he trusted God he trusted him completely, and his "Song of Victory" is an expression of what was to him a literal fact.

> The Lord is my rock, my fortress, and my deliverer—
> My God, my rock, in whom I seek refuge,
> My shield, the weapon of my deliverance, my tower,
>   and my refuge;
> My savior. (2 *Sam.* xxii. 2-3)

From the day when David first went out in the strength
of that conviction to face the ponderous armament of a
giant with five pebbles from the brook, there was only
one power he trusted, the power of God. He once tried
to make a military census of the men in Israel and Judah,
but he always afterwards counted it a deep sin that he
should have been tempted to build protection for his
kingdom out of the number of his warriors instead of his
faith in the power of God.

David did his best to impart this shining trust to his
son Solomon, the heir to a great throne and a united
kingdom.

> "Solomon my son, learn to know the God of your
> father and serve him with a perfect heart and a
> willing mind." (1 *Chron.* xxviii. 9)

But while Solomon was pleased to accept the throne and
the kingdom, there was nothing else his father could give
him that he was able to receive.

King Solomon was subsequently well loved by the
ecclesiastical historian of *Chronicles* because he erected
the temple at Jerusalem after David's plans, but in no
other way was Solomon a credit to the man that begot
him. He inherited a wide and prosperous kingdom,
gained as much by treaties as by the sword, and lavished
so much of its wealth on his own pleasure that it began
to disintegrate during his lifetime. He inherited the
allegiance of a free people who loved his father, and
found no better use for them than to burden them with
taxes. He inherited his father's God, the most precious

of all the legacies if he had known what to do with it, and slavishly worshipped in his old age the gods his foreign wives had brought with them from their own countries. He inherited the plans for a temple at Jerusalem and fulfilled them magnificently; but he understood so little why he was erecting those walls of cedar and floors of gold that he later built an altar for Moloch and worshipped there as well.

Only once, in David, did Israel have a completely satisfactory king, because he was the only one who wore the prophet's mantle of the love of God. After David's death, his spirit of divine curiosity and trust passed from the kings of Israel to its prophets, and it was the prophets who became the custodians of Moses' name for God.

Solomon was everything that a king of the Orient was expected to be. He ate from golden plates and the ships of Tarshish brought him ivory and peacocks, his cavalry numbered twelve thousand horsemen and he made silver as common as stones in the streets of Jerusalem. But Israel had once known something better than this, and the struggle began between the kings and the prophets because she did not propose to let her monarchs rob her of it.

It was her vision that had made Israel great; and when her kings were no longer able to sustain that vision, Israel looked elsewhere for rulers.

CHAPTER VI

There arose Elijah the prophet as fire.
Ecclesiasticus xlviii. 1

THE kings of Israel were not wholly successful when they tried to establish themselves as Oriental despots. Israel was a nation unlike her neighbors, and no king could hope to reduce her to their level. When Solomon's son candidly announced that he expected to play the tyrant, he was deposed; and when a later king attempted to establish a new state religion brought over from Tyre, he stirred up such powerful and determined opposition that his whole dynasty fell.

It was Solomon who first introduced the idea of an absolute monarchy into Israel, although in so mild a form that the neighboring kings would probably not have recognized it as such. Solomon was the son of the beloved David, and the people forgave him much. But even in Solomon's reign there was discontent, with at least one case of open rebellion, and after the king's death the discontent flared into organized revolt. The people of Israel definitely refused to let Solomon's son, Rehoboam, rule over them unless he offered some kind of guarantee that he would respect the rights of his subjects and rectify the abuses of his father's reign.

What the people wanted from Rehoboam was no more than a renewal of the covenant David had made with them, but this renewal Rehoboam considered it beneath his dignity to give. The older men who had been his father's counsellors, and who knew something of the temper of the people, urged the young king to give in to them; for the men of Israel were much more success-fully led than driven. "If you will be a servant to this

people today and will serve them, and when you answer
them, speak kindly to them, then they will be your servants forever." (1 *Kings* xii. 7) But young Rehoboam
could not resist the pleasure of acting in what he conceived to be the royal manner, and in this he was sec-
onded by the courtiers of his own age who had grown
up with him. Calling the people into his presence, he
gave them his answer. "My father made your yoke
heavy, but I will add to your yoke; my father chastised
you with whips, but I will chastise you as with scorpion
stings." (1 *Kings* xii. 14)

Rehoboam's enjoyment of his newly-assumed dignity
was short-lived. Instead of creeping in humble disappointment from the royal presence, his subjects promptly
and energetically raised the standard of revolt. They had
no ancient tradition that a man must be obeyed simply
because he was a king. The divine right of royalty was
no part of their philosophy. If Solomon's son would not
agree to their charter he was no king of theirs, even
though repudiating him meant repudiating the line of
David as well. King Rehoboam made one desperate attempt to assert himself; but the people stoned his deputy
to death, and "Rehoboam leaped into his chariot and
made off for Jerusalem." (1 *Kings* xii. 18)

The fugitive king was safe in Jerusalem; for Jerusalem was in the southern kingdom of Judah, and Judah
had never wavered in her almost emotional loyalty to the
house of David. But it could hardly have been a source
of much satisfaction to Rehoboam to feel that by his
general stubbornness he had lost half his kingdom and
destroyed any further possibility of a united and powerful Hebrew nation. He had split into two parts the kingdom that David had made one, and it was never re-
united.

The northern kingdom of Israel chose for her ruler an
Ephraimite named Jeroboam. The new king had rebelled

against Solomon in his youth and had lived for years as
a political exile in Egypt; and the people undoubtedly
hoped that a man who had himself struggled against
despotism would make them an ideal king. So it might
have been if their struggle for liberty had sprung from
nothing more fundamental than a general dislike of
tyranny. But the intense individualism of the people did
not come originally from any political conviction. It had
its roots in Moses' first commandment: "You must have
no other gods beside me." (*Exod.* xx. 3) You must have
no other ruler, no other authority, but One.

It is the fate of most religious principles that they
acquire a symbol; and the symbol may become so inextricably associated with the principle in the minds of
ordinary people that it ends by being substituted for it.
The symbol of Oneness in this case was the ark of the
covenant, which David had housed permanently in Jerusalem as one of the first acts of his reign. By the time a
temple had been built to shelter the ark, Jerusalem had
definitely become a holy city, and the idea of one God
had become firmly associated in the popular mind with
the idea of one temple. This confusion of the symbol
with the fact might not have greatly pleased Moses, but
it did at least serve to keep continually before the people
his conception of one God, the conception which a constant pressure of alien religions upon the Hebrews made
it only too easy to forget.

It is doubtful if Jeroboam, the new king of the northern kingdom of Israel, understood the fundamental truth
that lay behind the symbol of the ark and of a single place
of worship. All he could see was that it was highly in-
expedient from a political point of view that his people
should have acquired the habit of worshipping in a city
that now belonged to a rival king. "If this people go up
to make sacrifices in the temple of the Lord in Jerusalem,
then will the heart of this people return to their lord,

even to Rehoboam, king of Judah; and they will slay me, and return to Rehoboam, king of Judah." (1 *Kings* xii. 27)

To avoid so personal a catastrophe. Jeroboam took a step that must have seemed to him both intelligent and pious: he established some equally good altars in his own kingdom at which the people might worship. He put one altar at Bethel and one at Dan, and, since he could hardly supply another ark he gave his subjects two calves of gold, one symbol being quite as good as another to his practical mind.

The result was inevitable. Surrounded as they were by rich and important nations who believed as a matter of course in many gods, it had always been difficult for the average Israelite to remember the basis of all Moses' teachings:

"The Lord is our God, the Lord alone." (*Deut.* vi. 4)

As long as the symbol of this principle remained one, the people were able to keep to at least the letter of the law; but as the symbols began to vary and multiply they almost inevitably began to carry with them the idea of a multiplication of gods.

This multiplication would not have occurred if the majority of the Hebrews had made any effort to discover the God of Moses for themselves instead of worshipping him by rote. But the majority of the Israelites, like majorities anywhere, were content to let the properly constituted authorities do their thinking for them and to follow in religious matters wherever they were led. They were led to the ark, and they worshipped the ark. They were led to two golden calves, and they worshipped the calves. The ark had at least the sanction of Moses and the spiritual fact of Oneness behind it, but the calves were based on nothing more important than religious and political expediency. The symbol had already been confused with the fact, and it was only a step from many altars to many gods. It was for this reason that the later prophets of Israel so bitterly opposed the "high places."

The subsequent kings of Israel followed the religious precedent that Jeroboam had established, and time softened what had first been a startling innovation into a generally accepted orthodoxy. If the later rulers had been content with nothing further, they might have avoided many difficulties; but in an unlucky moment one of their number, King Ahab, took the final step and began to erect state altars for the worship of another deity entirely.

Ahab had married a foreign princess, Jezebel of Tyre, and she had brought with her from her own country an altar to the Tyrian Baal whose name was Melkart. Since the days of Solomon, most of the kings' wives had been foreigners, with their own foreign gods, and if Jezebel had been content to worship her Baal in private and leave Israel alone, nothing would have happened. But Jezebel, unfortunately, was a religious fanatic, firmly resolved that Israel should be taught to worship Melkart even if it meant killing off half the population.

With the unscrupulous cruelty that so often goes with religious zeal, Jezebel entered into a violent campaign on Melkart's behalf. She undertook a wholesale murder of the priests and prophets who constituted the opposition and succeeded in reducing the people to a state of terrified indecision, wavering unhappily between their old loyalty to the God of Moses and their extreme fear of the queen.

It was at this point in Israel's history that one of the greatest of her men appeared: Elijah the prophet. He had no political or military power, no authority, no soldiers.

He had only the conviction that Jezebel was trying to destroy the very life of Israel, faith in one God, and he set himself as resolutely against the danger as though he had fifty legions behind him.

Elijah succeeded in starting an avalanche that overwhelmed both the Tyrian Baal and the royal dynasty, and he succeeded because his determination was more than a match for Jezebel's. He fought her in the way of her own choosing, and defeated her with her own weapons.

Elijah as the public champion of Israel appears many times in the *Book of Kings*. Only twice does a different aspect of the prophet appear, the Elijah who fought a silent, secret battle and won through to a victory more important than any other in the Old Testament. It was not this aspect of his character that interested the historian of *Kings*. The spectacular champion of Israel against Jezebel and Melkart, the mighty hero who defied a queen and conquered the priests of the Tyrian Baal, was naturally of more interest to any historian than the lonely seeker after truth who found only one disciple to understand him.

The life of Elijah as recounted in the *Book of Kings* is extremely difficult reading. The whole account is abrupt, inadequate and confusing, and it is important that the point of view of the writer should be considered if the prophet is to emerge as a recognizable human being.

It is clear that the author of *Kings* did not mean his book to be an exhaustive history of the period. After the discussion of any given reign he habitually refers his readers to other books on the same subject that would give them additional information, source-books like the *Annals of the Kings of Israel*, the *Annals of the Kings of Judah* and the *Book of the Acts of Solomon*. All these books he expected his readers to use are now lost, and among them there must have been a *Life of Elijah*, since lost also but well-known at the time, from which the historian selected as he selected from the *Acts of Solomon*. There is no other explanation to account for Elijah's lack of ancestry, together with his abrupt appearances and equally abrupt disappearances, except the fact that the historian did not consider himself a biographer. He was writing against a background of common knowledge, and felt himself free to select from Elijah's life only those particular episodes that suited his purpose.

So great a man as Elijah deserves a more complete and careful account of his life than the fragmentary paragraphs in *Kings*, which confuse his character more often than they illumine it. It is not wholly impossible to reconcile the man who slew the five hundred prophets of Baal with the man who held with such love a dead child in his arms, since anyone who had Jezebel for an enemy was forced to resort to violent methods. But it is deeply to be regretted that the historian of *Kings* did not make a fuller use of his sources while they were still available.

Elijah appears most frequently in *Kings* as the warrior prophet whose influence finally overthrew Ahab's dynasty, since from the historical point of view this was his greatest contribution to the history of Israel. Yet the warfare he inaugurated was not primarily physical, in spite of the bloodshed. It was a war to gain the allegiance of the people, Elijah's influence in Israel against Jezebel's, his God against hers. The unlucky king Ahab was neutral; that is to say, he had an awed respect for both his wife and the prophet who opposed her, and hastily agreed with whichever one was nearer.

The story opens with a severe drought in the land which it was believed Elijah himself had caused. The king had spent three years searching for his troublesome subject, hoping that if Elijah could be disposed of the drought would come to an end. At the end of the third year the prophet entered the king's presence of his own accord, and calmly proposed a trial of strength between himself and the prophets of Baal on Mount Carmel, with all the people of Israel to act as witness. Each side would attempt to call down fire from heaven, the ancient and accepted sign of the response of a deity to his worshippers.

When all the people had gathered together at Mount Carmel, Elijah made a preliminary attempt that throws a strong light on his character. He tried to persuade the people to trust to their own powers of reason instead of to the superstitious belief that demanded miracles from heaven. As reasonable men they ought to be able to decide for themselves which was the true God, instead of being swayed by 'signs'; and Elijah apparently would have greatly preferred to reach them through their intelligence rather than through their religious awe. "How long are you going to limp upon two diverse opinions? If the Lord be God, follow him, but if the Baal, follow him." (1 *Kings* xviii. 21)

This was intelligent advice, too intelligent for the people to accept. They remained silent; and Elijah, like Moses, was left with no resource but to appeal to them in the only way they could understand.

The contest Elijah had arranged was strictly fair, except for the disproportion in numbers that left him alone to face four hundred and fifty prophets of Baal. Their turn came first, and they spent most of the day in a frantic but unsuccessful effort to call down fire from heaven on the unlighted altar. They cried upon the name of their god, they slashed themselves with knives and lances to work up the correct prophetic frenzy, they shouted and called and prayed; and behind them stood

the imperturbable Elijah, suggesting to the frantic prophets that their Baal must have gone travelling "or perhaps he is asleep." (1 *Kings* xviii. 27)

The God of Israel never slumbered or slept; and Elijah
was so sure of that fact that he saw no reason to work
himself up into the frenzy of the priests of Melkart.
When his own turn came, he soaked the altar and the
ground around it with water, convinced that if a sign
were needed a sign would come; and fire consumed not
only the sacrifice on the altar but the water itself. Then,
on a strict and needful basis of justice, the prophets of
Baal were killed as so many of the prophets of Israel had
been.

There still remained the drought. Elijah told the king
that he heard "the rushing sound of rain" (1 *Kings*
xviii. 41), but the sky remained cloudless. Nevertheless,
Elijah's faith was not of the kind that depends on outside
circumstances for support, and the fact that there was
no indication of rain in the sky did not alter his conviction that the drought was over. He ascended Carmel and
told his servant to go and look towards the sea; and the
servant came back to say there was not a cloud in the
sky. Elijah told him to look again, and six times the
servant came back to say there was nothing to report. The
seventh time he reported that a little cloud had come up
over the horizon. It was "as small as a man's hand," (1
Kings xviii. 44), but Elijah sent him down to tell Ahab
to harness up his chariot before the rain should prevent
his departure.

Elijah, of course, must have had some definite foundation for so colossal and unshakable a faith, and whatever it was that he trusted so unreservedly did not betray
him. "In a very short time the heavens grew black with
clouds and wind, and there was a great downpour." (1
Kings xviii. 45)

Jezebel was not one to take the loss of her four hundred and fifty prophets lightly, and she set out at once to kill the prophet who had conquered them. Elijah escaped into Beersheba, but he found himself weighed down by an almost unendurable sense of isolation. He was the only champion of God left in Israel, and apparently a useless one. "I, even I only, am left, and they are seeking to take away my life." (1 *Kings* xix. 10)

The lifting of Elijah's despair came on Horeb, the mountain of Moses. There he realized that there were thousands of other men in Israel who had remained faithful to the idea of one God, that a successor to the throne better than Ahab would arise, and that he himself would find a disciple to carry on his work. The historian gives this revelation in a different sequence, since the question of the royal succession naturally came first with him; but it is clear enough which answer came first with Elijah. He was not alone. He had no need to make God's honor his personal responsibility. Whatever the majority might do, there were still faithful men in Israel who would worship the God whose name Moses had discovered on Mount Horeb.

Elijah's next public appearance in *Kings* again represents him as the champion of Israel against Jezebel. As he had already stood for the idea of one God against many Baals, he now stood for the native idea of the people's rights against the foreign idea of the inalienable right of kings.

It happened that there was a vineyard near the palace that King Ahab wanted to buy and turn into a vegetable garden. He offered the owner, a man named Naboth, a fair price for the land or a better vineyard; but Naboth stood firm on his yeoman right to the land of his fathers and refused to sell. It did not occur to the king of Israel to force the land from his subject as a king of Tyre

would have done, but he sulked over the matter so visibly
that his wife finally asked what was troubling him. The
princess of Tyre was really shocked that a king should allow a mere subject to come between himself and his de-
sires, her convictions being as pronounced concerning
the divine right of kings as concerning the divine right
of Baals. She at once arranged to have Naboth officially
murdered through the use of bribed witnesses, and tri-
umphantly handed over the disputed vineyard to her
husband.

The unlucky Ahab had none of his wife's illusions
about the privileges of royalty in the kingdom of Israel;
and when Elijah appeared before him with an open
threat the king "lay in sackcloth, and went about quietly." (1 *Kings* xxi. 27) The king was frankly frightened
of Israel and her prophets, although he made a pathetic
attempt to banish his misgivings by gathering around his
person four hundred private prophets and making them
agree to prophesy only what he wished to hear.

With the exception of the curious story of Ahaziah's
captains, which cannot be explained on the basis of any
of the information available in *Kings*, the episode of the
vineyard was Elijah's last political appearance. In the
public life of the nation he was a great man and an influential one, although it cannot be said that his attempt
to institute social and religious reforms in the kingdom
was permanently successful. The governmental abuses
which the story of Naboth illustrates—the corruption of
justice in favor of the rich and the persistent draining
away of the rights of the individual—later became a
definite policy in the court circles according to the accounts of men like Amos. Ahab's dynasty might fall, but
the royal houses that followed were not an improvement
on it.

Nor were Elijah's efforts at religious reform much

more successful. Jehu, his personal choice for ruler, finally succeeded in destroying all the priests and followers of the Tyrian Baal in one of the bloodiest religious wars in history; but no amount of bloodshed could bring the nation back to unity of thought, any more than it could succeed in making Israel's rulers into enlightened constitutional monarchs. The days of a covenant between king and people were definitely over, and the only covenant upon which the individual could really rely was the covenant his ancestors had made with God.

It was in the fulfillment of this private covenant, born of a desire to know God, that Elijah accomplished something of more importance than all the achievements of his public career put together. The historian of *Kings* had very little concern with this aspect of the prophet's nature. Only twice does his book mention the man who searched for God. But these two allusions illuminate the inner life of Elijah like a flash of lightning, and make it clear why the Jews later regarded him as one of the greatest of their prophets, second only to Moses in stature.

The first of these two stories took place during the time of the three-year drought, while Elijah was staying at the house of a widow and her son in Zarephath. The child died, and his mother believed that the Lord had killed her son to punish her for her sins. She had him clutched to her breast when Elijah said, "Give me your son." (1 *Kings* xvii. 19) The prophet took the child and carried him upstairs to his own room, where he laid him upon the bed.

To understand the exact force of what the prophet did then, it is enlightening to compare his action with that of another great man who loved God as much as Elijah ever could. King David had a little son who became desperately ill, and David pleaded with God to be merciful and not take his child away from him. For seven days he prayed, refusing food and lying on the ground in sackcloth. If ever a prayer availed it should have been David's, uttered out of the depth of his great need and his loving trust in God.

On the seventh day, the child died. David's attendants were afraid to tell him what had happened, for fear of what he might do; but the king did nothing. "While the child was yet alive, I fasted and wept; for I said, 'Who knows whether the Lord will show himself merciful to me and let the child live?' But now he is dead; why should I fast? Can I bring him back again? I expect to go to him, but he will never come back to me." (2 *Sam.* xii. 22-23) No man had greater faith in the power of prayer than David, but the child was dead.

Elijah also loved a child, and the child died. David resigned himself to the fact that God had killed his son, but Elijah did not resign himself. He looked at the child on the bed and was shaken by a great wave of disbelief, so that he cried out in fierce incredulity: "O Lord, my God, hast thou also brought evil upon this widow, with whom I am staying, by slaying her son?" (1 *Kings* xvii. 20)

According to the best religious principles that Israel possessed such a question was blasphemy. Every great Hebrew, from Abraham to King David, reverently believed that God was the author of evil as well as of good, of death as well as of life. The correct attitude towards bereavement was the one expressed by Job at the beginning of his misfortunes:

> The Lord gave and the Lord has taken away;
> Blessed be the name of the Lord. (*Job* i. 21)

The prophet Elijah did not take the correct attitude. For one radical moment he refused to believe that his God was a bringer of evil and a murderer; and in that moment of fierce disbelief he achieved what King David had not been able to achieve by all his loving and reverent prayers. The child lived.

What was the origin of Elijah's sudden doubt it is impossible to say. The historian of *Kings* had no interest in the one quality that made Elijah great, and the story as he presents it stands isolated in the text without explanation or connective. All that is clear is that Elijah, the prophet whose name means in Hebrew 'My God is I AM,' once refused to believe that God was the author of death, and out of that disbelief raised a child to life.

Following this story is the political activity so dear to the historian of *Kings*, and then the subject of the conquest of death suddenly reappears. The last story told of Elijah is of his translation.

The narrative is presented on a curious note of sustained tension. Everyone knows that something is about to happen, although no one knows exactly what. The members of the prophetic guilds in Bethel and Jericho repeatedly tell Elisha, Elijah's single disciple, that he is about to lose his master, and Elisha answers them all desperately in the same words. "I know it. Hold your peace." (2 *Kings* ii. 3) He clings to his master with a tenacity that not even Elijah can break. "As the Lord lives and as you yourself are alive, I will not leave you." (2 *Kings* ii. 6)

The relationship between the two men was evidently very close, and no outsider felt at liberty to break in upon it. The men of the prophetic guild stood together at one side of the river Jordan, and the two prophets crossed the river alone. There Elijah stopped short and said to his disciple, "Ask, what I shall do for you, before I am taken from you." (2 *Kings* ii. 9)

Elisha had only one wish, to be like his great master.

"Let there be now a twofold share of your spirit upon
me!" (2 *Kings* ii. 9) "You have asked a hard thing," (2
Kings ii. 10) said Elijah, and then made a remarkable
statement, "Still, if you see me as I am being taken from
you, so shall it be with you; but if not, it shall not be so."
In other words, if Elisha could understand what Elijah
was going to do, his master's spirit would have descended
upon him.

If Elisha understood what happened next, certainly no
one else did. The historian of *Kings* reports picturesquely
that "suddenly a chariot of fire and horses of fire separated the two of them; and Elijah went up by a whirlwind to heaven." (2 *Kings* ii. 11) The fifty prophets on
the other side of the Jordan also thought that a high
wind was the only explanation, and they begged Elisha
to let them organize a searching-party. He finally gave
in to them, but when they returned empty-handed he
said, "Did I not say to you, 'Do not go'?". (2 *Kings* ii.
18)

Elijah's mantle had descended upon Elisha, and with
it an unconquerable faith in his great master. Armed
with this faith, Elisha was able to do to a certain extent
what Elijah had done, in a kind of reflected glow from
the greater prophet. It was apparently not on faith in
God that Elisha based his achievements. It was on faith
in Elijah.

The noblest example of this faith is the exquisitely
told story of the woman of Shunem. She was a very great
lady, with her courage and her courtesy and her unwavering faith in a power she only dimly understood. When
her only son was carried in from the harvest fields, dying, she held him in her arms until noon. Then she went
up to the room she had set aside for Elisha and laid the
boy on the empty bed, closing the door behind her. She
said to her husband quietly, "It is all right," (2 *Kings* iv.

23) and went out in search of the prophet. Her faith was very great, and so was his; and, between them, the child lived.

Elijah found only one disciple to follow him, and Elisha, though he spent much time with the prophetic guilds, found none at all. The only heritage that was left of the two men was a book of contradictory stories and a superstitious reverence for Elisha's body, which was once supposed to have revived a dead Moabite.

The story of Elijah would be capable of no explanation whatever if the matter of the conquest of death had ended there. But it did not. The prophets of Israel who followed Elijah began to teach of a time when God would destroy,

> The veil that veils all the peoples,
> And the web that is woven over all the nations—
> He will destroy death forever. (*Isa.* xxv. 7-8)

This destruction was to take place on the great "Day of the Lord," the day when God would be fully known.

Each prophet bent his strength to bring that day nearer, until a prophet came at last who knew God fully. This prophet conquered death. A whole new religion, in fact, was established on the basis that "death could not control him," (*Acts* ii. 24) and the whole of the New Testament unites to bear witness to this fact.

It is in the career of Jesus of Nazareth, not in the disjointed and fragmentary stories of the *Book of Kings*, that corroboration must be found for the reality and magnitude of Elijah's achievement.

CHAPTER VII

Where there is no vision, the people perish.
The Book of Proverbs xxix. 18

WHEN the kingdom of Israel grew quiet again after
Jehu's revolution, she was well on her way to becoming
a prosperous and successful nation. Her two great enemies, Egypt and Assyria, were too much occupied with
difficulties of their own to threaten her with war, and the
revival of trade over the caravan routes and across the
Red Sea had opened up the possibility of a mercantile
wealth greater than any since Solomon's. The country
had given up any attempt to re-establish a theocratic
form of government and was proud of a series of able
kings; a substantial merchant class and an aristocracy
had arisen to take the place of the more primitive institution of small land-holders with equal rights; and the religious institutions of the country were flourishing and
well-supported. Israel was fat, and she was bland, and
she was prosperous, a nation like other nations.

Or so it appeared on the surface. In actual fact, Israel
could never be a nation like other nations. She was the
"striver with God," dedicated not to material prosperity
but to a passionate, lonely search for the truth. Israel's
own nature would not allow her to play the traitor to
herself. The teachings of Moses were uncomfortable and
difficult to follow, but there was a quality in Israel that
made her still more uncomfortable when she was not following them. She was a nation with a conscience.

The spokesmen of this conscience were the prophets,
not the professional seers who went around in organized

groups and prophesied for cash, but the great line of philosophic poets born of the nation's deep but otherwise inarticulate desire for God. For two centuries they appeared, one after the other, and their work is one of the chief glories of the world's literature.

Only Israel could have produced men like the prophets. She was the one nation that wanted, not a state deity, but the truth; and it was because the greatest of the prophets were content with nothing less that they surpassed each other in the steadily widening search. From the first of them to the last they were the direct product of Moses' command: "You shall love the Lord your God with all your mind and with all your heart and with all your strength." Israel had always clung to this ideal, but never more tightly than when it seemed, in the days of her prosperity, to be most seriously threatened.

By any civilized standards except her own there was nothing wrong with Israel's prosperity. It was true that the wealth of the upper classes had been acquired largely at the expense of the farming population, who had seen their land gradually being taken away from them to be incorporated in large estates; but this was considered, especially by the upper classes themselves, to be a sign of progress and the development of a more centralized state. As for Israel's religious condition, that was agreed to be above reproach. The temples were thronged and the people in a most admirable state of piety. Every morning they brought sacrifices to the altars, and every three days their tithes.

Nothing could have been a more profound shock to the community than the appearance of a commoner named Amos who told the country to its face that its religious observances were worse than useless, and that the only offering which would find favor in the sight of God was justice and national decency.

This man who took all political and religious official-
dom for his antagonist was by trade a shepherd and a
dresser of sycamores. He said he was not a prophet, by
which he meant a member of one of the professional
prophetic guilds. He was a son of Israel, and his God
could not be bought and sold across an altar.

Amos declared that the only way in which a God of
righteousness could be worshipped was by righteousness,
and that if the people tried anything else they were de-
ceiving themselves. They were putting their trust in a
future Day of the Lord, but when it came they would
find it a day of terror instead of joy, because they had
never striven to know God aright but had been content to
cheat their neighbors and then to buy absolution with a
temple sacrifice. It is not surprising that Amos was unpopular. He made it his business to tell Israel that her
present standard of business, social and religious morality would mean national ruin unless it was promptly and
drastically changed.

The standard which Amos denounced was the inevitable one of sudden prosperity. A man was judged by his
outward success rather than by his inward worth, being a
wise man if he were rich and a good man if he supported
the temple. If he could add to his wealth by making a
few preliminary arrangements with the judge in a law-
suit or by trading off the worst of his grain first, this was
only a sign that he was a clever man and deserved to succeed. And if he could earn enough to build himself a palace of stone and take his ease on a couch of ivory, the
exact manner in which he had gained his wealth did not
greatly matter. It was enough that he was a rich, a
powerful, and therefore a worthy citizen.

Amos wrote his book to deny that a man could shelter
himself behind success. However he might try to surround himself with the safeguards of wealth and posi-

tion he was still an individual, still directly responsible to the God "who tells man what is his thought." (*Amos* iv. 13) No amount of public success could alter the fact that the man who played the cheat in Israel was trifling, to his own ultimate destruction, with an ethical principle that was unchanging: God himself.

The *Book of Amos* is written in the usual prophetic manner, in the first person and in the name of God. Even the least of the professional prophets prefaced his addresses with "Thus says the Lord," and Amos, who possessed a really great vision, could hardly do less. The book is also written in poetry, which was the characteristic medium of Hebrew prophecy; and it has the kind of timelessness which comes partly from the perennial youth of all good writing and partly from the fact that the sins of Israel have been shared by every other prosperous nation on earth.

The sins against which Amos hurled himself were not, he knew, common to Israel alone, and his book opens with a denunciation of all the nations. Yet it is on Israel that the heaviest responsibility must fall, since Israel is the only nation who had already been taught that God is a righteous God.

> "You only have I known,
>   Of all the families of the earth;
>   Therefore, will I punish you
>   For all your wrongdoing." (*Amos* iii. 2)

The other nations could not betray what they had never known, but Israel knew and therefore betrayed. Her very zeal for religious observances was a transgression, since the poor man had been robbed of his wheat and the innocent man condemned in the courts. As long as this kind of thing continued, there was no merit in crowded temples and laden altars.

"I hate, I spurn your feasts,
And I take no pleasure in your festal gatherings . . .
Take away from me the noise of your songs,
And to the melody of your lyres I will not listen.
But let justice roll down like waters,
And righteousness like a perennial stream."
(*Amos* v. 21-24)

The nation has forgotten its love of truth and turned instead to love of gold. Its great men lie at their ease and lead gracious lives, eating the finest calves and anointing themselves with the most precious oils. They compose beautiful songs as David did, "but they are not heart-sick for the breach of Joseph." (*Amos* vi. 6) They look on willingly while the poor man is being destroyed, and because of this they shall go into exile, "and the shout of the revellers shall pass away." (*Amos* vi. 7) Those who should have led Israel have betrayed her, and in so doing they have brought about their own destruction.

There was nothing at all arbitrary about the judgment Amos foresaw. A law had been broken, and the consequences were as inevitable as the attempt to defy any other natural law.

Does a bird fall to the ground, unless there be a snare
    for it?
Does a trap rise up from the ground, when it has
    taken nothing at all? (*Amos* iii. 5)

If Israel is destroyed, will it not be because she has forsaken God?

Amos was right, of course. It was Israel's vision that had made her great, and if she betrayed her vision she would lose her greatness. She might still seem to be rich and impregnable, but her palaces and gardens and vineyards were only a splendid shell masking the hidden corruption within. At the first pressure from an outside power they would crumble, as Amos knew. He wrote his book in a desperate attempt to expose the dishonesty and hypocrisy that were being practiced in Israel under the name of good business and good religion before it was too late.

The prophet's warning was not successful, and in the nature of things could not be. It is easy now to see that Amos was right, since everything that he feared for his country actually occurred; but it was less easy in the days of apparent safety and prosperity in which he wrote. All he gained was thorough dislike, since the popular mind naturally ignored the great ethical conception on which his argument was based and saw in Amos only a trouble-maker who threatened the citizens of Israel with exile from their own land. Along with every other great prophet, Amos found that

> They hate him who reproves in the gate,
> And loathe him who speaks the truth. (*Amos* v. 10)

Amos could offer his people very little comfort. It was only the few who had held themselves steady and un-moved under Israel's prosperity that might expect safety, and he promised that these men would eventually return to rebuild the ruined cities that corruption had torn down and to share a prosperity that would be based on right-eousness and therefore not subject to decay. Yet before this happened there would be a famine in the land, the most terrible that Israel would ever be called upon to bear.

> Not a famine of bread,
> Nor a thirst for water,
> But for hearing the words of the Lord.
> And they shall wander from sea to sea,
> And run from north to east,
> To seek the word of the Lord;
> But shall not find it. (*Amos* viii. 11-12)

Amos had a clear understanding where the people had

erred, but the prophet who followed him had a clearer. Amos assailed the symptoms of decay, but Hosea assailed the cause. Amos accused Israel of having broken the Law that was One, but Hosea knew that such a thing could never have happened if the idea of Oneness had not itself become adulterated.

It was for this reason that Hosea centered his attack squarely upon the multitude of altars that had grown up over the land. Amos mentions them only in passing, but to Hosea they were the very root of the difficulty.

As has been said before, the golden calves set up by Jeroboam I as a political expedient, to keep his people from worshipping at Israel, had been the origin of much religious confusion. The God of Moses was still nominally worshipped at these and other shrines; but when Hosea was writing, in the reign of Jeroboam II, the images put up in honor of God were being treated almost as if they were gods themselves. They were kissed as worshippers kissed the feet of Baals, and all the piety and wealth of the land were lavished on newer and more splendid altars.

> Israel is a spreading vine;
> His fruit renders him confident;
> The more his fruit increased,
> The more altars he made;
> The more prosperous his land became,
> The finer did he make his sacred pillars. (*Hos.* x. 1)

Hosea understood perfectly that all this was being done with the best of intentions; but he knew also that through it the idea of one God was becoming so adulterated in the land that it hardly existed at all. Nominally the Israelites were still worshipping the God of Israel, but actually, as Hosea says, they were calling him Baal. Such ignorance of the nature of God might be well-meant, but it constituted a deadly danger to Israel. If Hosea had gone no further than this he would still be a great prophet. But Hosea did not stop with Amos' conviction that God was a Law which to break meant destruction. God was more than a Law. He was a Love that would eventually draw Israel back to himself in spite of all her transgressions. However Israel might stumble along darkened ways she would eventually find the light, and her very losses would become the means of her ultimate salvation.

Hosea opens his book with this conception of God, expressed with clearness and beauty in the emblem of the harlot. God's love for adulterous Israel is acted out in symbolism when the prophet takes for himself an adulterous wife. The first child of the union is named Jezreel, the town where Naboth was slain by royal tyranny and where Jezebel was killed in savage retaliation. The second child is named Lo-ruhamah, "She-who-is-unpitied"; "for I will not again have pity upon the house of Israel, that I should ever forgive them." (*Hos.* i. 6) The third child is called Lo-ammi, "Not-my-people"; "for you are not my people, and I am not your God." (*Hos.* i. 9) These three names were the three consecutive steps in the spiritual disaster that Hosea was able to recognize where Amos saw only a moral and political danger.

Yet Hosea was convinced that God's love could never really be turned away from Israel, and, by the very impulsion of this fact, Israel could never really be turned away from God. As in the emblem of the harlot, she might go whoring after her lovers, sure that it was they who gave her corn and wine and oil and silver and gold; but God, her one true husband, would hedge her path with thorns so that she could not find them. At last she would grow weary of searching for what she cannot find,

> And she shall say, "I will go back to my first husband,
> For it was better with me then than now."
>
> *(Hos.* ii. 7)

Israel's punishment will come when she learns that it was
God who gave her all her glory, and that her festivals,
her sabbaths and her ritual feasts will avail her nothing
for her sin of not having understood God. When she
realizes this, she will be "as in the days of her youth,"
(Hos. ii. 15) in her bridal days when she first came up
out of Egypt.

> "In that day it shall come to pass," saith the Lord,
> "That you will call me, 'My husband,'
> And you will no longer call me, 'My Baal.' "
>
> *(Hos.* ii. 16)

As for the harlot's children, with their tragic names of
estrangement, their names will be changed.

> "And I will pity 'Her-who-is-unpitied';
> And I will say to 'Not-my-people,' 'You are my
> people';
> And he shall say, 'My God.' " *(Hos.* ii. 23)

Hosea's conviction, set forth so beautifully under the
emblem of the harlot, that the love of God was sufficient
to draw all Israel back to himself, is the cornerstone of
all the prophet's work. It is the first thing in his book,
and it is also the last. But Hosea did not intend his book
to be a comfort to the already overly satisfied citizens of
Israel. He intended it for a direct reproof; and most of
the book consists of a clear explanation to Israel of the
fact of her own harlotry.

The reason for Israel's coming downfall is that she
never really understood the God she worshipped at her
multitude of altars. "My people are destroyed for want
of knowledge." *(Hos.* iv. 6) For this state of affairs the

priestcraft is at least partly responsible, since its members have grown wealthy on the people's ignorance. Their numbers have increased, but their spiritual perception has not.

> "The more they increased, the more they sinned
>   against me.
> They have exchanged their glory for shame.
> They feed on the sin of my people." (*Hos.* iv. 7-8)

The temples are filled with physical as well as spiritual adultery, and a "fat ox" (*Hos.* iv. 17) has become deity.

When the rulers and the people of Israel finally discover that they have been moving towards their own destruction, they will not find repentance difficult. But it will be a facile, surface repentance, inspired rather by fear of consequences than by love of God.

> "Come, let us return unto the Lord;
> For he has torn, and he will heal us.
> He smote, and he will bind us up.
> He will revive us after two or three days . . .
> As soon as we seek him, we shall find him."
>   (*Hos.* vi. 1-3)

The prophet's scorn of this easy philosophy is most humanly evident. Like all the great men of Israel, he himself had trod the hard and lonely road of the "striver with God" and knew by experience how much of labor and consecration was needed. Yet here was Israel, finding herself a little hurt and a little unhappy, and childishly convinced that if she promised to be good everything would be forgiven her. She felt that she had to make only the least of gestures towards finding God to find him at once and without difficulty.

It was because Israel had never understood what it meant to follow one God that she should think a gesture in his direction was sufficient. If she had understood him, she would never have tried to make her orgy of ritualistic worship and her sacrifices into a substitute for finding him. "For I delight in piety, not sacrifice; and in the knowledge of God, rather than burnt-offerings." (*Hos.* vi. 6)

In an effort to save herself, Israel has turned to everything except to her one real hope of safety. She has conducted herself "like a silly dove, without sense" (*Hos.* vii. 11) looking first to Egypt and then to Assyria to protect her, and all this to her own ultimate destruction. For God himself cannot save his people as long as their own foolishness stands in the way.

> "Can I redeem them,
>   While they speak lies against me?" (*Hos.* vii. 13)

There is something almost sad in Hosea's knowledge of the human heart. He has the pitying forbearance of Moses in his recognition of the weakness of the people, the Lord's own people who "do not cry unto me from their hearts, but wail upon their couches for grain and new wine." (*Hos.* vii. 14)

As long as Israel had so strange an idea of her God as to worship an image which had no meaning, since "a mechanic made it; and it is not God," (*Hos.* viii. 6) then she was continuing to sow a wind that would reap her the whirlwind. She had betrayed the God Moses had taught her to follow in the wilderness, and no pious attendance at the temples or intensification of ritual could be a substitute for the truth she had abandoned. Israel trusted to her armed might and to the strength of her chariots; and because she believed in the power of the sword, the sword would destroy her.

Even more than they had hated Amos the people hated Hosea, who spoke from a watch-tower higher than any they could ever climb. "Great is the opposition to the watchman." (*Hos.* ix. 8) They hated him for the strong words he used in an effort to shock them out of their false sense of security. They were convinced that they were the happy members of a rich and splendid nation, with a fine army and good kings and holy priests; and it needed harsh words to make any impression on the smooth wall of their complacency.

Hosea mocked their boasted military strength.

> "You have eaten the fruit of lies,
>   In that you trusted in your chariots." (*Hos.* x. 13)

He heaped scorn upon the holy images that they revered so faithfully.

> "Men kissing calves!" (*Hos.* xiii. 2)

He even belittled the great royal dynasty.

> "Where now is your king that he may deliver you?"
>   (*Hos.* xiii. 10)

There was still hope for the people if they were willing to turn to God and renew the force that had in literal fact made Israel a great nation. But if they did not, the truth they had betrayed would stand in their path like a devouring lion, to destroy them utterly.

Yet even while he wrote this, Hosea did not believe it. Israel might leave God, but God would never abandon Israel. She might attempt to play the harlot, but the truth she had once known was stronger than she was and would save her in the end in spite of herself. The nation had one true lover, one husband, and in the end the people would turn to him through the very force of that fact, and so be cured.

> "I will heal their backsliding;
>   I will love them voluntarily." (*Hos.* xiv. 4)

In that day should Israel be safe forever, with a beauty beyond all telling.

> "I will be like the dew to Israel,
> So that he will blossom like the lily,
> And his roots will spread like the poplar . . .
> His beauty will be like the olive tree,
> And his fragrance like that of Lebanon."
>
> (*Hos.* xiv. 5-6)

To neither Amos nor Hosea was there anything capricious in the doom that was to come upon Israel. To Amos the cause of it was simple: Israel had broken the elementary law of social righteousness, the law given by God, and she would suffer for it just as surely as the man who tries to walk on air falls to the ground. The breaking of the law brought with it automatically its own punishment.

To Hosea, the cause was less simple but more fundamental. Israel's greatness as a nation had been built entirely on her trust in one God; and when she began to put her trust elsewhere, whether in foreign nations, in her own wealth, or in her elaborate altars, she betrayed the highest thing she knew and signed the warrant of her own destruction. "It is your destruction, O Israel, that you are against me, against your help." (*Hos.* xiii. 9) Yet Hosea was convinced also that the truth to which Israel had once been loyal, because it was the truth, was stronger than Israel's disloyalty and would triumph in the end.

It is remarkable that men like Amos and Hosea, surrounded as they were by so many evidences of wealth and peace and foreign conquests and domestic piety, should neverthless have been able to see with such unwavering clearness that this apparent security was quicksand and its beauty rottenness. So clear was their vision that they could see the truth even while they themselves

were living in the worst of all confusions, the confusion
of national prosperity.

The two prophets were hated and feared for what they
said: Amos that the fabric of the national life had come
to be formed of inhumanity and corruption, Hosea that
Israel was spiritually bankrupt; yet it is clear today that
both men were right in what they taught. No political
structure could long endure that furnished wealth and
easy living for a few people at the expense of the pov-
erty of thousands. A system founded on the denial of the
rights of the individual in a nation that had once been
democratic would eventually fall of its own inherent
weakness. And Israel had been much more than a nation
of independent freeholders. She had been the only nation
in the world to honor God, and now she was betraying
him.

Since Amos and Hosea could see so accurately the rottenness of Israel's political, social and religious foundations, it was inevitable that they should also foresee her
fall; but the end came with a suddenness and violence
that even they could hardly have expected.

The first outward sign of decay was the one customary
in the East, the disintegration of the royal dynasty. After
the death of Jeroboam II, only one of his successors was
able to hand the throne over to his own son. The rest
were all murdered by usurpers, each one keeping a precarious clutch on the throne until he was disposed of in
his turn. The apparently sturdy political fabric of the nation crumpled with such dismaying rapidity that anyone
could see how unstable its foundations had been.

All that was needed to complete the destruction of the
kingdom was pressure from some outside power, and it
was Assyria who struck the final blow. Sargon, the great
Assyrian, finally captured the capital city of Jerusalem,
successfully completing the siege of Samaria that his pred-

ecessor had begun and which the men of Israel had
withstood with gallant desperation for three years. With
Samaria taken, Israel's life as a nation was over. Her people were sent into exile in Assyria, and strangers came
to repeople the land.

Hosea had been right in his sorrowful prediction.

> Assyria shall be his king . . .
> The sword shall begin upon his cities,
> And make an end to his fields,
> And shall devour his fortresses. (*Hos.* xi. 5-6)

But Hosea had been right also in his unconquerable hope
for the future. Israel as a political entity with king and
court might rise or fall; but its varying fortunes would
leave untouched the real Israel, the "striver with God."
It was the spirit that made the nation, not the nation the
spirit. Israel was an idea, not a geographical location,
and Sargon might overrun the land but he could never
destroy the idea.

When Hosea, the last of the northern prophets, fell
silent, it was not the end. The prophets of the southern
kingdom of Judah received his spirit, held it and carried
it forward. Isaiah and those that followed him were natives of Judah; but all history has united in calling them,
and correctly, men of Israel.

CHAPTER VIII

Behold, this dreamer.

Genesis xxxvii. 19

FOR a long time after the northern kingdom of Israel
had fallen, the so ithern kingdom of Judah remained a
nation. Judah wa more protected geographically, she
had always been careful not to antagonize Assyria, and
she had remained consistently faithful to the house of
David while the northern kingdom was undergoing
frenzied changes of dynasty. But everything for which
Amos and Hosea had reproached Israel was to be found
also in Judah: wealth and dishonesty and flourishing
altars at which there was no knowledge of God.

There was also to be found in Judah, as in Israel, the
great men who saw the apparent security and the religious zeal of the nation for the shams they were, and
who continued alone the search for God that the nation
as a whole seemed to have abandoned. There was much
to criticize in the Judah of the eighth century, nearly as
much as there had been in Israel; but the fact that she
was capable of producing a man like Isaiah is sufficient
glory to lighten greater sins than hers.

Unlike Amos, Isaiah was not a country prophet. He
was a citizen of Jerusalem, closely connected with court
life, and his friendship was valued by more than one
ruler of Judah. King Ahaz went to Isaiah for reassurance
when a coalition between Syria and Israel temporarily
threatened the life of the southern kingdom, and King
Hezekiah did the same when the Assyrians came to con-

137

quer Jerusalem. The situation with the Assyrians would
not have arisen if the king had taken Isaiah's advice in
the first place; but while Hezekiah was one of the best of
Judah's rulers, he never acquired half of Isaiah's wisdom
in statecraft.

As a statesman of the highest type Isaiah had very
few equals, so perfectly equipped was he to see beyond
the immediate future and not to be deceived by the obvious. He was perfectly aware that Judah was strong
when she trusted to the spirit and weak when she trusted
to chariots and allies, and he was capable not only of
stating this fact in great poetry but of proving it as a
matter of practical politics.

Isaiah knew that the great contemporary empires
would fall, as all empires must, and that if Judah expected to outlast them she would have to build with
something stronger than gold and iron. It was only the
knowledge of God that would enable Judah to endure,
and Isaiah strove to show his country that ritualistic worship was insufficient for a God who demanded, not sacrifices and not money, but understanding. The prophet
had a philosophy of world history that could see even the
greatest of empires under the control of a force mightier
than any they could comprehend, and that could see the
desire for God of a diminutive kingdom like Judah out-
lasting all the military strength of the world.

It was because Isaiah knew the importance of this
spiritual strength that his work is so vehement and sometimes so harsh. He wanted to shock the nation out of its
complacency, its bland conviction that it was doing all
that could be expected from a religious point of view if
its citizens crowded the Temple with their offerings and
paid their tithes regularly. Isaiah could see so great a
reward available to Judah for the asking that he could
not endure to see the nation falling short of the truth,

and he tried almost by main force to hold the people to the path that would make them great.

The tragic "Dooms" of Assyria and Egypt and Babylon, written by the prophet, it must be remembered, when all three nations were great powers in the land, are epics in miniature of the ultimate collapse of physical force; and Judah appears in them also because she has imitated the empires around her in their worship of material power and can only expect to share their destruction. Isaiah's Dooms of the Nations were not intended as a prophecy, but as a warning. They were written in the hope that they might make Judah turn back to God, through fear if nothing else, before it was too late.

There is, however, another side to the prophet Isaiah, and a more important one. He was a statesman wiser than it is given to most men to be, but he was also the possessor of a dream; and he gave more to the sons of Israel out of his dream than out of all his clear, sad wisdom.

This side of the prophet Isaiah went untouched by the turmoil and terror of his own day: the threat of Assyria, the apostasy of Judah, and his own responsibility to hold to the truth that everyone else seemed to have deserted. All these things might exist for a time, but in the end none of them would matter. Israel would not desert the truth, because the truth would not desert Israel.

In the end, the whole face of the world would be changed through that fidelity. The nations that now strove together like animals would learn that peace was possible. Even Egypt the idolatrous and Assyria the bloody conqueror would be gathered in to share with the sons of Israel the blessing of the God who made all the nations. The only leader would be the man who could rule justly and keep peace, and all men would learn the truth from one, correct source. On that day there would come, not only the ending of wars, but the ending of sin, the ending of mistakes, the ending of death itself; and there would be one God only.

The warning statesman in Isaiah's nature was obliged to promise this future peace only to a remnant of his people which should be saved after great tribulation. It was not his business to reassure further a nation already smug with self-satisfaction. But the great visionary in Isaiah did not write with one eye cocked in anxious consideration at the moral welfare of the people. Both eyes gazed straight ahead at the glory of his dream, and whatever might of necessity come before its fulfillment was a smiting "only to heal." (*Isa.* xix. 22)

The *Book of Isaiah* in its present form is a collection of fragments rather than a single literary unit; and nothing is more interesting than to trace in it the two sides of Isaiah, the almost pendulum-like swing between the two points of view. What may seem like an inconsistency is nothing of the sort. It is the conscientious teacher that was a definite part of the prophet's nature warring with the conviction that there was only one Teacher who could say,

"This is the way; walk in it!" (*Isa.* xxx. 21)

Isaiah was a practical man, and he was at the same time one of the greatest prophets Israel ever had; in a writer of such power, the result is deeply stirring.

It is hardly necessary to add that Isaiah was also a great poet. His work has become necessarily much mutilated in translation, and the subtle overtones, rhythms and connotations that are the very garments of poetry are now lost; but it is impossible to read the *Book of Isaiah* without recognizing his mastery of poetic expression. He has in particular the painter's art of giving the

whole picture in a few lines: of a bale of hay catching
fire and sinking down into the flame, of a nest moved so
carefully that of its occupants not one

> moved a wing,
> Or opened the mouth, or chirped, (*Isa.* x. 14)

or of the midsummer stillness of "shimmering heat in
sunshine." (*Isa.* xviii. 4) He could bring before his
readers the Nile itself in the very act of drying up, with
the channels stagnant and the sedge-grass withering. As
for the spirit of Isaiah's poetry, which is so much greater
than its manner, it raises him among the highest; for his
dream is the very soul of poetry, the Golden Age when
all dreams end.

The book is opened by Isaiah the teacher, the lineal
descendant of the two troubled prophets of the northern
kingdom. Even the ox and the ass have enough sense to
recognize their own masters, but Israel and Judah have
entirely forgotten to whom they owe allegiance. They
trample their temple courts and load the altars with their
offerings; but

> "Of what use is the multitude of your sacrifices to me?"
> Says the Lord . . .
> "Who demands this of you—
> The trampling of my courts?" (*Isa.* i. 11-12)

There is no avail in the blood of bullocks, the holding of
sabbaths and assemblies, the observance of new moons
and appointed seasons. If the people wish to worship a
God of righteousness they can do it only by becoming
righteous themselves.

Out of this very fine but purely local admonition comes
one of those sudden expansions so characteristic of Isaiah's
work. Because the sons of Israel have known the truth
and remained faithful to it, the hill of Zion will eventu-

ally be exalted over all the earth and all nations will come to it to learn of the one true God. There will be no need of fighting, for the word of the Lord will be a judge for all the nations.

> Nation will not lift up sword against nation,
> And they will learn no more the art of war.
>
> (*Isa.* ii. 4)

Then Isaiah the teacher returns, directing his shafts against everything that Judah wanted to trust. He attacks his nation's superstitious faith in fortune-tellers and diviners, her confidence in horses and chariots, her pride in her fat treasury and in her images of gold and silver. All such trust was a weakness, and Isaiah warned Judah of the day when she found it out, when her towers and battlements would be brought low, and when men would fling their idols to the bats and moles and seek refuge under stones from the terror of the presence of God. Because they had countenanced tyranny and dishonesty and pride, the citizens of Jerusalem had become, in the bitter symbolism of the Song of the Vineyard, like carefully tended grapevines that in the end yielded only wild grapes. The only possible end for so useless a vineyard was destruction, and Isaiah did not hesitate to let the nation know it.

It was not only the obvious sins of Judah that worried the prophet. There was the more subtle betrayal of "those who are wise in their own eyes, and in their own sight intelligent." (*Isa.* v. 21) There is no man more difficult to convince than one sure of his own righteousness, sure that the standard of morality to which he has drifted must be right because it is his. Only Isaiah, to whom it had been said:

> "Naught that this people call holy
> Shall you call holy," (*Isa.* viii. 12)

was able to see with uncomfortable clearness how faulty this standard was. He had for his consolation at this point only the conviction that when this lofty tree of false pride was cut down a new and unquenchably living shoot would spring from the stump of it.

The next prophecy in the *Book of Isaiah* has been the source of much confusion, largely because the historical events that called it into existence are ignored.

The king of Syria and one of the last rulers of the fading northern kingdom of Israel formed a military alliance against King Ahaz of Judah because he refused to join them in revolting against Assyria. Isaiah told Ahaz that the two armies encamped outside the city walls would not overthrow Jerusalem; but Ahaz was so frightened that he sent an imploring message to the king of Assyria, "I am your servant and your son; come up and deliver me from the hand of the king of Syria and from the hand of the king of Israel." (2 *Kings* xvi. 7) Judah's own strength having proved insufficient, she now proposed to trust to the strength of Assyria; and it was exactly this sort of thing that Isaiah so strongly condemned.

It is Isaiah's prophecy for this period of Judah's history that first introduces the famous sign of Immanuel, or 'God is with us.' At first the choice of the name has no very profound significance. A young woman is to have a son and Isaiah is to have a son, and the names of both boys are to stand as emblems for the fall of Syria and Israel. Isaiah's son is to be named 'Speeding to the spoil, hastening to the prey,' and before he is old enough to talk "the wealth of Damascus and the spoil of Samaria [the capital cities, respectively, of Syria and Israel] shall be carried away before the king of Assyria." (*Isa.* viii. 4) The other boy is to be named 'God is with us,' and before he is old enough to distinguish right from wrong "the land before whose two kings you stand in dread will be forsaken." (*Isa.* vii. 16) Both names at this point mean substantially the same thing.

But the name 'God is with us' comes back again with a wider application. After Assyria has conquered Judah's enemies in the north, she will turn upon Judah herself, laying waste the nation that has turned to her for aid. Because Judah has not trusted to spiritual strength, "the waters of Shiloah, that flow gently," (*Isa.* viii. 6) she would find more savage waters coming to overwhelm her, those of the Assyrian river Euphrates.

> The waters of the River, mighty and many,
> Even the king of Assyria and all his glory;
> And it shall rise over all its channels,
> And shall pass over all its banks,
> And shall sweep on through Judah in an overwhelming
>   flood. (*Isa.* viii. 7-8)

And yet it shall not prevail; for the unexpected climax to this torrent of destruction is the reappearance of the name Immanuel.

> His outspread wings shall fill the breadth of your land,
> O "God is with us!" (*Isa.* viii. 8)

Whatever Assyria might do, there still remained the protection that the name of Immanuel symbolized. Since "God is with us," even the invasion itself would be a step in the working out of God's salvation for his people. Whatever happened to Judah was no wanton accident but a purging to make her worthy, the beginning of the separation of the wheat from the chaff.

Then Isaiah turns back to his emblem of the child, and makes it, as he makes the name, a symbol of Judah's redemption. When the child is born, the nation that has been walking in darkness will see a great light, all wars will cease, and the bloody war cloaks will be burned.

> For a child is born to us, a son is given to us;
> And the government will be upon his shoulder.
>
> *(Isa.* ix. 6)

His title will be prince of peace, and of that peace there will be no end.

This is Isaiah at his greatest. As a statesman he was able to see how dangerous trust in Assyria had become to his people, and in his emblem of the flowing river he was actually foretelling the invasion that occurred during the next reign and in the prophet's own lifetime. Yet, in spite of this clearness of perception, Isaiah was not in the least afraid of what Assyria might do. He did not believe that any empire could consciously dictate the course of history. "Shall an axe boast over the man that hews with it?" *(Isa.* x. 15) Whatever power of destruction might be let loose, it had one purpose and could have only one result: to turn the people back to God. In no other way could they learn to "no more lean on the enemy that smote them," but to "lean in loyal trust on the Lord." *(Isa.* x. 20)

When this day of complete confidence and complete understanding of God finally arrived, a perfect world would result from it. In this world there would be neither destruction nor possibility of destruction. The lamb would lodge safely with the wolf and the calf with the young lion; and a little child would lead them.

> They will do no harm or destruction
>   On all my holy mountain;
> For the land will have become full of the knowledge
>   of the Lord,
>   As the waters cover the sea. *(Isa.* xi. 9)

On this day the sons of Israel will no longer be like the cowards who ran to Assyria for help, but they will be able to say, and mean it,

"God is my salvation—
I will trust, and will not be afraid;
For the Lord is my strength and my song,
And he has become my salvation." (*Isa.* xii. 2)

Believing that such a result would come from the worst that military tyranny could do, it is no wonder that Isaiah had no fear of Assyria or any other physical power. The only thing he feared was the apostasy of his own people, and he spent his life warring against it.

The next group of prophecies in the *Book of Isaiah* is a general "Doom of the Nations." The first concerns Babylon, whose gradual rise to power in the East had as yet had no effect on Judah, and it is the custom to say that this prophecy must therefore be the work of a later writer. This conclusion is not necessarily correct. The *Book of Kings* (2 *Kings* xx. 12-21) tells how the King of Babylon sent gifts to Hezekiah of Judah, who could not resist the pleasure of showing the messengers through his own armories and treasuries. Isaiah thereupon told him that his whole realm would eventually go into exile in Babylon, and the king comforted himself with the somewhat reprehensible but very human reflection that this event would not occur in his own lifetime and might therefore be endured with equanimity.

As poetry, Isaiah's doom against Babylon is of a very high order, especially the latter part that turns directly on the king.

How still has the tyrant become,
How still the terror! (*Isa.* xiv. 4)

As he descends into Sheol, all the earth breaks into singing with joy and relief because he is gone, and underground the shades rise up, half in mockery and half in awe, to greet his coming.

"How are you fallen from heaven,
    O Lucifer, son of the morning!
How are you hewn to the earth,
    Who laid waste all the nations!" (*Isa.* xiv. 12)

All the sepulchered kings lie in honor, each in his own
house. It is only the tyrant who built his throne on
slaughter that is cast out tombless,

Like a hateful abortion,
Clothed with slain men gashed by the sword,
Who go down to the stones of the Pit—
    Like a trampled corpse. (*Isa.* xiv. 19)

The next doom is against Assyria, the chief threat of
Isaiah's own day and another of the great empires who
put her trust in the sword. Next comes a warning against
Philistia, and then the beautiful prophecy against Moab,
with its note of personal grief.

"With my tears I drench you,
    O Heshbon and Elealeh!
For the battle-shout has fallen
    On your fruits and on your harvest,
And joy and gladness vanish
    Out of the garden-land." (*Isa.* xvi. 9-10)

Concerning Damascus, the rich capital of Syria, it is pre-
dicted that she will become a heap of ruins, with her
daughter cities a pasture for sheep; and on that same day
will the glory of Israel vanish, because she stocked her
garden "with vine-slips of an alien god." (*Isa.* xvii. 10)
Egypt of the ancient magic is also doomed; her spirit
will be emptied out of her, and her strength will shrivel
and decay.

All this is written by Isaiah the teacher; but at this
point the other Isaiah breaks in and almost destroys the
effect that has been so carefully and vividly created.
God's salvation is for everyone. It is as much for Egypt
and Assyria as it is for Judah, if only they will accept

it. "Though the Lord may smite the Egyptians, he will smite only to heal: when they turn to the Lord, he will listen to their entreaties, and will heal them." (*Isa*. xix. 22) When the day of perfect understanding comes, all the nations will share it together. "On that day will Israel be a third with Egypt and Assyria as a blessing in the midst of the earth, which the Lord of hosts has blessed in these terms, 'Blessed be Egypt my people, and Assyria the work of my hands, and Israel my heritage!' " (*Isa*. xix. 24-25)

That Isaiah should have been able to write such a thing as this, while as a statesman he was wholly occupied with trying to force Judah away from her faith in these countries, is not the least of the prophet's achievements. Himself in the thick of contemporary politics and deeply concerned by them, he was able to stand off and recognize a spiritual warfare in which Assyria and Judah, Egypt and Israel, were all being betrayed by the same enemy, the lack of knowledge of God, and from which they might all be saved together.

The reason for the wholesale destruction pictured in Isaiah's various dooms is that the inhabitants of the earth must pay the inevitable penalty for having "broken the everlasting covenant." (*Isa*. xxiv. 5) It is for this reason that the mirth of the harp is stilled and the whole earth hides its face in terror. But when the purging is finished that ignorance and disloyalty have made necessary, all the nations will share a perfect understanding of God. The symbol of this understanding is Jerusalem, the city David established as a memorial to the truth, and at Jerusalem a deathless world will be created.

> He will destroy on this mountain
> The veil that veils all the peoples,
> And the web that is woven over all the nations—
> He will destroy death forever. (*Isa*. xxv. 7-8)

When a perfect God was understood, a perfect world would also appear and there would be no more death. This was Isaiah's conviction; and with such a vision before his eyes it is no wonder that he fought so desperately to keep his nation advancing along the path where Moses had first set her feet. His nation must keep faith, since through her the whole world might be redeemed.

Isaiah knew that this keeping faith was no easy thing, since no amount of human labor could of itself procure salvation.

> "We were with child, we writhed in pain,
> But we gave birth only to wind;
> No deliverance we wrought for the land,
> No inhabitants of the world came to birth through
> us." (*Isa.* xxvi. 18)

Yet it was in this fact that Isaiah found reassurance; for if it was not man's labor that brought deliverance to the world, then it was through God alone that it came. Isaiah knew that the fulfillment of his vision did not depend on Judah, the arrogant, faithless nation with whose sins he was so thoroughly familiar. The Day of the Lord was God's and it would come, even in spite of Judah if need be.

The Isaiah of the "Dooms" saw the nations of the earth being destroyed by their sins, but the Isaiah of the vision can see the sin as something quite distinct from the people. When the Lord comes "to punish the inhabitants of the world for their guilt," (*Isa.* xxvi. 21) it is not the inhabitants he punishes; it is the guilt, under its ancient and familiar symbol of a serpent.

> On that day will the Lord punish,
> With his sword that is hard and great and strong,
> Leviathan the fleeing serpent, Leviathan the coiled
> serpent;
> And he will slay the dragon that is in the sea.
>
> (*Isa.* xxvii. 1)

It is not the vineyard that will be destroyed, but only the weeds that have choked it.

> "Wrath have I none;
> But should I find briers and thorns,
> In war would I march against them,
> I would burn them altogether." (*Isa.* xxvii. 4)

Free from all hindrance, Israel and Judah would at last "fill the face of the world with fruit," (*Isa.* xxvii. 6) a poetic re-statement of the ancient promise to Abraham that in his seed should all the nations of the world be blessed.

The final group of prophecies in the *Book of Isaiah* has no very clear structure. The one consistent thing about them is the alternation in mood between the two Isaiahs, the teacher who must warn the nation of its danger and turn it into the right path, and the prophet who knows that the responsibility is God's and that he can be trusted to finish what he has begun. Isaiah could see the sins of his people with reproachful steadiness; but almost in spite of himself there is a clearer light interposing, until in the end the reproach dies away and only the light remains.

Ephraim is a drunkard. His glorious beauty is a fading flower beaten down by a storm of hail. Yet after his own beauty is gone the Lord will be "a beautiful crown and a glorious diadem" (*Isa.* xxviii. 5) to him.

The priests and prophets of Judah are crazed as though with strong drink. They have made a refuge of lies, which will be broken and themselves with it. Yet this threshing will not go on forever, but only until the wheat is separated from the chaff.

Jerusalem's enemies have compassed her about with terror. Yet when the Lord comes, "their siege-works and forts and storming-parties shall be like a dream, a vision of the night." (*Isa.* xxix. 7)

The people are blind to all spiritual things, and have degraded their approach to God into a ritual.

> "This people draw near me with their mouth,
> And honor me with their lips,
> While their thoughts are far from me,
> And their reverence for me is a commandment of
>   men." (*Isa.* xxix. 13)

Yet the day will come when they shall learn a better way, and "out of gloom and darkness shall the eyes of the blind see." (*Isa.* xxix. 18)

Judah has trusted to her own strength and cleverness, and has said to her prophets: "Speak to us smooth things; prophesy delusions!" (*Isa.* xxx. 10) "Trouble us no more with the Holy One of Israel!" (*Isa.* xxx. 11) She has trusted to the power of her chariots, and it is therefore in chariots that she will be obliged to flee. Yet the day of her understanding will come nevertheless.

> "Your eyes will behold your Teacher.
> And when you turn to right or to left,
> Your ears will hear a voice behind you, saying,
> 'This is the way; walk in it!' " (*Isa.* xxx. 20-21)

The women of Jerusalem have been very complacent over the wealth and beauty of their land, and they will lose it. They will see the vines destroyed and the earth yielding only briers. Yet in the end the people will find safe gardens and secure resting-places.

The final prophecy of the *Book of Isaiah* is unlike any of the others. It is a carefully unified and exquisitely wrought piece of literary art written from the point of view of the Babylonian Exile. This Exile occurred many generations after Isaiah lived and wrote, and the book belongs so intimately to this period that it even mentions by name the great Persian conqueror Cyrus, whose military exploits were the immediate cause of the book's being written. It is most unlikely that it could have been a product of the eighth century, since its purpose would be intelligible neither to Isaiah's contemporaries nor to his immediate descendants. It identifies itself so closely with Isaiah's great spirit that it is easy to see why it should have been attributed to him, but it nevertheless cannot be considered jointly with his work. It belongs to the time of the Babylonian captivity and it is there it must be considered, if only in fairness to the book itself.

Of Isaiah's own work it is not possible to make a comprehensive judgment. It can easily be said that Isaiah was a great poet, and that his statesmanship had influence with the best of Judah's kings; but the mental range of the prophet is so colossal that it is difficult to see him as a whole.

Isaiah believed that the one force that gave permanent life to a nation was the desire to find God, and that against this force not even the mightiest of armaments could prevail. He believed that the truth about God was so near and so free that it was available to any nation willing to accept it. And he believed that the truth was so powerful that, once it was understood, it was capable of destroying war and hate and even death itself.

The whole of this vision was not original with Isaiah. All the prophets up to his time contributed something towards it, and it may have been in part no more than a re-statement of the best in contemporary thought. His picture of all the nations turning to the hill of Zion for instruction is repeated almost word for word by another prophet of the eighth century named Micah. (*Isa.* ii. 2-4; *Mic.* iv. 1-3) But the beauty and the magnitude and, above all, the persistence of the vision are Isaiah's own, and make him one of the greatest of all the men of Israel.

Isaiah was one of the very few prophets to be honored

in his own day, but not for the greatness of his teaching. He was honored because he had been instrumental in the turning back of Sennacherib's hosts from the gates of Jerusalem, and his promise that the Chosen People would never be destroyed later became an integral part of the national life of Judah. The people did not understand in the least the spiritual foundation upon which Isaiah had based his promise, but the fact itself was a comfort to them when they needed it most, and it later became a burning conviction that no discouragement could entirely quench.

Isaiah knew that he was not understood. He sometimes felt that he would have to "bind up his testimony" (*Isa.* viii. 16) since only he and his disciples honored the truth and the nation as a whole had thrown it over for lies. Yet he never did. Even though the people remained deaf and blind, Isaiah continued to tell them what he knew to be true: that their God was the only reality and that

The whole earth is full of his glory. (*Isa.* vi. 3)

CHAPTER IX

> It was little by little and in different ways that
> God spoke in olden times to our forefathers through
> the prophets.
>
> *Letters to the Hebrews* i. 1

WHEN Isaiah protested against the idolatry of Judah, he
was, if anything, understating the case. The Hebrews
were a small nation, surrounded by very old and very
cultured civilizations, and it was natural that they should
try to imitate their neighbors. As a result, there had developed in Judah such a confusion of foreign religions
and such a consequent corruption of their own that it is
not remarkable the subject should have occupied a large
share of the prophets' attention.

Part of the responsibility for this apostasy rested with
the court circles, who were in particularly close contact
with the great cosmopolitan centers of the Eastern world
and yearned to imitate them all. A characteristic example
of the royal point of view was the eagerness with which
King Ahab borrowed the pattern of an Assyrian altar so
that he might have one like it made for his own use.
This particular altar would probably seem foreign and
heathenish to the people in general of the king's own
generation, but the passage of time would eventually
soften the innovation until it became first familiar, then
respectable, and then holy. As a result of this almost un-
controllable tendency, the land became full of enthusi-
astic worshippers who performed their devotions before
a medley of shrines. The God of Moses still remained the
chief god of the Hebrews, but he was only one god
among many.

King Hezekiah made an earnest attempt to correct
this state of affairs in Judah by forcibly disposing of as

many of these foreign altars as he could; but they were all rebuilt when his son Manasseh came to the throne, and it is obvious that Hezekiah did not have the support of the people in his measures.

After this one brief excursion into reform, the inhabitants of Judah continued placidly on their way in the exercise of their confused religion. They worshipped the sun and they worshipped the moon, they practiced the old fertility cults, they sacrificed to Moloch, they bowed before Ishtar, Milcom, Chemosh and a great quantity of others, secure in the conviction that they had every authority for their worship of these old gods. Solomon himself had established a temple for Milcom, the god of the Ammonites, as warrant of its respectability.

It was natural that these gods should be worshipped in a spirit of profound orthodoxy in the eighth century B.C. It was men like Isaiah who were the misfits, with their revolutionary and difficult ideas. Their insistence that the God of Israel was not a god but the only God, that he belonged not only to Judah but to the whole world, and that true worship of him was not primarily outward but inward, was so unorthodox and even apparently so irreligious that it is not strange their words fell on deaf ears. To the prophets such a doctrine was elementary, but to the people in general it was so hopelessly advanced as to be almost unintelligible.

The religion of the prophets was mental and that of the people physical, so that there was really no point of contact between the two. The common mind has never cared to mix reason with its religion, and Isaiah's command, "Come now, and let us reason together," (*Isa.* i. 18) was cold and unattractive to the worshippers at the colorful and emotionally exciting altars of Ishtar and Moloch.

The strong language of the prophets finds its full

excuse in this attitude on the part of the people. Even
the heaviest threat was hardly sufficient to shake them
out of the mental lethargy that was rapidly undermining
their existence as a nation.

Micah, a contemporary of Isaiah, blamed the preva-
lent and unabashed worship of foreign gods largely on
the influence of the two capital cities of Israel and
Judah.

> What is Jacob's transgression?
> Is it not Samaria?
> And what is Judah's sin?
> Is it not Jerusalem? (*Mic.* i. 5)

It was naturally in the big cities, with their wealthy,
travelling merchant class and their somewhat decadent
courts, that the gods of the foreign nations should be
first accepted, especially under the system of royal inter-
marriages that had first worked such havoc in Solomon's
day. It was also the urban men of the upper classes who
would attempt to consolidate their position at the expense
of the old yeoman population and, in Micah's words,
would "covet fields and seize them, and houses, and
carry them off." (*Mic.* ii. 2)

What chiefly angered Micah about the situation was
the fundamental dishonesty of men who worshipped
where they pleased, imposed on the common people, perverted the justice of the courts, used oracles to bring
them a profit, and then blandly put their trust in the fact
that they were the Chosen People.

> Her chiefs pronounce judgment for a bribe,
> And her priests declare oracles for hire,
> And her prophets divine for cash.
> Yet they lean upon the Lord, saying,
> "Is not the Lord in the midst of us?
> No misfortune can befall us." (*Mic.* iii. 11)

When Micah pointed out to these people that they

were putting a heavy strain on their relationship to God, they exasperated him further by their bland conviction that the responsibility for the welfare of Judah belonged to God only. They themselves, the rulers and the priests, had nothing to do with the matter, which it was really better not to discuss.

> "Do not keep on harping," they harp;
> One should not be harping upon such things . . .
> Is the Lord's spirit impatient,
> Or are such things his deeds?
> Do not his words mean good
> To his people Israel?" (*Mic.* ii. 6-7)

Faced with a point of view like that, it is not surprising that the writings of the prophets are filled with dooms and visions of coming judgment. Into such crass smugness nothing else could penetrate.

Furious at the hard indifference of the authorities to the condition of the lower classes, Micah constituted himself the champion of the oppressed against the privileged. In his version of the Day of the Lord, it was the lame and sick and afflicted who were to be gathered together into a "strong nation." (*Mic.* iv. 7) Each man should sit under his own vine and fig tree, and no one would have the power to take his property away from him. A new and good ruler would come, not from the proud and rich cities that might fairly expect to claim the honor, but from little Bethlehem, "too little to be among the clans of Judah." (*Mic.* v. 2) And this ruler should rule at last with justice and not as a tyrant.

Micah was no Isaiah. He had nothing whatever of the wide illumination of the greater prophet's vision, and his conception of an ideal future was no more than of a time when his nation should be exalted over all others because of the covenant that had been made with Abraham. Yet he was firmly convinced that the God of Israel

could be worshipped in none of the usual ways, neither
with gifts nor with sacrifices nor with ceremonies.

Micah incorporated this conviction in a miniature
drama that is a masterpiece, written so clearly that even
the most thick-witted could grasp its point. Israel faces
the Lord and the Lord faces Israel, with the mountains
for witness. "For the Lord has an argument with his
people, and a controversy with Israel." (*Mic.* vi. 2)
Israel, called upon to answer her Lord, is greatly confused. Shall she come before the Lord with burnt-offerings and yearling calves? Shall she please him with
thousands of lambs, and myriads of streams of oil? Would
he like her sons offered up as a sacrifice, "the fruit of
my body for the sin of my soul"? (*Mic.* vi. 7) She waits
for an answer and the answer comes back instantly, with
all the force of Micah's simplicity and honesty behind it.

> What does the Lord require of you,
> But to do justice, and to love kindness,
> And to walk humbly with your God? (*Mic.* vi. 8)

A younger contemporary of Micah was the prophet
Nahum, but to judge by the single fragment of his work
that remains, Nahum possessed neither Micah's ethical
principles nor his capacity for clear thinking.

Nahum cannot strictly be classed among the real
prophets at all, but he is a very effective poet. As a
painter of vivid pictures he can hardly be surpassed, except possibly by the writer of the *Book of Joel*, with its
wonderful picture of the horde of locusts advancing like
an army; but when it came to an analysis of the fundamental problems of his own day, Nahum was helpless.

It does not seem to have occurred to Nahum that there
was anything wrong with Judah. He believed that all
her difficulties could be directly traced to the baleful influence of Assyria, and it was at Assyria rather than at

his own people that Nahum hurled his denunciations. He was correct in predicting the ultimate downfall of the Assyrian empire, but he seems to have been moved by hopefulness rather than by any trace of the true prophetic spirit.

Nahum's book opens with an attempt to give the case sober and impartial consideration. It is clear that the Lord "is good to those that wait for him" (*Nahum* i. 7) and equally clear that he "lays up wrath for his foes." (*Nahum* i. 2) This was a commonplace of the prophetic doctrine, but the great prophets knew that the "foes" were mental evils rather than physical empires.

This view of the situation did not occur to Nahum. To him the foe was Assyria, and as soon as Assyria was destroyed the vine of Israel would be restored to its former glory. His imagination ranged to the fall of Nineveh and at once the poet in him took the upper hand; he plunges into a series of vivid battle pictures, almost revelling in the opportunity given by his subject to use his powers of description.

The first scene is Nineveh, in all the pride of the city's military strength, trying to arm itself against the danger that threatens it. Nahum tells of the watchfulness along the walls and the guarding of all the roads, the gathering together of the mighty warriors, clothed in bright scarlet "like the flame of torches." (*Nahum* ii. 4) He tells of the impatient prancing of the war horses, the milling about of the chariots in the narrow streets, "dashing to and fro in the open spaces," (*Nahum* ii. 5) the gathering of the nobles who stumble in their haste as they come running, and the setting-up of the battering ram on the thick walls.

Then, with the skill of a good writer who knows the dramatic value of contrast, Nahum shifts to the still and hopeless desolation of Nineveh after its defeat.

> The gates of the rivers are opened,
> And the palace melts away. (*Nahum* ii. 6)

The queen of the city is carried away into captivity,
while her maidens beat their breasts and mourn with a
moaning like doves. Nineveh, in the vivid simile, "is like
a pool of water, whose water escapes." (*Nahum* ii. 8)
"Halt! Halt!" is the cry in the city, but no one turns
back, not even for plunder. In all that proud city there
is nothing left but emptiness and desolation.

Then the poet turns to a brief, violent picture of the
city in the actual throes of the battle, with a piling-up
of the images of wholesale slaughter until they rise to a
bloody climax.

> The crack of the whip, and the noise of the rumbling
>   wheel;
> And the galloping horse, and the jolting chariot.
> The charging horseman, and the flashing sword,
> And the glittering spear, and a multitude of slain,
> And a mass of bodies, and no end to the corpses!
>   (*Nahum* iii. 2-3)

This is good vivid poetry, and it is impossible to feel
that Nahum is not enjoying his subject. Equally lively
are his next lines, his very human jeer at the city who
thought herself so great. Did Nineveh think she was any
better than Thebes, who was walled in by ramparts of
water but who perished nevertheless? The city might
strengthen her forts and multiply her merchants; but in
the end her protectors would vanish as the locusts vanish
when they settle in the hedges to escape the strength of
the rising sun.

> Your shepherds slumber, O king of Assyria;
>   Your nobles sleep!
> Your people are scattered upon the hilltops,
>   With none to gather them. (*Nahum* iii. 18)

Here there is a faint note of pity, but it vanishes at once with the uncharitable assertion that "everyone who shall hear the news about you will clap his hands." (*Nahum* iii. 19) There is no doubt that Nahum was a good poet, but there is equally no doubt that in his spiritual development he had a long way to go.

An interesting contrast to Nahum's childish spirit of gleeful destruction is the attitude taken towards the same city of Nineveh in the *Book of Jonah*. The date of the actual writing of the book is unknown, but the hero of the book apparently lived in the days of Jeroboam II. Unlike the other prophetic books, the *Book of Jonah* is a prose narrative rather than a poetic discourse; and the point of the narrative is how Jonah was taught a truth that men like Nahum greatly needed to learn.

The story begins when Jonah has received a call to go to the city of Nineveh and preach against its wickedness. Unwilling to go, he shipped for Tarshish, hoping that the "presence of the Lord" (*Jonah* i. 3) would not be able to follow him there. The first climax of the story occurs when Jonah discovers that God is as much present on the water as on land, a discovery made after the prophet has been tossed into the sea by the frightened sailors to appease a storm. A poetic interlude, supposed to be given in Jonah's own words, tells how narrowly he escaped drowning:

> "The waters closed in over my life; the deep surrounded me.
> Sea-weed was wound around my head.
> To the roots of the hills I went down. . . .
> But thou didst bring up my life from the pit, O Lord, my God!
> When I was losing consciousness, I remembered the Lord:
> And my prayer unto thee entered thy holy temple."
> (Jonah ii. 5-7)

Out of this experience Jonah discovered that "deliverance belongs to the Lord." (*Jonah* ii. 9) But the sequel shows that he had not yet made this discovery thoroughly his own.

Once more Jonah was called upon to go and preach against Nineveh, and this time he went. He proclaimed to Nineveh that in forty days, because of her wickedness, she would be overthrown. The king and people at once abandoned their former ways, repenting in sackcloth and ashes, and on this account the judgment against Nineveh was annulled by the Lord. Jonah was furious. "Are you so very angry?" asks the Lord (*Jonah* iv. 4) and proceeds to give his prophet an object lesson that Nahum would have done well to share.

Jonah, still hopeful that the vengeance which he had prophesied would come to pass, went outside the city walls and sat down to see what would happen. As he waited, a gourd vine grew up to shade him from the hot sun, and Jonah was very pleased to have the gourd over him. But the next day the gourd wilted and the sun smote Jonah's unprotected head, so that he wailed loudly over the destruction of the vine.

> Then God said to Jonah,
> "Are you so very angry over the gourd?"
> And he replied,
> "I am angry enough to die!"
> Then the Lord said,
> "You have had pity on the gourd . . . which grew in a night, and perished in a night. And should not I, indeed, have pity on Nineveh, that great city, wherein are more than a hundred and twenty thousand infants, that cannot distinguish between their right hand and their left?" (*Jonah* iv. 9-11)

Another minor prophet who found it difficult to believe that any foe of the Chosen People should be spared was Obadiah; and it was against the point of view of men like himself that the parable of Jonah was directed. Obadiah's brief battle-shout over Edom, a neighboring country that had been tactless enough to be pleased with Judah's difficulties, is a natural enough expression of human nature. But Obadiah failed to notice that he himself had fallen into the sin he deprecated so strongly in Edom, the sin of rejoicing over another's downfall.

It doubtless pleased Obadiah's listeners to hear of a time when Judah would be exalted and Edom brought low, but the popularity of his doctrine hardly contributed to the stature of Obadiah as a prophet. Neither he nor Nahum was a seeker. They both had it firmly settled in their own minds that Judah was good and all her enemies were evil; Isaiah would never have recognized their narrow world of black and white.

The prophet Habakkuk was a different kind of man altogether. He was no local patriot but an honest, if perplexed, seeker. His book is largely a record of the difficulty he had in reconciling his own lofty conception of God with the evil he saw about him. Since God was too pure to behold evil and refused to countenance wrongdoing, why was it that sinful men were allowed to go on oppressing those more righteous than themselves?

The first part of the *Book of Habakkuk* is cast in dialog form, and opens with the prophet's anguished cry for enlightenment. He is standing in the midst of a nation perverted in all her ways, with her law courts paralysed and the wicked harming the innocent.

"How long, O Lord, must I cry for help,
And thou not hear?" (*Hab.* i. 2)

The answer comes to the prophet that Judah will not lack for punishment. The Chaldeans will sweep down upon it with a fury that nothing can withstand.

Yet the prophet is still confused and unsatisfied. **Why**

should the good God use an instrument that is obviously
evil? Will the conqueror of Judah "keep on emptying
his net forever" (*Hab.* i. 17) like some gigantic and successful fisherman, with none to prevent him?

> "I will take my stand upon my watch-tower,
>   And station myself upon the rampart;
>   And watch to see what he will say to me,
>   And what answer he will make to my complaint."
>   (*Hab.* ii. 1)

The prophet was sure he would receive an answer if
he asked honestly, and the answer came. No unright-
eousness, whether of an empire or of an individual, could
endure. Those that indulged in it wrote their own doom,
whether it was an outside power that destroyed them or
not. If anyone "enriches himself with what is not his
own" (*Hab.* ii. 6) he has contracted a debt that has to
be paid, whether he knows it or not, and in the end his
creditors will rise up and destroy him. If anyone builds
his house on unjust gains and sets it high to be free
from the danger of reprisal, will not the very stones and
woodwork of the building he has made cry out against
him?

So confident was Habakkuk of the correctness of this
answer, that evil cannot endure because it must eventually fall of its own weight, that he closes his book with
a psalm of thanksgiving that was eventually set to music
and used in the temple services. Even though the prophet
may not see the answer to his question fulfilled in his
own lifetime,

> "Yet I will exult in the Lord . . .
>   He makes my feet like the feet of hinds,
>   And makes me walk upon my heights."
>   (*Hab.* iii. 18-19)

Habakkuk mentions scornfully in passing the idols
which the people have made out of dead wood and stone

and worshipped as gods, but he does not make them his primary consideration as Micah did. It was Zephaniah, a lineal descendant of the king who first tried to abolish foreign altars in Judah, who made the most wholesale denunciation of the religious practices of the people.

In Zephaniah's day of doom, the first nation to receive the wrath of God is Judah herself, because of those who have been priestlings to Baal, because of those who prostrate themselves on the roofs of the city and pray to the moon and the stars, because of those who bow before the Lord and swear by Milcom, and because of those who have committed the negative but equally grave sin of not looking for God, "those who have not sought the Lord, nor inquired after him." (*Zeph.* i. 6) From Judah, the judgment speeds over the whole earth, to include all its inhabitants; and the result is to teach all the nations of the world

> a purified speech;
> So that all of them may call upon the name of the
>   Lord,
> And serve him unanimously." (*Zeph.* iii. 9)

There were other prophets also who fought against Judah's religious failings, but their work is now lost. The *Book of Chronicles* mentions the *Records of the Seers*, in which was incorporated, among other things, the rebuke the prophets directed towards King Manasseh, a dazzled believer in necromancy who went so far as to set up an altar to one of his private gods inside the Temple itself.

The citizens of Judah did not lack for warnings against their love of worshipping idols, or against their method of worshipping the God of Israel when they did worship him; but it was a long time before the teachings of the prophets had much effect. The gods that the people wanted to worship were the ruling deities of great and powerful nations, and how should the God of little Judah be greater than they?

Even when the God of Moses alone was worshipped, as he probably was more often than the prophets imply, it was much easier to honor him in the usual way than in the way the prophets demanded. It was in every way easier and more satisfying to bring a fine fat bull to the Temple where everyone could see it than "to do justice, and to love kindness." (*Mic.* vi. 8) Moreover it was an arrangement more satisfactory to the priests, who, if they were given the choice between a private reformation and a substantial temple payment, would naturally be biased in favor of the payment.

If it had no effect on the people, the prophets' unceasing attack on the smooth wall of Judah's orthodox piety finally had its effect on Judah's kings. Manasseh's son was as bad as his father, but the grandson, Josiah, was apparently deeply impressed by the teachings of the prophets. In the twelfth year of his reign King Josiah began a systematic destruction of the altars both in Jerusalem and in the surrounding countryside, and in six years' time the work had progressed so far that the Temple was already beginning to be viewed by the popular mind as the one proper place to worship. Thereupon Josiah set some workmen to mend and restore the Temple, parts of the building having been torn down by his royal ancestors.

It was while the work of restoration was going on that someone discovered a "book of the law" in the Temple debris. (*2 Kings* xxii. 8) Both king and court were deeply moved by this sounding of a voice out of the remote past, and the book was ordered read in a solemn convocation before representatives of all the people.

Immediately a great wave of reform swept over the

land. The people had been annoyed by the wisdom of their own prophets; but over the book of Moses there rested the sanctifying glow of the past and of a great tradition, and the people could hardly be quick enough to fulfill its demands.

A large part of this zeal was undoubtedly rooted in the fact that Moses had promised prosperity and a firm anchorage in the land of Canaan if his laws were obeyed. The people were eager to collect their reward, and it was only the prophets who were not deceived. One of their number, a woman named Huldah, told the men of Jerusalem that the book of the law was genuine, but she told them also that it was too late to expect results from their sudden reformation and that Judah might expect the fulfillment of its threats rather than its blessings.

The people did not believe Huldah, but it was not long before they found out she had been right. Josiah was killed in battle by the king of Egypt, who put the dead man's son, Jehoiakim, on the throne of Judah as his vassal. When the balance of power shifted from Egypt to Babylon after the battle of Carchemish, the king of Judah was obliged to shift his allegiance with it; but he kept one eye hopefully on Egypt and finally plucked up sufficient courage to withhold his regular payment of tribute money to Babylon. Jehoiakim escaped punishment by dying suddenly, but the three months' reign of his youthful son came to an abrupt end when King Nebuchadnezzar of Babylon marched on Jerusalem.

Nebuchadnezzar took the royal family back with him to Babylon as captives, together with some ten thousand of the leading families in Judah. He left as nominal ruler the king's young uncle, Zedekiah, who eventually revolted against his Babylonian overlord. Nebuchadnezzar, his patience exhausted, laid final siege to Jerusalem, capturing the city after months of agonized resistance on the part of her inhabitants. He broke down the walls, burned the buildings, razed the Temple and sent the remaining citizens into exile in Babylon, crushing all further opportunities for revolt and the kingdom of Judah with it.

The Southern Kingdom went to her end in the dust of desolation, to the accompaniment of one of the greatest of funeral dirges.

> How lonely the city sits, once so crowded with people!
> She has become like a widow, once so great among the
>   nations;
> She that was a princess among the cities has become
>   a vassal. (*Lam.* i. 1)

The *Book of Lamentations*, the tragic acrostic that closed forever Judah's history as an independent nation, saw little hope for the future. The past was still too near, and the memories of the past too terrible. The Holy City of the poet's joy had been reduced to ashes, her sanctuary violated and her people dragged into captivity. Everything to which she trusted had betrayed her.

> "I called on my lovers, but they repudiated me;
> My priests and elders perished in the city,
> When they sought food to keep themselves alive."
>   (*Lam.* i. 19)

The pictures of the siege are too vivid to be anything but first-hand, the dying children begging for food in the city squares, the young men of great houses like skeletons in the streets, the people frantically searching the dunghills for food and longing to die in battle rather than of starvation; and all this taking place in Jerusalem, the city that had been called "the crowning joy of all the earth." (*Lam.* ii. 15)

The mood of the dirge, whether it be one elegy or many, vibrates mournfully between the knowledge that Jerusalem's punishment is just and a wild passion that she alone, of all the nations of the earth, should be singled out for torture; between the hope that the Lord would "not willingly afflict" (*Lam.* iii. 33) and the conviction that he would; between a prayer of compassion towards Judah and a desire that all the other cities of the earth should be punished too, the moods shifting uneasily and without logic in the half-delirium of pain. The closing lines forsake the elegiac rhythm to give the wail of the exiles themselves. Overworked, degraded, ruled over by servants, and with the memory always behind them of a Mount Zion that lies desolate with jackals prowling upon it, they send up a prayer for return to their land that has no breath of hope in it.

Lamentations was traditionally assumed to have been the work of Jeremiah, although anything more unlike the point of view of that great prophet can hardly be imagined. *Lamentations* is the confused despair of all Judah crystallized into elaborate poetry, a Judah woefully convinced that the thunderous warnings of the prophets have come true at last and that the line of Israel, for its sins, will sink into oblivion.

The poet need not have been afraid. The search for God that was Israel's whole reason for existence was not so frail a thing that it could not flourish in Babylon as well as in Judah, or so weak that it would disappear because a few bricks had been torn down. The nation as a whole had never been the keeper of the covenant; it had always belonged to the individual. And if Judah's prosperity had not helped the individual in his search for God, it was not likely that the sudden collapse of that prosperity would hinder him.

No outside influence could make Israel, the striver with God, forget her search. The only betrayal could come from within, and any danger of that the prophets had averted by the very fact of their existence.

CHAPTER X

O land, land, land,
Hear the word of the Lord!
Book of Jeremiah xxii. 29

THE otherwise tragic record of the last days of the kingdom of Judah contains one name worthy to stand beside
the greatest of Israel's prophets. It belonged to Jeremiah,
of a priestly family at Anathoth, who for forty years
stood in opposition to all the priests and prophets of
Judah. No one was more grieved than Jeremiah over
what he had to do; but he did it nevertheless.

To understand the exact quality of Jeremiah's courage
it is necessary to remember what it was that he was opposing. The Jerusalem of his day was not the openly
idolatrous city that Isaiah had condemned. The discovery of the "book of the law" had brought about Josiah's
great religious reformation, and the Temple had been
restored, purified and dedicated to the worship of only
one God. All other altars had been destroyed, and the
services in the reformed Temple were as righteous and
enlightened as it was possible to make them.

This state of affairs was very reassuring to the inhabitants of Judah. Jerusalem had always been a holy city
but now she was doubly so, since she contained the true
Temple of God and the only one. As a result she was
under God's protection, and, however Babylon might
threaten her, its power would not avail. As the Lord had
swept away the Assyrians in the days of Isaiah, so would
he now destroy the Babylonians if they dared to march
against his chosen city.

Priest and prophet gave this doctrine to the people,

and the people believed them. Emotionally, the apparently miraculous destruction of Sennacherib's Assyrian hosts in Isaiah's day, at the very gates of the city, had had a profound effect on her inhabitants; and they naturally believed the priests who told them in the name of God that the city built on Mount Zion, the city blessed through his Temple and made for his glory, was also fully protected by his power. "Ah, Lord God! the prophets keep saying to them, 'You shall not see the sword, nor shall famine visit you; but assured peace will I give you in this place.' " (*Jer.* xiv. 13)

Against this doctrine, so soothing and apparently so holy, stood Jeremiah, alone.

It was his terrifying responsibility to tell the people of Jerusalem that they were putting their faith in a lie, and that if they believed the priests and prophets who spoke in the name of God they would lose their last chance of safety. Jerusalem was not of itself holy; neither was the Temple; neither was the ark. The only thing that was holy in itself was the individual's understanding of God, and it was this, rather than temple services or circumcision, that could save the city. If this understanding of God was lacking, as it apparently was, Jerusalem would fall as surely as Samaria had fallen, and nothing could save her. The priests and the prophets were trusting to a tradition rather than to a fact, still talking of peace when war was already at the gates.

However bitter this doctrine might be, it was the truth; and it was a truth about which Jeremiah could not keep silence as long as there remained any hope of saving the city. The prophet was like a surgeon making a bloody knife-thrust at the root of the disease while everyone else had gathered around to soothe the patient and assure him that he might expect a long and prosperous life.

Jeremiah had a clearer vision than any of his contemporaries, and he loved Jerusalem more than they. As a result he was scourged and imprisoned and stared death in the face all his life. His only reward was the reward of a real prophet; he knew that he was speaking the truth.

So great a man was Jeremiah that he could understand the point of view of the men opposing him even while he knew that it was wrong. He saw the tragedy of their position as clearly as he saw the tragedy of his own, and he pitied them from the bottom of his heart on the day when they would find it out for themselves. "On that day the courage of the king and the princes shall fail, the priests shall stand aghast, and the prophets shall be dazed with horror. They shall say, 'Ah, Lord God! thou hast certainly deceived this people, and Jerusalem, saying, "All shall be well with you," when the sword was reaching the heart.' " (*Jer.* iv. 9-10)

Only Jeremiah could see the sword, and the deadly wound it was making. Everyone else thought the evil could be cured by ignoring it.

> "The wound of the daughter of my people
>   They lightly heal,
>   Saying 'All is well, all is well,'
>   When naught is well." (*Jer.* vi. 14)

On Jeremiah alone fell the responsibility of saying, "Naught is well," and as a result there was never a man more thoroughly and universally hated.

Jeremiah was born of a priestly family, and the greatest enmity to him came, of course, from the men of his own class. To the priests, Jeremiah could lay no claim to being a true prophet. He was simply, according to them, a "madman who plays the prophet," (*Jer.* xxix. 26) a dangerous firebrand who upset the people and called the wisest men in the nation liars. For the sake of the peace of Judah it was necessary that he should be put out of the way, especially since he dared to present his blasphemous theories in the name of God and to follow the formula of "Thus says the Lord" which none but a true prophet had the right to use.

It was the men of Jeremiah's own town of Anathoth who made the first attempt to kill him. "You shall not prophesy in the name of the Lord, lest you die by our hands!" (*Jer.* xi. 21) They were not the only group of self-appointed spiritual leaders in the nation who decided that the only way to quiet Jeremiah was to murder him.

> "Come and let us hatch a plot against Jeremiah,
> For instruction shall not pass from the priest,
> Nor counsel from the wise, nor the word from the
>   prophet;
> Come and let us smite him for his speech."
>
> (*Jer.* xviii. 18)

Even the high priest himself finally interposed and tried to silence Jeremiah by humiliating him publicly with a scourging and the stocks. Ridicule was the strongest weapon in his armory. But however Jeremiah may have been shaken inwardly, he did not change his message.

Among those who gained an uneasy immortality by opposing Jeremiah was the prophet Hananiah. This prophet was apparently a man of high personal character and much influence. He faced Jeremiah in the Temple, before the throng of priests and worshippers, and told him that Jerusalem would never be destroyed. "Thus says the Lord of hosts, the God of Israel: 'I have broken the yoke of the king of Babylon. Within two years will I bring back to this place all the vessels of the house of the Lord which Nebuchadnezzar, king of Babylon, took away from this place.' " (*Jer.* xxviii. 2-3)

This was exactly the sort of thing everyone liked **to**

hear, and Jeremiah himself hoped that it might come true. But he added rather sadly that "the prophets who preceded you and me" (*Jer.* xxviii. 8) had never found any reason to promise the people safety and prosperity, and that if Hananiah were right he would have to prove it. Then Jeremiah went away, thought over what he had said, and regretted that he had seemed to half-consent to Hananiah's statement. At once he went back to his influential opponent and told him bluntly to his face, "Hear now, Hananiah! The Lord has not sent you, but you are making this people put their trust in a lie." (*Jer.* xxviii. 15)

Nothing would have made Jeremiah happier than to be able to say with the priests and the prophets, "All is well." Instead, he was obliged to tell the people that the reassurances of their leaders were "a lying dream, an empty superstition, a deceptive invention of their own minds." (*Jer.* xiv. 14) This was not pleasant news either to the prophets or to the people, and least of all was it pleasant to Jeremiah. These men were close friends of his, and of his own class. The leadership of the people was their responsibility. But they had put their trust in a tradition instead of trying to understand God.

> "I sent not the prophets, yet they ran;
> I spoke not to them, yet they prophesied.
> But if only they had stood in my council,
> And had listened to my words,
> They would have turned my people from their evil
>   course." (*Jer.* xxiii. 21-22)

Because of this lack of understanding of God, Jerusalem was betrayed. Her leaders contented themselves with prophesying peace, and there could be no peace for the city.

Nor was there peace for Jeremiah. It was a difficult

thing he was forced to do, and all his life he rebelled against the necessity of doing it. The opening of the *Book of Jeremiah* finds him protesting against such a responsibility when the call first came to him.

> "Ah, Lord God! I cannot speak;
> For I am only a boy." (*Jer.* i. 6)

His reassurance was that he had the truth on his side, and on that account need fear neither the princes nor the priests of Judah. He had complete authority to "root up and to pull down, to wreck and to ruin," and, what is so often forgotten of Jeremiah, "to build and to plant." (*Jer.* i. 10)

Nevertheless, Jeremiah hated what he was obliged to do. "My heart is broken within me." (*Jer.* xxiii. 9) He would have given much to be able to leave Jerusalem behind him and forget the warnings he was obliged to deliver to an unheeding city.

> "Oh, that I had in the desert
> A traveller's inn,
> That I might leave my people,
> And be quit of them!" (*Jer.* ix. 2)

The prophets might not be able to see the sword that was reaching the heart of Jerusalem; but Jeremiah could see it, and he felt it like a sword in his own heart. "For the wound of the daughter of my people I am wounded with grief, I walk in mourning, horror has seized me." (*Jer.* viii. 21) "My pain is incurable, my heart is sick within me." (*Jer.* viii. 18)

Bitterest of all to Jeremiah was the apparent futility of his mission, since no one believed him. The people decided that the prophet must want to see the city destroyed since he prophesied its doom so insistently.

> "Lo! they continue saying to me,
> 'Where is the word of the Lord?
>   Pray, let it come!'
> Yet I never urged thee to bring trouble on them,
> Nor longed for the fatal day—
>   Thou knowest!" (*Jer.* xvii. 15-16)

Jeremiah knew that he had become a laughing-stock, and his message a mockery. Yet he could not keep silent. "If I say, 'I will not think of it, nor speak any more in his name,' it is in my heart like a burning fire, shut up in my bones; I am worn out with holding it in—I cannot endure it." (*Jer.* xx. 9) So he spoke out, preferring even the threat of death to the denial of his mission.

The principle upon which Jeremiah based his message was a simple one, and might have been clear to the people if they had been willing to listen to it. The whole message of the professional prophets was that Jerusalem was a holy city, and it was on this conviction that they based their reiterated "All is well, all is well." Jeremiah contended that Jerusalem was not a holy city, however reformed her Temple might be, however holy her ark; and it was on this contention that he based his "Naught is well." The safety of the city was not a matter of bricks and mortar, however sanctified by tradition they might be. The safety of the city rested on the understanding of God possessed by its inhabitants, and where this understanding did not exist there was no safety to be found in Jerusalem.

That there should be no lack of clearness on this point, Jeremiah went and delivered his message inside the actual confines of the holy Temple itself. He told the worshippers there that the buildings would be forsaken as utterly as Shiloh was forsaken, unless they gave less thought to burnt-offerings and more to inward purity. What was the use of trusting to the holiness of the Temple while they themselves were unholy? "Thus says the Lord of hosts, the God of Israel. 'Amend your ways and your doings, that I may establish your home in this place. Trust not in deceptive words, such as, "The temple of the Lord, the temple of the Lord, the temple of the Lord is this!" For only if you amend your ways . . . will I establish your home in this place.' " (*Jer.* vii. 3-7)

Josiah's religious reformation made no difference to Jeremiah. He distrusted wholesale public movements, believing as he did that all spiritual responsibility rested with the individual rather than with the state. He was disposed to rate a reformed Jerusalem no higher than Samaria, the capital city of the northern kingdom of Israel, whose fall had become almost a by-word for the punishment of following more than one God.

> "In the prophets of Samaria I saw an offensive thing—
> They prophesied by the Baal, and misled my people Israel.
> But in the prophets of Jerusalem have I seen a horrible thing—
> They commit adultery and walk in lies."
>
> (*Jer.* xxiii. 13-14)

Israel had betrayed God by following idols, and because of that the kingdom was divorced and put away; but her sister Judah did a worse thing. Although she finally turned to the worship of one God, she did it not "in sincerity, but in sheer hypocrisy." (*Jer.* iii. 10) For this reason, "apostate Israel has proved herself more in the right than faithless Judah." (*Jer.* iii. 11)

It is easy to see how insulting Jeremiah's doctrine was to a Judah that considered herself reformed and holy, and how deeply it would antagonize the priesthood. It was sufficiently difficult for the authorities to hold the people to their religious obligations at any time; and the matter was certainly made no easier by the teachings of

a man who ignored the sanctity of ritual and had so little
respect for outward observances that he talked of cir-
cumcising the heart as well as the body. Jeremiah did
not even reverence the ark of the covenant, which had
been a holy object even in the days of the country's worst
idolatry and which reposed in the innermost sanctuary
of the Temple. He declared that when Jerusalem finally
did return to God there would no longer be any need for
an ark. "Men shall no more speak of 'The ark of the
covenant of the Lord'—it shall be neither remembered,
nor mentioned, nor sought after, nor made anew." (*Jer.*
iii. 16)

In their furious hatred of Jeremiah and his teachings,
the priests and prophets of Judah acted with the blindness of men completely sure of the righteousness of their
own position. They attacked Jeremiah, when they should
have attacked the danger he was pointing out to them.
"This man deserves to die; for he has prophesied against
this city." (*Jer.* xxvi. 11)

Never in his life did Jeremiah prophesy against the
city. He prophesied against trusting to the city, against
trusting to anything except God. He prophesied against
even wisdom and power, if they prevented a man from
seeking out God for himself.

> Thus says the Lord:
> "Let not the wise man boast of his wisdom,
> Nor the strong man boast of his strength,
> Nor the rich man boast of his riches!
> But if one must boast, let him boast of this,
> That he understands and knows me."
> (*Jer.* ix. 23-24)

Naturally a nation that had grown "fat and sleek" (*Jer.*
v. 28) with riches, and that lavished expensive foreign
incense on its altars, preferred to misunderstand its one
great prophet.

Jeremiah attempted to take his case to the common people, "the poor folk, who are without sense." (*Jer.* v. 4) He tried to free them from their stubborn faith in astrology and their only half-suppressed fear of the gods of the other nations, so powerful and so malign. Jeremiah told them there was no reason to believe in the power of the stars just because other people did; and as for the great gods of Assyria and Egypt, they were no more than blocks of wood overlaid with metal.

> They stand like scarecrows in a garden of cucumbers,
>   and cannot speak;
> They have to be carried, for they cannot walk.
> Be not afraid of them! for they cannot do harm,
> And also to do good is not in their power."
>   (*Jer.* x. 5)

The gods of the other nations had to be framed of wood by their worshippers; but the God whom Jeremiah implored the people to understand was himself "the framer of all things." (*Jer.* x. 16)

Jeremiah took over the familiar prophetic device of acting out his warnings, so that even the least intelligent might understand his message before it grew too late—

> Before it grow dark,
> Before your feet stumble
> On the twilight mountains. (*Jer.* xiii. 16)

He showed them a clay jar that had been spoiled in the making, "as clay is apt to do in the potter's hand," (*Jer.* xviii. 4) and reminded his listeners how easy it was for the potter to turn the jar into some other shape than the one originally intended. Even though they were the Chosen People, so might God do to the citizens of Judah. He called together the priests and elders and broke a flask before their eyes. "Thus says the Lord of hosts: 'As the potter's vessel is broken and cannot be mended

again, so will I break this people and this city.' " (*Jer.*
xix. 11) He even used as an object lesson the terrible
period of the drought, when all the cisterns ran dry, and
the wild asses stood on the bare heights with gasping
breath and lusterless eyes "because there was no green
thing." (*Jer.* xiv. 6)

Jeremiah's efforts were useless. Almost without exception, the prophets were preaching a Jerusalem that
could never be destroyed, since it was the home of God
and under his protection; and naturally the people preferred to believe these prophets rather than Jeremiah.
They brought comfort, and he brought woe. They brought
peace, and he, in his own bitter words, was "a man of
strife and a man of contention to all the earth." (*Jer.*
xv. 10) They told the people in the name of God: "You
shall not see the sword, nor shall famine visit you; but assured peace will I give you in this place." (*Jer.* xiv. 13)
Jeremiah found himself obliged to tell the people in the
same name: "You have kindled my wrath to a fire which
shall burn forever." (*Jer.* xvii. 4)

Not only the priests were Jeremiah's enemies but the
patriots as well, since his political convictions were as
unpopular as his religious principles. Jeremiah was
strongly opposed to the disastrous idea of an Egyptian
alliance and said so, thereby alienating the anti-Baby-
lonian party in Jerusalem which included most of the
influential men of the city. The court circles were anxious to see Judah freed from her overlord, Babylon, and
had the theory that an alliance with Egypt would give
her the military strength that would make revolt prac-
ticable. Jeremiah knew that any revolt which depended
on Egypt for assistance would never be a success, and he
strongly advised the people not to be influenced by the
pro-Egyptian party. "Do not listen to them, but serve
the king of Babylon, that you may live." (*Jer.* xxvii. 17)

Preaching such a doctrine, Jeremiah only narrowly escaped being murdered; but he succeeded in drawing about him a small group of influential men who believed, as he did, that trust in Egypt was a mistake, chief among these being the aristocratic and very splendid house of Shaphan.

King Jehoiakim sided with the pro-Egyptian party in ignoring Jeremiah's teachings and was also disposed, rather unwisely, to ignore Jeremiah himself. When some of the princes forced a scroll of Jeremiah's prophecies on his attention, he permitted them to be read but, as each column was finished, he cut it off with his knife and tossed it into the brazier that was warming the room. Unlike his father Josiah, Jehoiakim had no respect for prophets. He considered them no more than rather inconvenient private citizens, to be executed out of hand if they became too troublesome. The king did actually direct the murder of a prophet named Uriah who had prophesied against the city in a manner similar to Jeremiah's. But Jeremiah was equally undeterred by Uriah's death and by his own very narrow escape. He only added to his book a swift character sketch of the royal tyrant, and mocked his capacity for building houses rather than for ruling righteously. "Would you play the king, forsooth, by vying with others in cedar?" (*Jer.* xxii. 15)

Zedekiah, the last king of dying Judah, lacked entirely his older brother's strength of character. He feared the pro-Egyptian party, but he also feared Jeremiah; and he spent his whole reign in a futile attempt at compromise between the two. He finally yielded to the court party because it was the stronger, and then had his worst fears realized when King Nebuchadnezzar of Babylon started towards the city on a punitive expedition.

King Zedekiah hastened at once to Jeremiah to inquire if the Lord in his loving mercy was going to be graciously inclined to spare Jerusalem, and Jeremiah told him bluntly that the city would fall. Events, however, discredited the prophet, for the king of Babylon was obliged to raise the siege on Jerusalem to meet the Egyptian army, which had also marched into Palestine. The party of the opposition seized on this opportunity to get the prophet imprisoned; but the unhappy Zedekiah sent for him secretly to inquire, "Is there any word from the Lord?" (*Jer*. xxxvii. 17) Unmoved by his apparent failure, Jeremiah replied, "There is. You shall be given into the hand of the king of Babylon." (*Jer*. xxxvii. 17)

Almost at once, Jeremiah was proven correct. Nebuchadnezzar defeated the Egyptians and returned to the siege of Jerusalem, this time to complete it. During the long months of the siege, Jeremiah earned such unpopularity by his pacifistic speeches that the patriots finally demanded the king's permission to put the prophet to death. Zedekiah replied meekly, "He is in your hand; for the king can do nothing against you," (*Jer*. xxxviii. 5) and allowed Jeremiah to be thrown into a muddy cistern in the guard-court to die. When one of Jeremiah's friends protested, the king with equal meekness allowed the prophet to be rescued from the cistern; but although Jeremiah escaped death, he remained imprisoned in the guard-house for the rest of the siege.

It was then that Jeremiah showed the real beauty and gentleness of his spirit. All his prophecies, heretofore mocked as wild visions, had come true, and everyone could see that the holy city was doomed. There was no longer any reason to threaten and to warn, and the promptness with which Jeremiah dropped the role that had been forced on him shows how foreign it was to his real nature.

Jeremiah wrote no more of terror and destruction. He wasted no time in congratulating himself on his own wisdom. He wrote instead what has been called the little book of consolation.

Jerusalem would rise again. Her citizens might go into exile, but only to find grace in the wilderness, and when they returned they would be prepared to rebuild their city on a new foundation, that of understanding. The new Jerusalem would really be safe and indestructible, because it would be founded on the truth, and out of it would go songs of thanksgiving to the God that satisfies "the weary spirit." (*Jer.* xxxi. 25)

In the new city no one would be under the necessity of trying to teach a knowledge of God to unheeding ears. The heart that Jeremiah had once called "treacherous above all things, and desperately sick" (*Jer.* xvii. 9) would be forever healed, and each man would know God fully for himself. "They shall teach no more every one his neighbor, and every one his brother, saying, 'Know the Lord'; for all of them shall know me, from the least of them to the greatest." (*Jer.* xxxi. 34)

Even the covenant of Moses, the old covenant of which the priesthood had been so proud, would no longer be necessary. A new covenant would be made with each individual, each in his own heart, and would never be broken. It would be no public pledge, based on compulsion, but an inward law, based on the spirit. "I will make a new covenant with the household of Israel and with the household of Judah, not like the covenant which I made with their fathers . . . I will put my law within them, and will write it on their hearts; and I will be their God, and they shall be my people." (*Jer.* xxxi. 31-33) The city to be built under this covenant would be born of the complete understanding of God, and it would therefore be "a joy and praise and glory among all the nations of the earth." (*Jer.* xxxiii. 9)

Jeremiah wrote this while he was shut up in the guard-

house and the defences of the besieged city were slowly
crumbling before the Babylonian troops. Yet to testify
that he spoke the truth, the prophet bought a plot of
land in the stricken countryside and had the deed of pur-
chase witnessed by all the men who were in the guard-
house at the time. There could be no claim made to the
land in his own lifetime; but Jeremiah ordered the deed
placed in an earthenware jar, where it might be kept safe
as a witness to the truth of his prophecy. "For thus says
the Lord of hosts, the God of Israel: 'Houses and fields
and vineyards shall once more be bought in this land.' "
(*Jer.* xxxii. 15)

The details of this transaction were carried out by
Baruch, the young man who had constituted himself
Jeremiah's secretary, his friend, and almost his son. Born
of an influential family and normally destined for "great
things," (*Jer.* xlv. 5) Baruch left them all to throw in
his lot with the unpopular prophet whom he loved. He
once risked his life reading Jeremiah's prophecies aloud
in the Temple courtyard after Jeremiah himself had been
forbidden to enter there again.

It is to Baruch that the *Book of Jeremiah* is largely
owing. He gathered together the scattered prophecies and
memoirs that his great master had dictated to him, and
incorporated them with what he himself remembered
to make the most personal and most dramatic of all the
prophetic books of the Old Testament. Baruch did not
arrange his notes in historical sequence, a fact which
makes the book confusing on first glance. But he dated
each section so carefully with the year of the reigning
king that it is not difficult to put the book into its historical order and to follow Jeremiah's life very much as he
lived it.

Jeremiah was still in prison when the walls of the
starving city were breached and Nebuchadnezzar entered

the city at the head of his troops. The commander of the guard was ordered to let Jeremiah do as he wished; he might stay in the half-ruined city, move to the country, or follow the exiles to Babylon. "Go wherever you think right and proper." (*Jer*. xl. 4) Jeremiah decided to stay in Jerusalem and cast in his lot with the new governor, Gedaliah.

Gedaliah was a member of the house of Shaphan, and an intelligent, enlightened ruler. He might very possibly have succeeded in building a new kingdom on the ruins of the old if he had not been murdered, while he sat at dinner, by a Jewish princeling whom he trusted. The remnant that remained in Judah were terrified by the outrage, knowing that Nebuchadnezzar would hold them responsible for the murder of their governor; and they gathered together all the rest of the people and fled to Egypt.

As a preliminary, however, they went respectfully to Jeremiah and asked him what the Lord wanted them to do, promising to obey whatever might be asked of them. "Whether it be pleasant or unpleasant, we will obey the voice of the Lord our God." (*Jer*. xlii. 6) Jeremiah told them to stay in the land, and not to be afraid of the king of Babylon, whereupon the petitioners decided that Baruch had persuaded the prophet to give them the wrong answer out of a desire for revenge. They went into headlong flight into Egypt, taking Jeremiah with them.

Once in Egypt the refugees committed the final act of betrayal. They began to reorganize the cult of "the queen of the heavens," an excellent example of Jeremiah's contention that much of the great religious reformation had been "sheer hypocrisy." (*Jer*. iii. 10) As the refugees told Jeremiah, it was only when they agreed to worship at the altar of his God that they had met disaster, while the queen of heaven had always protected them. "For then we had plenty to eat, and were well, and met with no trouble; but since we gave up offering sacrifice to the queen of the heavens, and pouring libations to her, we have been destitute of all things, and have been consumed by sword and famine." (*Jer.* xliv. 17-18)

If Jeremiah's heart could ever have been broken by his people's complete lack of understanding, it would have broken then; but he had apparently ceased long since to expect anything of them or to be troubled by what they might do. Jeremiah had always known that he would have a long time to wait before his covenant, the inward covenant of understanding, came into existence, and as he grew older he was content to let that day come of itself and without his striving. He told the scattered remnant of his people in Egypt that they might do as they liked and offer sacrifices to whomsoever they would; but in the end they would know "whose word shall stand—mine, or theirs." (*Jer.* xliv. 28) Then he left them, to disappear from their sight and also from history.

In the book which remains as a memorial to one of the greatest of Judah's prophets, it is not so much Jeremiah's honesty that stands as the most important thing about him, or even his invincible moral courage. It is primarily the steadiness and patience with which he fought for the principle of individual obligation.

Jeremiah would admit no sort of a mediator between a man and his God, neither a temple nor an ancient covenant nor a priest. The understanding of God was not a matter of ecclesiastical organization but of individual responsibility; and no man could hope to escape that responsibility by the piety of his outward observances.

This doctrine of the individual was implicit in the teachings of the prophets of Israel long before Jeremiah was born. But he was the first to give it in clear and un-

mistakable language, and it was on that account that he
made an open and avowed enemy of the most enlightened
religious institution of his day, the Jewish Temple. Jeremiah believed that neither Abraham's covenant, Moses'
law nor David's city could be used as a substitute for individual righteousness, and his attitude was a death-blow
to an organization which depended for its existence on
the people's faith in all three.

To Jeremiah, there was no such thing as a vicarious
at-one-ment. Both the search and the obligation to search
were individual, and no institution, no matter how sanctified by tradition or the work of great men, was sufficient
to bring its believers into the "new Jerusalem" of the
knowledge of God.

CHAPTER XI

Could we sing the songs of the Lord
In a foreign land?

The Book of Psalms cxxxvii. 4

WHILE Jeremiah was preaching the unpopular doctrine of individual responsibility in Jerusalem, another Hebrew prophet was doing the same in Babylonia. Ezekiel, also the son of a priest, had been among the ten thousand exiles of the first captivity; and he had settled in a small colony among his own people on the banks of one of the great Babylonian canals, to teach there what Jeremiah was teaching in Jerusalem.

Although the two prophets resembled each other in some things, Ezekiel never stirred up the intense opposition in Babylonia that Jeremiah met with in Jerusalem. Himself a lesser man, he was addressing a more intelligent group of people and one unlikely to be swayed by mob spirit. It was the best men who had been taken away from Judah in the first captivity, as Jeremiah bitterly reminded the rest in his parable of the bad and good figs. In any case, it was less painful to hear a prediction of Jerusalem's fall in far-off Babylonia than in the doomed city itself; and Ezekiel had no angry priestcraft to contend with, since there was no solidly entrenched temple for the Jews on the banks of the Chebar.

Moreover, Ezekiel was an attractive orator, and his method of delivering his prophecies was both colorful and enlivening. Jeremiah was accustomed to write out a collection of harsh but necessary truths on a scroll and then read them to the assembled worshippers in the Temple when they were in an emotional rather than a logical state of mind. His interest centered on the fact itself rather than on the method of its delivery, and it is probable that neither he nor his disciple Baruch was a very successful orator. Ezekiel, on the other hand, was both orator and actor, and his audience thoroughly enjoyed listening to him.

Ezekiel himself was too honest a prophet to be pleased that this was so. He also was more interested in the truth than in the manner of its delivery, and the fact that he was a colorful speaker is no reflection on his sincerity. He himself complained that the people treated him as though he were "a singer of love-songs, with a beautiful voice." (*Ezek.* xxxiii. 32) They came and listened with the most eager attention to everything he said, and then went away and acted as though he had never spoken. Ezekiel did not speak to enjoy the act of oratory. There was a serious purpose behind everything he said, as serious as Jeremiah's, and the people would have done well to listen less to his delivery and more to his meaning. "They listen to your words, but they will not obey them. Only when the hour comes—and it is coming—they shall know that a prophet has been in the midst of them." (*Ezek.* xxxiii. 32-33)

The central idea of Ezekiel's teachings bears a close resemblance to that of Jeremiah's. Judah once made a covenant with God, and she should have guarded it more jealously than her very life. Because she had betrayed it, wilfully losing what was of more importance to her than her existence, she would lose her existence as well. Yet in the end, when she understood that this covenant was not of the flesh but of the spirit, she would be reinstated as a nation and regain all that she had lost. Judah's sin was lack of understanding; it was because she had misunderstood the covenant that she had lost it.

Jeremiah told this to the people of Jerusalem, and they hated him for it; but the exiled elders in Babylonia flocked to Ezekiel to hear the same thing.

It would be an injustice to the exiles to suppose that they went to Ezekiel only for the pleasure of listening to him, but there can be no doubt that his message was made much more forceful by the way he delivered it. The emblem of the married woman playing the harlot had been used by nearly all the prophets to symbolize the nation's adultery, but no one else succeeded in putting into the well-worn simile the vividness, the coarseness and the dramatic force with which Ezekiel endowed it. No man among his listeners could fail to feel angry contempt for the young slut of Ezekiel's picturing who clutched at her husband's gifts of fabrics and jewels and used them to bribe other men to lie with her, having not even the prostitute's excuse that she did it for hire. Every husband in the audience would be willing to agree that no punishment could be too heavy for such wanton adultery, and Ezekiel would have his listeners exactly where he wanted them. For no one could deny that Judah's adulteration of the truth had been as wanton as any harlot's, or that she had made the religions of Assyria and Babylon her lovers in disobedience to a covenant more binding than any marriage vow.

Ezekiel instinctively saw everything in pictures; in his writings the old prophetic symbols come vividly to life. The fall of Tyre had for him no conventional setting of rapine and disaster. In his discourse Tyre is a great ship, every detail of which he lovingly describes. Her decks are made of larch, her mast of cedar, and her sails are of richly embroidered Egyptian linen. Her awnings are purple and blue, and rows of shields and helmets glitter along her sides. Heavily laden with merchandise from all over the world, ivory and rubies and wine and spices and fine white wool, she meets an east wind while she is moving in the heart of the sea and sinks. With her goes all her store of jewels and spices, her traders and soldiers and mariners; and at the last cry of her steersmen, the coastlands tremble in terror.

Ezekiel describes the king of Egypt as a great dragon lying in the midst of the Nile and exulting,

> "This stream of mine is mine own
> It was I that made it," (*Ezek.* xxix. 3)

only to be dragged out by a hook, all the fishes clinging to his sides, and left to die on the dry land. Egypt's military defeat is like the pain of a broken right arm, on which neither "healing applications may be used" nor "bandages put on, to make it strong enough to grasp the sword." (*Ezek.* xxx. 21) The faithless rulers of Judah are like rams who trample the pasture grass beneath their feet and muddy the clear water so that the lambs cannot drink it, or like shepherds who shear the flocks at their pleasure but forget to protect them from the dangers of night and the wild beasts. Samaria looking towards the Assyrians for help is a young girl falling in love with the beautiful Assyrian gentlemen, "lords clothed in purple, governors and deputies, all of them handsome young men, knights riding on horseback." (*Ezek.* xxiii. 6) And her sister city Jerusalem turns towards the religion of the Babylonians because she sees "portraits of men on the walls—figures of Chaldeans portrayed in vermilion, with girdles round their loins, and flowing turbans upon their heads, all of them looking like officers." (*Ezek.* xxiii. 14-15)

Ezekiel saw everything in such vivid and literal pictures that the sudden caution that comes upon him when he tries to put into words his vision of the glory of God is doubly interesting. Each symbol which he uses he labels as a symbol, a precaution very unusual with him. "Upon the semblance of a throne was a semblance like that of a man sitting above it. From the appearance of his loins upward I saw something with a luster like that of shining metal; and from the appearance of his loins downward I saw something resembling fire, with a radiance round about it, resembling the bow that appears in the clouds on a rainy day." (*Ezek.* i. 26-28) Ezekiel, the vivid painter, does not call this confused picture the glory of the Lord; he calls it "the semblance of the glory of the Lord." (*Ezek.* i. 28) Even though his listeners were well acquainted with the Oriental use of imagery and were not likely to take him literally, Ezekiel was unwilling to let even the dullest suppose that when he spoke of God he meant a glorified man.

Another quality in addition to his picturesqueness that endeared the prophet to his audiences was his acting ability. All Hebrew prophets occasionally suited the action to the word, but Ezekiel's skillful use of this device raised the practice to the level of a fine art. Much can be said with a gesture, especially in the Eastern countries, but Ezekiel expanded his gestures until they became miniature dramas in themselves.

One day the prophet would pack up his belongings as though he were going on a journey, mimic the digging of a hole in a city wall, and cover his face so that he could not see the ground while he was doing it. Then, when his fellow countrymen, consumed with curiosity, asked him what he was doing, he would enter into his discourse, explaining that his action was an omen for the citizens of Jerusalem. "As I have done, so shall they have to do; they shall go into exile—into captivity. And the prince who is in the midst of them shall carry his baggage upon his shoulders, and go out in the dark; he shall dig a hole through the wall, to go out by it; he shall cover his face, so that he may not see the ground with his eyes." (*Ezek.* xii. 11-12)

Or Ezekiel would draw his sword, and make it the

sword of the king of Babylon, "the sword of the slain, the great sword of the slain . . . which is made to flash as lightning, and is whetted for slaughter!" (*Ezek.* xxi. 14-15) He would sketch with its point in the dust the two roads that lay before the king of Babylon, one of them leading to Judah, and picture him standing at the crossroads practicing divination to find out which road he should take. "Into his right hand falls the lot marked 'Jerusalem,' calling for slaughter," (*Ezek.* xxi. 22) and Ezekiel whirls the sword of slaughter aloft and then plunges it suddenly into its sheath. Even so simple an idea as the ultimate union of Israel and Judah was acted out, two sticks held wide apart and then dramatically joined.

Yet Ezekiel could be blunt enough when he wished to be. He had recourse to no imagery when he denounced the prophets "who prophesy out of their own imagination" (*Ezek.* xiii. 17) or the outwardly pious men who "set up idols in their minds." (*Ezek.* xiv. 3) He was as plain-spoken as Jeremiah when it came to the doctrine of individual responsibility.

> What mean you by quoting this proverb in the land of Israel:
>> The fathers eat sour grapes,
>> And the children's teeth are set on edge?
> (*Ezek.* xviii. 2)

No man can be held responsible for any but his own sins, except that a true prophet is responsible if he does not warn a man in time. Nor can a man sin and then claim exemption because of past virtues, although if a man resolutely puts his wrong-doing behind him, he will not be punished for that which he has truly forsaken. " 'Have I any pleasure at all in the death of the wicked?' is the oracle of the Lord God; 'and not rather in this, that he turn from his way and live?' " (*Ezek.* xviii. 23)

Men dare to say that the ways of the Lord are not fair; but "is it not your ways that are not fair?" (*Ezek.* xviii. 25)

For a long time, as a corollary to this doctrine of individual responsibility, Ezekiel had been predicting the fall of the supposedly holy city of Jerusalem. The exiles were beginning to say to each other, "The vision which he sees is for many days hence; he is prophesying of times far off;" (*Ezek.* xii. 27) but one day a messenger arrived with the news that his warning had come true. "The city is smitten." (*Ezek.* xxxiii. 21)

When he heard the news, Ezekiel did not stop to exalt his own wisdom, as he might so naturally and forgivably have done. Instead, like Jeremiah, he turned to console his people, although the comfort he offered was no easy one.

The people of Judah had believed for a long time that their national safety was founded on Abraham's covenant with God, and that as long as the covenant endured the land would be safe. Moreover, they were thousands where Abraham was only one. "Abraham was but one man, yet he received possession of the land; now, we being many, the land will surely be given to us as a possession." (*Ezek.* xxxiii. 24) They had failed to understand that the only real covenant with God depended neither on Abraham nor on numbers, but on the understanding of the individual. And so they had lost the land. They would regain it when they made a new covenant with God, one which God himself would give them in honor of his own name. "I will give you a new heart, and will put within you a new spirit; I will remove the heart of stone out of your flesh, and will give you a heart of flesh; and I will put my spirit within you, and will make you follow my statutes and keep my ordinances and obey them." (*Ezek.* xxxvi. 26-27) "It is not for

your sake that I am about to act, O household of Israel,
but for my holy name." (*Ezek.* xxxvi. 22)

Ezekiel reinforces this prophecy with a description of
a vision. The prophet finds himself in a valley filled with
dry bones and is asked,

"O mortal man, can these bones live?"
(*Ezek.* xxxvii. 3)

He is told to give the bones the word of God, and as
he does so he hears a rustling; the bones come together
one by one, are clothed with sinews and flesh, catch their
breath from the winds and become living men. The
prophet is told that "these bones are the whole household
of Israel." (*Ezek.* xxxvii. 11) Israel may appear dead,
but the word of God can nevertheless restore her. "I will
put my spirit into you, and you shall live." (*Ezek.*
xxxvii. 14)

One last picture closes the *Book of Ezekiel,* that of an
ideal temple and a rebuilt Jerusalem. Ezekiel is as exact
as a carpenter in his dimensions, giving measurements
for the temple rooms, the gates, even the city itself, and
it is quite possible that he intended his vision to serve as
a kind of chart for the exiles in that far-off day when
they returned to rebuild the ruined city.

Each number had a specific meaning to the Hebrews,
and Ezekiel's vision is an explanation in pictures and
figures of how the new city should conduct herself. The
prophet arranged for no political or ecclesiastical leader;
the king is given no power and the office of high priest
is not recognized. The chief emphasis is on the dimensions of the rebuilt temple, the dimensions of the altar,
the regulations for its worship and the qualifications of
the priests who are to minister to it. The vision ends with
a mention of the famous springs which rose on Zion and
flowed out of the temple, springs which would become

so holy by contact with that holy place that when they reached the Dead Sea its water would revive and become fresh.

It is obvious that Ezekiel, even if he had remained in Jerusalem, would never have become involved with the hostility of the priestcraft as Jeremiah did. Ezekiel was the son of a priest, and his minute arrangements for the details of temple worship in the new Jerusalem show how thoroughly he identified himself with the priestly point of view.

So greatly was Ezekiel concerned for the honor of the altar that he would not permit the Levites (the priestly class as a whole) to administer to it because they once went "astray." (*Ezek*. xliv. 10) Only one branch of the Levites, the sons of Zadok, were to have that privilege. Ezekiel himself was one of the sons of Zadok, and the heritage undoubtedly colored his point of view. He would have been incapable of going into the Temple, as Jeremiah once did, to say that the building which the people trusted was not worthy of trust. Jeremiah also belonged to a priestly family, but he cast the relationship from him. Ezekiel remained essentially a priest always, and it is partly for that reason that he is the lesser prophet.

Another Hebrew prophet was in Babylonia at the same time as Ezekiel, the prophet Daniel; but while Ezekiel was allowed to settle in a colony composed of men of his own faith, Daniel was taken to the capital city to be surrounded, as Joseph had once been, with strange customs and hostile gods.

Very little is known with certainty about the career of Daniel, except that he was evidently a very great man and the memory of his deeds was treasured by his own people. When a Jewish writer four centuries later wanted to comfort and sustain his people in a period of bitter religious persecution, he almost instinctively chose the name of the prophet Daniel to carry his message. Daniel was the prophet who had trusted completely and successfully to the power of God, and who had been afraid of nothing.

The *Book of Daniel* as it now stands is a product of this period of persecution that took place four centuries after the Babylonian Exile, and it is difficult to say how much may be attributed to Daniel of Babylonia and how much to a later hand. The fact that the book is written in two languages, Hebrew and Aramaic, may indicate that the author was working from an Aramaic fragment, consisting of Daniel's life in Babylon and a single prophecy, to which he added an introduction, alterations, and a group of subsequent visions in late Hebrew. Or it is equally possible that the author of the book in its present form relied on verbal traditions of the life of the prophet Daniel and did all the writing himself.

It is by the four "visions" in the *Book of Daniel* that the book may be dated. Each vision begins at the same point, with a warfare among empires and the return from exile, and each vision ends at the same point, with a very evil king who will set up an abomination of desolation in the temple of the Most High and who will eventually be destroyed. That there shall be no doubt in anyone's mind as to the identity of this great force for evil, each vision gives the historical events previous to the throning of this ruler and also the events of his reign. The fourth vision is the longest and most explicit, and is therefore the most useful in identifying the particular blasphemy against which the *Book of Daniel* is directed.

The fourth vision is introduced with the greatest solemnity of the four. An angel that is almost a vision in fire comes to the prophet and announces his mission:

"I will tell you what is inscribed in the book of truth—here and now I will tell you the truth." (*Dan.* xi. 1-2)

What follows is undoubtedly the truth. It is a survey of ancient history beginning at the time of the return from the Babylonian Exile and continuing for the subsequent four centuries.

> There shall arise three more kings in Persia, then a fourth, who shall be far richer than all of them; and when he has grown strong through his riches, he shall set all his forces in motion against the kingdom of Greece. Then a warlike king shall arise, who shall rule with great power, and shall do as he pleases. But when he has grown strong, his kingdom shall be broken up, and divided towards the four winds of the heavens; it shall not pass to his posterity, nor shall it retain the power with which he ruled. (*Dan.* xi. 2-4)

Persia was the nation that conquered Babylonia and permitted the Jews to return and rebuild Jerusalem. Persia in its turn was conquered by Alexander of Greece, who built a great empire which dissolved again at his death. He had no heir, and the lands he conquered were split among his four generals.

> Then the king of the south shall be strong; but one of his captains shall be stronger than he, and shall rule over a kingdom greater than his. After a number of years they shall form an alliance; and the daughter of the king of the south shall come to the king of the north, to seal the treaty of peace. But her influence shall be of no avail, nor shall her influence last; for she shall be given up, together with her suite.
> (*Dan.* xi. 5-6)

One of Alexander's four generals, Ptolemy, acquired Egypt, and became the "king of the south." An officer of his, Seleucus, eventually acquired Syria and founded the Seleucid dynasty. To cement an alliance between the two kingdoms, Ptolemy's granddaughter Berenice was sent north to marry Antiochus II of Syria; and there she was murdered. The vision continues with the lengthy wars that resulted between the two kingdoms, wars that were of particular importance to Judah, since whichever side won the war won Judah as well.

> There shall arise in his place a scion from her roots, who shall come with an army, and shall enter the stronghold of the king of the north, and shall throw him and his people into a panic . . . For a number of years he shall refrain from attacking the king of the north. Then the latter shall invade the kingdom of the king of the south, though he shall return to his own country. But his son shall bestir himself, and shall muster an array of great forces. (*Dan.* xi. 7-10)

The "scion from her roots" was Berenice's brother, Ptolemy III, who marched north to avenge her murder. He was successful in his invasion, and sacked Antioch. Then there was a lull of sorts, until Antiochus III came to the throne of Syria and mustered a large army to take his revenge on the Ptolemys.

> Then the king of the south, moved by fierce rage, shall march out and fight with him—that is, with the king of the north—who shall raise a great army. But the army shall be given into his hand, and shall be carried away captive. Then his heart shall be lifted up, and he shall put down tens of thousands, though he shall not make good his success. For the king of the north shall raise another army, greater than the former one . . . and the forces of the south shall make no stand against him—even their picked troops shall have no strength to stand. The invader shall do as he pleases, with none to stand against him; he shall stand in the glorious land, holding it all in his hand.
> (*Dan.* xi. 11-16)

Ptolemy mustered his forces against Antiochus, and defeated him at the inconclusive Battle of Raphia. The king of Syria then raised another army "greater than the former one." and conquered the Egyptians in the year 200 B.C. After this victory the Syrians controlled Palestine, and Antiochus II stood "in the glorious land, holding it all in his hand." It is with Antiochus that the vision continues.

> Then he shall set his face to advance against the king of the south with the full strength of his kingdom, but shall have to make terms with him; and he shall give him his daughter in marriage. . . . Then he shall turn his face towards the coast-lands, and shall take many of them; but a certain commander shall put an end to his insolence. (*Dan.* xi. 17-18)

An alliance was concluded between the two warring kingdoms when Antiochus gave Ptolemy V the hand of his daughter, Cleopatra of Syria, in marriage. Then Antiochus turned his attention towards Thrace and the "coastlands" of Asia Minor, where he collided with the power of Rome in the Mediterranean. A Roman commander, Scipio Africanus, defeated him at the battle of Magnesia.

> In his place there shall arise one who will send an exactor of tribute through the most glorious part of the kingdom; but within a few days he shall be broken, though not by open violence, nor in battle.
>
> (*Dan.* xi. 20)

The Romans put a heavy indemnity on the defeated Syrians, and the next Syrian ruler, Seleucus IV, was obliged to tax Judea heavily. It was no regret to the Jews when they heard that Seleucus had met death at the hands of his chief minister, Heliodorus.

> In his place there shall arise a contemptible person, on whom the royal dignity has not been conferred, but who shall come by stealth, and shall win the kingdom by intrigues. Armed forces shall be utterly overwhelmed before him, and the prince of the covenant shall also be broken. (*Dan.* xi. 21-22)

Thus enters the evil king of the *Book of Daniel*, the king who tried to destroy the religion of the Jews.

His name was Antiochus IV, and he was a brother of the King Seleucus who was murdered. The Seleucids all thought they were descended from the Greek god Apollo, but Antiochus IV went a step further and decreed that he should be worshipped as a god in his own lifetime, adding to his name the title of Theos Epiphanes, or God Manifest.

Antiochus Epiphanes decided that his Jewish subjects should also worship the Greek gods, among whom he numbered himself, and he undertook to convert the country by main force as Jezebel of Tyre had once tried to do before him. The king had a statue to Zeus erected in the holy inner sanctuary of the Temple at Jerusalem and ordered swine's flesh to be sacrificed before it, the most appalling blasphemy of which the Jewish mind could conceive. Then he began a reign of terror in Judea, putting to torture and death anyone who opposed him, and making it a capital crime to observe the Jewish Sabbath or to own a copy of the Jewish Scripture.

Even at the beginning of his reign there was preliminary trouble, when Onias, the high priest of the Temple, the "prince of the covenant" mentioned above, was murdered.

> By means of a great army he shall raise his might and courage against the king of the south. . . . Then he shall return to his own land laden with goods; and his mind being set against the holy covenant, he shall work his will. (*Dan.* xi. 25-28)

Antiochus Epiphanes undertook a successful campaign against Egypt, and then returned through Judea. There had been a minor revolt against him in Jerusalem, and he repaid it by plundering the Temple and massacring some of the inhabitants.

> At the time appointed he shall again invade the south;
> but this time it shall not be as in former times, for
> Roman ships shall come against him, and he shall be
> cowed. Then he shall be inflamed once more with rage
> against the holy covenant; and having come to an un-
> derstanding with those who have forsaken the holy
> covenant, he shall once more work his will.
>
> (*Dan.* xi. 29-30)

When Antiochus tried another invasion of Egypt the
following year, he was less successful. Rome had no intention of letting the balance of power in the Eastern
Mediterranean be upset by Syria. Her naval power
forced Antiochus to renounce any hopes he may have
had of extending his empire, and he had to be content
with Palestine as his southern frontier. It therefore became especially important to make Judea a stronghold of
loyalty to the "God Manifest," Antiochus himself, and
to eradicate the worship of the God of Judah. In this
work Antiochus had the support of many Hellenistic
Jews who had "forsaken the holy covenant" and who
admired the Greek religion so much that they even attempted to have the marks of circumcision removed arti-
ficially.

> Armed forces shall be raised by him, and they shall
> desecrate the stronghold of the sanctuary, and shall
> abolish the continual offering, and shall put in its
> place the desolating abomination. By his intrigues he
> shall corrupt those who have violated the covenant;
> but the people who know their God shall be steadfast
> and shall accomplish exploits. Such as are wise among
> the people shall bring understanding to the multitude,
> though for many days they shall fall victims to sword
> and flame, to captivity and plunder. (*Dan.* xi. 31-33)

Since Antiochus had the help of the Hellenistic Jews, he
probably thought he could carry out his program easily
enough when he marched into Jerusalem, abolished the

Temple offerings and erected his statue to Zeus inside the innermost sanctuary. Instead, the crowning insult of a heathen statue inside their holy Temple roused the Jews to a fury of desperate courage, and the result was the Maccabean War.

The revolt against Syria was prolonged and bitter, as the *Books of the Maccabees* attest, with their stories of torture and slaughter and of the bitter, reckless courage of the loyalist Jews. There were few darker periods in Jewish history, and it was at this time that the *Book of Daniel* was written, to reassure the loyalist Jews and to promise them that their religion, the religion of one God, could never be lost.

The writer of the book expressed this conviction in the name of Daniel, because Daniel had maintained his religion in a court of alien gods, and because neither fear nor loneliness nor the strength of his enemies had shaken his faith in the power of God. Daniel had eventually triumphed and the writer of the four visions promises that again the Jews will triumph as he did, to shine "like the stars forever and ever." (*Dan.* xii. 3)

It is not a political or military victory that is promised in the *Book of Daniel*. Its author believed that the war against Antiochus Epiphanes was a holy war and that the archangel Michael would himself rise against the evil king who had tried to destroy the religion of the Jews. As soon as he was destroyed there would be a final Day of Judgment and "those who sleep in the land of dust shall awake, some to everlasting life, and others to everlasting reproach and contempt." (*Dan.* xii. 2)

The *Book of Daniel* is in many ways a distinguished piece of work, and it is certainly a courageous one. It is not, however, a book of much spiritual value. Its writer made the familiar mistake of believing that a single man could become the embodiment of all evil, so that if this single man were destroyed all evil would cease with him.

This was not the kind of mistake Isaiah would have made, but it was characteristic of the narrower point of view of the men of the Return. They came to believe that "evil" meant faithlessness to the Law, and that "good" meant unquestioning acceptance of the God of Judaism. They were the lineal descendants of the men who thought Jeremiah a blasphemer because he questioned the religious traditions of the forefathers. They themselves worshipped God without question, reverently and blindly; they were not of the race of Israel, the "striver with God."

As far as the knowledge of names goes, Jeremiah was the last prophet of the Old Testament to belong to that great race of iconoclasts and builders who deserve the honor of the name of 'Israel.' But there was at least one great prophet in the days of the Babylonian Exile who was the equal of Isaiah and Jeremiah, although his name is now lost. He is sometimes called the "second Isaiah" because his prophetic work now appears as the last twenty-seven chapters of the *Book of Isaiah;* and, whatever his name, he was both prophet and poet.

His great drama of Israel's redemption is a fitting climax to Old Testament prophecy. It gathers up all the discoveries of the earlier prophets into a unified whole and it expresses, in poetry that for sustained beauty is matched by nothing else in the Bible, the final meaning of Israel's search for God.

CHAPTER XII

Then shall the glory of the Lord be revealed.
The Book of Isaiah xl. 5

EACH Hebrew prophet went on his own way, occupied with the problems of his own time, and each gave in the name of God the measure of his own striving. But there was one prophet, the last of the line and the greatest, who paused long enough to gather together all the discoveries that had been made by the men before him, and to combine them into a philosophy that was neither Hebrew nor contemporary, but universal.

In the Bible this prophet is given the last twenty-seven chapters of the *Book of Isaiah,* and it may be that the man who lived in the days of the Babylonian Exile had the same name as the great prophet before him. His work is the distilled essence of the spirit of the first Isaiah, and of the most inspired of the other prophets as well, so that his book becomes the final achievement of prophetic vision in the Old Testament.

As a poet, he belongs among the great ones of the earth. His only rivals among the Hebrews are some of the Psalmists and the author of *Job.* Like them, he subordinates his magnificent lyric gifts to the value of his ideas and gives his poetry something deeper than a magic of form and phrasing. It was only because the jewel itself was of such great worth that he lavished his art on a setting that would match it in loveliness.

Like *Job,* his book is a mental drama, but, unlike *Job,* it does not deal with individual men and their ideas. The whole world is his subject, the universe his stage, and the

almost cosmic assurance of his manner is not only suitable
to his subject but also characteristic of his race.

The men of Israel never acknowledged that there was
any conceivable limitation to what the mind of man
might do; and as long as they kept that conviction and
refused to accept any limits, there were none. It was for
this reason that the prophets found themselves the friends
and familiars of ideas so vast in their scope and their possibilities that the rest of the world has never succeeded
in catching up with them. The narrow room in which
most men are content to live they abandoned for the open
air.

The subject of the drama that concludes the *Book of
Isaiah* may be briefly summarized as the coming of freedom into an imprisoned world, of light into darkness.
The way of its approach is through Israel, since it was
Israel, of all the nations of the earth, who set out alone
to look for God and was determined to seek him until he
was found. The final discovery of God is the light, and
because of the importance of its attainment history itself
will draw together to that end. Israel has constituted herself the servant of God, the light-bringer. Because she
has dedicated herself to that service it will be her ultimate privilege to find God and to teach all the nations
what she has discovered, greeting them as her guests in
the New Jerusalem that is the knowledge of his presence.

This drama of the spirit of man opens with a lyric
prelude, a foreshadowing of the drama and of its result.
It opens with the word of God spoken "to the heart of
Jerusalem," (*Isa.* xl. 2) promising that her struggle is
nearly finished and her time of service ended. A voice
cries out that a highway is to be made across the desert
places, raising the valleys and levelling the mountains to
make a straight road for all men to travel to see the glory
of God. The voice says, "Call!" (*Isa.* xl. 6) and is met by

the despairing answer, like a momentary shadow, that there is nothing to call, that men die like grass and their beauty fades like the flowers of the field. To this comes the instant, superb reply:

> The grass withers, the flower fades,
> But the word of our God shall stand forever,
>
> *(Isa.* xl. 8)

and all the voices break out together in a chorus of rejoicing.

> On a high mountain get you up,
> O heralds of good news to Zion!
> Lift up your voice with strength,
> O heralds of good news to Jerusalem! *(Isa.* xl. 9)

For the Lord is coming as gently as a shepherd, leading the young sheep and carrying the lambs.

After this lyric introduction comes the drama itself, which may be divided into seven movements.

The first movement discloses all the nations of the world gathered together in silence before the Lord; and the words of God are prefaced by one of those beautiful hymns to his glory that the Hebrews alone were able to write because they alone meant what they said. The hymn is reminiscent of the voice of the whirlwind in *Job*, with its evocation of the might that dwarfs the empires of the world into nothingness, that protects the stars in their courses, and that protects, also, the men who trust it.

> They that wait upon the Lord shall renew their strength,
> They shall mount up with wings as eagles,
> They shall run and not be weary,
> They shall walk and not faint. *(Isa.* xl. 31)

With this the drama opens, and the Lord turns to the nations who stand before him.

"Listen to me in silence, you coast-lands." (*Isa.* xli. 1)

The occasion for this speech, the immediate occasion, in fact, for the whole drama, was the sudden appearance in Asia of the Persian conqueror, Cyrus. To the Eastern world he seemed a senseless and terrifying force of destruction; to the unmoved author of this drama he was a small but necessary step in the discovery of the truth, since it was through him that Babylon would fall and the Jews be released to go back to Jerusalem. Cyrus did not know God, but God knew Cyrus; and this was the one fact that mattered about the great Eastern conqueror. The whole structure of the first movement is designed to make this point clear and to show how important was the work that Cyrus had been selected to do.

Although Cyrus is later mentioned explicitly by name, he is at first introduced in veiled language. He is "one from the east, whom victory meets at every step." (*Isa.* xli. 2) The nations tremble at his coming, but Israel is to have no fear; "for I, the Lord your God, have hold of your right hand." (*Isa.* xli. 13)

Then comes a challenge to the gods of the other nations to produce some evidence of power if they can. "Do good or do evil, that, when we see it, we may all be dismayed." (*Isa.* xli. 23) There is a pause, but no answer to the challenge, and the gods are dismissed from all consideration, scattered into non-existence.

"Lo! you are naught,
And your work is a blank." (*Isa.* xli. 24)

Then the speech swings back to the nations again, and Israel is presented to them as the servant of God in an extremely beautiful statement of his mission. His striving has not been for his own benefit. It has been for a

"set purpose" (*Isa.* xlii. 6) so that through his knowledge of God he may become

"A light to the nations—
In opening blind eyes,
In bringing prisoners out of the dungeon,
Those who sit in darkness out of the prison."
(*Isa.* xlii. 6-7)

He is the servant of the truth, and through him the truth
will free the world from darkness.

At this point the speech is interrupted by a lyric that
fairly shouts for joy, as though no one could keep silent
before the glory of such a promise.

Sing to the Lord a new song,
His praise from the end of the earth;
Let the sea roar, and that which fills it,
The sea-coasts, and those who dwell in them!
(*Isa.* xlii. 10)

These lyric insertions are frequent throughout the drama,
songs of gratitude and praise that comment on the action and intensify it.

Then the words of God continue. Israel, his servant,
has shared the blindness of the other nations, and on that
account he has been subject to them, "a prey, with none
to deliver." (*Isa.* xlii. 22) But now he will be redeemed,
"created and formed and made for my glory." (*Isa.*
xliii. 7) He will be freed from the yoke of Babylon, not
by virtue of his own strength but by the power of the
truth itself. "I, I am he who for my own sake blots out
your transgressions." (*Isa.* xliii. 25) Like streams in a
thirsty land, God will pour out his spirit upon the children of Israel and they will flourish like willows beside
running water.

When the people leaned towards the idea of many

gods they were indulging in an unconscious self-decep-
tion. They were like a man "led astray by a deluded
mind, so that he cannot save himself, nor confess, 'Am
not I holding to a delusion?' " (*Isa.* xliv. 20) Yet because
Israel is God's servant, all these former transgressions
will be blotted out and no longer have power to mislead
the nation.

Again comes a lyric interruption.

> Sing, O heavens, for the Lord has done it,
> Shout, O depths of the earth;
> Break into singing, O mountains,
> O forest, and every tree in it!
> For the Lord has redeemed Jacob,
> And is revealing his glory to Israel. (*Isa.* xliv. 23)

The address now turns to the Persian conqueror whose
advent in the East inspired the drama.

> Thus says the Lord to his anointed one,
> To Cyrus. . . .
> "For the sake of Jacob my servant,
> Israel my chosen one,
> I have called you by name,
> I have surnamed you, though you knew me not . . .
> I will gird you, though you knew me not,
> That men may know, from the east
> And from the west, that apart from me there is none.
> I am the Lord, and there is no other." (*Isa.* xlv. 1-6)

It is because Cyrus will be unwittingly helping to build
something stronger than any empire when he frees the
Judean captives that the Lord will go before him to break
down the heavy bronze doors of the gates of Babylon. No
man orders history through the exercise of his own will,
or can forecast the results of his actions. "Does the clay
ask its potter, 'What are you making?' or a man's work
say to him, 'How handless you are!'?" (*Isa.* xlv. 9) It
is God who orders all things, and there is no other power.

The city of Babylon against which Cyrus is marching has trusted to her own strength and her own wisdom.

> "Your wisdom and your skill
>   Have led you astray,
>   So that you said to yourself,
>   'I am, and there is none but me.'"
>
> (*Isa.* xlvii. 10)

The nation had great faith in her astrologers, "those who map out the heavens, and gaze at the stars," (*Isa.* xlvii. 13) but those who cannot save even themselves will never be able to save Babylon. Babylon was only the temporary means whereby Israel was purified "in the furnace of suffering" (*Isa.* xlviii. 10), and now Israel is ready to go free. A third lyric is interposed, a development of the others.

> Go out from Babylon, flee from the Chaldeans!
> With voice of singing tell, announce this—
> Send forth the news to the end of the earth!
> Say, "The Lord has redeemed his servant Jacob."
>
> (*Isa.* xlviii. 20)

And the first movement ends.

The second movement concerns Israel's struggle for redemption. It is an inward struggle, since Cyrus can only free her from Babylon; he cannot free her from herself. This spiritual warfare is typified by two speakers: one the now-familiar servant of God, fully awake to the greatness of his mission and bearing the name of Israel, and the other the unhappy and doubting nation as a whole, carrying the name of Zion.

Israel the servant is the triumphant "striver with God," and he stands up proudly before the assemblage of nations to announce himself.

> "Listen, you coast-lands, to me;
> Hearken, you peoples afar!" (*Isa.* xlix. 1)

The servant of God has at last discovered what it is that he has been sent out to find, not a salvation for himself or a salvation for his nation, but a salvation for the whole world.

> "My God has become my strength—
> He says, 'It is too slight a thing for your being my servant
> That I should but raise up the tribes of Jacob,
> And restore the survivors of Israel;
> So I will make you a light to the nations,
> That my salvation may reach to the end of the earth.' " (*Isa.* xlix. 5-6)

It is because this is Israel's great obligation to the world that the nation is to be freed from captivity and allowed to return to Jerusalem; and again a lyric breaks in to rejoice in the coming event.

> Sing, O heavens, and exult, O earth;
> Break into singing, O mountains!
> For the Lord has comforted his people,
> And has had pity upon his afflicted ones.
>   (*Isa.* xlix. 13)

Israel is triumphant, but Zion wails aloud. "Zion says, 'The Lord has forsaken me, the Lord has forgotten me!' " (*Isa.* xlix. 14) Yet this is wholly impossible. A mother might forsake her child and forget the son of her womb, but "even should these forget, I will not forget you." (*Isa.* xlix. 15) Zion, however, is only partly reassured by this promise, since Babylon is so powerful a nation that it seems impossible that the promise will ever be fulfilled. "Can prey be taken from a warrior, or a tyrant's captives be rescued?" (*Isa.* xlix. 24) Back comes the instant answer: "Is my hand too short to redeem, or have I no strength to save?" (*Isa.* l. 2) Zion is silenced, and Israel, who has never questioned the power of God, comes forth proudly to assert it again.

"I have set my face like a flint,
And I know that I shall not be ashamed."

(Isa. l. 7)

The third movement concerns the struggle to arouse Zion, the trembling nation that thought herself forsaken, and that feared the chariots of the Babylonians because she dared not trust the power of God. Zion has completely failed to understand the fulness of this power, which nothing physical can either help or hinder, and which is eternal.

"The heavens shall vanish like smoke,
And the earth shall wear out like a garment . . .
But my salvation shall be forever,
And my deliverance shall be unbroken."

(Isa. li. 6)

Here a shout of praise interposes, and a call to the Lord to assert his strength as he did in the days of old. Then the reassurance continues, for if Zion has the teaching of God in her heart she need not be afraid of anything that men can do.

"I, I am your comforter;
Of whom are you afraid?
Of man that dies, of mortal man
That becomes like grass?" *(Isa.* li. 12)

Another lyric shout interrupts, a call to Zion to arouse herself, she who has drunk the cup of God's fury and now has it removed from her. She can be free, if only she will shake herself from the dust and arise.

Awake, awake, put on your strength, O Zion;
Put on your beautiful garments, O Jerusalem, the
holy city! *(Isa.* lii. 1)

For the word of the Lord is: "See! here I am." *(Isa.* lii. 6)

With this, Zion awakens. Her watchmen are able to

see on the mountain tops the heralds coming in swift beauty to bring tidings of peace and salvation, and the good news to Zion that her God is her king. At the joyfulness of this promise, the watchmen lift up their voices and sing, and the waste places in ruined Jerusalem join with them in a song of rejoicing; for all the earth will now be able to see the glory of God's salvation.

In the fourth movement, the nations of the world speak for the first time. The servant of God is presented to them, and they are told that he "shall be exalted, and lifted up, and shall be very high." (*Isa.* lii. 13) The nations answer in awed acknowledgment, overcome with wonder that one whom they had scorned should be raised to so high a position. They had accounted him afflicted, unhandsome, and they had despised him. But now they learn that he was afflicted for their welfare, so that through his stripes they might be healed. It was through the suffering he had endured that the servant of God, the righteous one, was able to "bring righteousness to many"; (*Isa.* liii. 11) and the vision ends with the concluding words of God in his praise.

The fifth movement is the ultimate statement in lyric form of the "covenant of love" (*Isa.* lv. 3) that will redeem Jerusalem, and, through Jerusalem, the world. The emblem used is the familiar one of the forsaken wife, who is now called upon to rejoice, for she that was once barren will repeople the world. No more will she remember the reproach of her widowhood; for God is her husband, and his love is everlasting.

"Though the mountains should remove,
    And the hills should waver,
    My love shall not remove from you." (*Isa.* liv. 10)

Jerusalem, the storm-tossed and uncomforted, will be built of precious stones, her foundations of sapphire, her pinnacles of rubies, and all her encircling walls of jewels. Her sons will all be taught of God, and neither tyranny nor destruction will ever come near her again.

Then the word of God goes forth, calling on all men to cease their striving after what cannot satisfy them, and to buy instead the real milk and grain for which no money is asked. He who listens to the word of God will "eat what is good" (*Isa.* lv. 2) and through it he will find real life. There is an everlasting covenant between God and the men who seek to know him, "the covenant of love which I faithfully promised to David." (*Isa.* lv. 3) Through it they shall be able to call to nations yet unknown, "and nations that know you not shall run to you." (*Isa.* lv. 5)

God's ways are not the ways of man.

> "But as the heavens are higher than the earth,
> So are my ways higher than your ways,
> And my thoughts than your thoughts." (*Isa.* lv. 9)

As rain and snow come down from the sky and do not return until they have watered the earth and made it fruitful, giving seed to the sower and bread to the eater, so does the word of God go forth and does not return until it has accomplished the purpose for which it was sent. Therefore the people shall go forth in joy and peace. The mountains will break out in singing before them, and all the trees of the fields will clap their hands.

The sixth movement has for its subject redemption in Zion, and how it will be brought about. This redemption is not for the Chosen People only. It has nothing to do with any one race. The alien will find no difference in his reward if he loves God, for God's temple is "a house of prayer for all the peoples." (*Isa.* lvi. 7) Nor should the eunuch mourn and consider himself a barren tree, for he will receive a surer immortality than that of

sons, "an everlasting name that shall not be cut off."
(*Isa.* lvi. 5) Even the nations who warred against Israel
will share her eventual salvation.

> "I will yet gather to them
> Those who were gathered against them."
> > (*Isa.* lvi. 8)

Nevertheless, Zion herself has not yet proved herself
worthy to be admitted to this peace. The watchmen she
has chosen are without sense and lie dreaming like dogs;
her leaders are false shepherds who care nothing for the
flocks. Why did Zion attribute such power to idols that
she worshipped them under every green tree? "Of whom
were you in such fear and dread that you played the
traitor?" (*Isa.* lvii. 11) Idols cannot save even themselves,

> "But he who takes refuge in me shall inherit the land,
> And shall enter into possession of my holy mountain."
> > (*Isa.* lvii. 13)

In the heart of the repentant there is perfect safety; for
while God is enthroned on high, he is "with him also
that is contrite and humble in spirit." (*Isa.* lvii. 15) It
is through their own acts that the wicked are like a
restless sea in which is neither peace nor safety.

The people must be clearly shown wherein they have
erred, for they think they have been doing the will of
God when they have only been following a series of
religious ordinances. It is in complete bewilderment that
they cry out,

> "Why have we fasted, and thou seest not;
> Why have we humbled ourselves, and thou heedest
> not?" (*Isa.* lviii. 3)

Truly they have abased themselves. They have bowed
their heads like bulrushes and groveled in sackcloth and

ashes. But "will you call this a fast, a day of pleasure to the Lord?" (*Isa.* lviii. 5) The kind of fast he chooses is the one that lets the oppressed go free, that shares its bread with the poor and gives shelter to the homeless. It is this kind of fasting only that brings a man nearer God; for God would have heard the people of Zion when they called if their sins had not raised up a barrier between them.

The men of repentant Zion suddenly recognize this fact.

> "Therefore is redress far from us,
> And deliverance does not reach us." (*Isa.* lix. 9)

It is because of this that the citizens "grope like blind men along a wall" and "stumble at noonday as in the twilight." (*Isa.* lix. 10) But the very fact that the people can say, "Our iniquities we know" (*Isa.* lix. 12) indicates that Zion has had a change of heart, and with this change comes the conviction that the Lord can save her from herself. "To Zion shall he come as a redeemer, and shall remove transgression from Jacob." (*Isa.* lix. 20)

With this, the scene suddenly brightens. One of the loveliest of the lyrics interposes to picture the glory of the New Jerusalem, the city of all men who have learned to know God.

> Arise, shine! for your light has come,
> And the glory of the Lord has risen upon you.
> (*Isa.* lx. 1)

In the reflection of that glory the whole world will be illuminated; "Nations shall walk in your light, and kings in the brightness of your rising." (*Isa.* lx. 3) The gates of the city will be forever open, so that all may enter, and its wall will be called Salvation, its gates Praise.

"And Peace will I make your government, and Righteousness your ruler." (*Isa.* lx. 17) There will be need of neither sun nor moon to light the city, for the presence of God will be its unfailing light and God its glory.

The final speaker is Israel, the exultant servant of God whom the people are now ready to accept. The spirit of God is upon him, to comfort the broken-hearted and proclaim liberty to the captives. He is arrayed in garments of salvation as a bride is adorned with jewels, and it is as a bride that Jerusalem will go to meet God.

> As a young man marries a maiden,
> So shall your Builder marry you;
> And as a bridegroom rejoices over his bride,
> So shall your God rejoice over you. (*Isa.* lxii. 5)

The seventh and last movement of the drama is the day of actual fulfillment, the Day of the Lord. It is prefaced by a short, dramatic dialog between two speakers.

> "Who is this that comes all reddened,
>   In garments more crimson than those of a wine-
>   treader . . . ?"

> "It is I, who have promised deliverance,
>   And am mighty to save."

> "Why is thy clothing red,
>   Thy garments like his who treads in the wine-press?"

> "The wine-trough I trod alone . . .
>   For a day of vengeance was in my heart."
>   (*Isa.* lxiii. 1-4)

This vision of judgment unnerves the exiles, although the sole purpose of crushing grapes is to make wine. They begin a long speech to the Lord, a frantic and frightened attempt at reconciliation. They point out to God that he once led the nation safely in the days of Moses and plead with him to do it again, even "though

Abraham know us not, and Israel acknowledge us not."
(*Isa.* lxiii. 16) They inquire pathetically why the Lord
has permitted evil men to trample on his holy sanctuary
and has allowed Jerusalem to become a desolation. They
implore him to rend the heavens apart and come down
to exact vengeance on their enemies; and the speech ends
with a loud wail of self-pity.

> "Our holy and beautiful house,
> Where our fathers praised thee,
> Has been burned with fire,
> And all that we cherished has been laid waste.
> For these things, O Lord, wilt thou restrain thyself;
> Wilt thou keep silent, and afflict us beyond measure?"
>
> (*Isa.* lxiv. 11-12)

This speech is the essence of unintelligent piety, having
within it everything that the drama as a whole condemns. It is because this state of mind still persists that
the Day of the Lord must be one of judgment as well
as salvation; and the answer that comes to the unhappy
and questioning people is swift and terrible.

> "I was ready to be consulted by those who asked me
>   not,
> I was ready to be found by those who sought me not;
> I said, 'Here am I! Here am I!'
> To a nation that called not upon my name."
>
> (*Isa.* lxv. 1)

It is only for the sake of those few who looked for
God that the whole will not be destroyed. Those only
will be able to inherit the land who are servants of God
and able to "pray by the God of truth." (*Isa.* lxv. 16)
For these, the servants, a new heaven and a new earth
will be created, and none of the past will be remembered.
No longer will there be sorrow or injustice or tyranny.
There will be no laboring in vain, and all men will be
near to God.

> "Before they call, I will answer;
> While they are yet speaking, I will hear." (*Isa.* lxv. 24)

The wolf and the lamb will feed side by side, with neither fear in their hearts nor the desire to destroy; and as for the serpent, that ancient symbol of evil, "its food shall be dust." (*Isa.* lxv. 25)

Then comes a memory of Zion's wail that her "holy and beautiful house," the temple at Jerusalem, has been destroyed, and scorn is heaped on the whole principle of visible worship.

> "The heavens are my throne,
> And the earth is my footstool;
> What manner of house, then, would you build for
> me,
> What manner of place as my residence?"
> (*Isa.* lxvi. 1)

Even further than this is the scorn carried. An offering of the mind and the spirit is the only kind that will ever be accepted, and any attempt at visible worship is no better than the lowest form of idolatry.

> "He who slaughters an ox, as well as he who slays a
> man . . .
> He who makes a memorial-offering of frankincense,
> as well as he who blesses an idol—
> These men choose their own ways,
> And delight in their abominations." (*Isa.* lxvi. 3)

When Zion at last realizes the implications of this new and astonishing conception of worship, her travail begins and a new nation is born.

> "Who has seen the like?
> Can a land pass through travail
> In a single day?
> Can a nation be brought to the birth
> All at once?
> But as soon as Zion travailed,
> She gave birth to her children." (*Isa.* lxvi. 8)

It was not through Zion's own efforts that the birth came. It was God himself who brought it about.

"Shall I bring to the birth and not give delivery?"
Says the Lord. (*Isa.* lxvi. 9)

This birth ends the drama. All who love Jerusalem and what she stands for may now come with rejoicing to drink the milk of consolation from her breast. Through Jerusalem all the world will be comforted, and gather together at the holy mountain of her understanding to see the glory of God.

This great book of the redemption of Israel was written during the Babylonian Exile and found its immediate inspiration in the career of Cyrus; but the purely historical implications vanish from the drama almost as soon as they are stated. It was no rebuilding of a physical city that occupied the attention of the poet. He used the city of Jerusalem as a symbol for an attainment of the full understanding of God, the city where there would be no temple and the Lord was the only light.

It was the prophet's hope that the exiles would in truth be able to build such a city, if they had fully learned in their exile the doctrine of Jeremiah, that the true Jerusalem was a city of the spirit and none other was safe. If they had learned this fact, as the poet himself had learned it, they would be able to build a new heaven and a new earth out of the understanding of God they possessed, and would be able to release the whole world from its bondage as they had released themselves.

The man who wrote this greatest of spiritual dramas was the heir of all the prophets who had preceded him. He owed a great deal to them all, and most, perhaps, to Isaiah, whose name his book now bears. Like Isaiah he was convinced that the truth, because it was the truth, would triumph eventually and constitute a light in which all darkness would be dispelled. He was like Isaiah, too, in a philosophy of world history that saw all empires as the unconscious instruments of a mental power stronger than they, in his scorn of any strength save that of the spirit, and in his conviction that a perfect world would ultimately appear. He resembled Amos in the loftiness of his ethical standards, Hosea in his deep sense of the love of God, and Jeremiah in his contempt for the outward paraphernalia of worship, his scathing denunciation of the fundamental foolishness of idolatry and his sense of the nearness of God.

He was nevertheless no imitator. He made all these ideas his own, and added to them his own greatness of spirit; and the result is one of the most perfect and important works of art ever to be created.

This prophet was the final spokesman of ancient Israel, the line of the search, and it is fitting that it remained for him to illuminate the importance of the search itself. It was "too slight a thing" for all those centuries of labor that Israel should save only herself. Instead, she would save the whole world, not by force, not by teaching, but by proof. She would not make her voice heard in the streets. She would not "cry, nor shout." (*Isa.* xlii. 2) The bending reed would not be broken, nor the flickering wick quenched. There will be only one function for the servant of God, to "bring forth right," (*Isa.* xlii. 3) and by that would Israel be known.

This is the whole foundation of the drama. It is for this "set purpose" that the nations are summoned before God at the beginning to hear the real reason behind the threatened Persian conquest. Everything in the action of the poem looks towards a single conclusion, towards the time which is both foreshadowed and summarized in the lyric prelude.

> Then shall the glory of the Lord be revealed,
> And all flesh shall see it together. (*Isa.* xl. 5)

To the poet, this was the real Jerusalem. No geographical location could have anything to do with the God who filled heaven and earth, and no temple with the God who refused all outward signs of worship. It was a city of the spirit that the children of Israel were to strive for when Cyrus let them go free, and the poet of the Exile was convinced that this city could be attained and the glory of the Lord fully revealed. Once known, the truth would prove itself invincible, and the world that learned it of Israel would be freed forever from the darkness of the prison house.

This had been the dream of all the great prophets of Israel; but never before had it been expressed so beautifully, so clearly, or with such recklessly magnificent assurance.

CHAPTER XIII

With his whole heart he sang praise,
and loved him that made him.

Ecclesiasticus xlvii. 8

GREAT poetry is the result of great desire. Genius may
be based on a love of the craft itself, but only as an instrument is beloved since through it a man can make
the music in him heard. It is not the perfection of the
craft that makes poetry, the obedient shapes and colors
of words and the precise interlocking of phrases. It is
rather the striving heart that uses the craft to express
its own desire and that makes the instrument the willing
servant of the dream. If the desire is lacking, there is
no real poetry.

This desire is for one thing only. It is the need to
reach and then to express in terms the outer world can
understand some secret inner illumination of the spirit
that only the poet himself knows. It may illuminate for
him anything, a blade of grass or a memory or a star,
but his one desire is to tell the world what he has felt
so that everyone may share it with him.

The greatest poetry, therefore, is usually love poetry,
since love is almost by definition the power to see things
beautifully. Sometimes it is love of nature, so that trees
and stones become intimate and almost holy under the
lover's touch. Sometimes it is love of people, so that even
their fears, their pathetic good intentions and their
stumbling confusion in a dark world are touched with
glory and given a meaning. Sometimes it is the love
of a woman, who becomes mother and mistress and comforter in its light. And once, to some of the greatest
poets who ever lived, it was the love of God.

If the poets of Israel had not loved God and found in that love both beauty and delight, they would never have been able to produce the collection of poetry called the *Psalms*. All the delicacy of their craftsmanship has been lost in translation, the curve of the rhythms, the balance of the lines, the color of the words; and, to our loss, there has disappeared also the musical accompaniment of voices and stringed instruments that must have given the songs so large a part of their original beauty —since songs were meant to be sung and not to be read. Yet in spite of all this vanished loveliness, there still remains the love and the desire to share it which are at the heart of all great poetry, so inextricably associated with the lines that nothing can separate them. It is this quality, which nothing can destroy, which makes the Hebrew Psalter one of the most beautiful books of poetry in the world.

It is impossible to mistake this quality of love. It is possessed even by the elaborate anthems and the artificial, complicated acrostic meditations; and those psalms which have it least are the least beautiful. Masterpieces like the familiar twenty-third psalm are so full of love that the poet's trust and happiness are like a dancing light across the page.

It is natural that so many of the psalms should have been attributed to King David. With his sensitive artistic perception, his desire for happiness, and, above all, his capacity for loving, David was exactly the kind of man who could have written them. Any kind of dishonesty is quickly evident in poetry; a man cannot successfully write that he trusts God unless he does, or that the search for God has brought him happiness unless it has. David's life attests to his love of God; and while not one man but many produced the Hebrew Psalter, it is pleasant to know that there were many men in Israel who were like King David, great poet and great lover.

The search for God which is fundamentally the subject of all great Hebrew literature had both a public and a private life. Its public life found expression in the work of the prophets, in the visions and dramas which contained the discoveries about God that they had made. Its private life found expression in the psalms, in the lyrics that give not the result of the striving but the striving itself, not the discoveries that rewarded the long years of the search but the struggles and the happiness which accompanied it. They are the living expression of Israel's conviction that what she was doing was worth doing, that not only the goal was important but the way also.

Only one love song in the formal sense of the word is contained in the Psalter, and this is the least loving of them all. The forty-fifth psalm is a celebration of the wedding of a king of Israel and a princess of Tyre, and while the poet writes with a lavish spread of words and says that he enjoys his theme, the result is not the love song it calls itself. There is more of real passion in one line of the sixty-third psalm,

> O God, thou art my God; I seek for thee;
> My spirit thirsts for thee; my flesh yearns for thee,
> As in a dry and parched land where no water is.
> (Ps. lxiii. 1)

than there is even in the impassioned imagery and jewel-hung splendor of the *Song of Songs*.

It is not possible to speak adequately of the great Hebrew psalms. Each one is worth a chapter of comment and such comment would be useless, since each lyric is its own best interpreter. All that any comment can do is to point out certain qualities that the reader might overlook either through too-hasty a reading or through too great a familiarity with the sound of the words.

The most obvious single quality in the psalms is their happiness. Whenever the dramatic symbols of terror and distress are introduced, the inward enemies of pain and fear or the outward enemies of war, they are used only to throw into brighter relief the peace that almost invariably ends the poem. It is not they that set the mood. They are present only to intensify the final deliverance.

While the psalms have none of the mournfulness of much great poetry, there is nothing childlike about the happiness that most of them show. It is no easy achievement to look at sorrow and refuse to be made sorrowful, nor is it easy for a man of intelligence to win through to a peace that can be trusted. The marks of the struggle are apparent in nearly all the psalms, in their sobriety, their passion and their humanity; and it is their victory that has made them so dear to a struggling world.

The joy of the psalms is not that of innocence, but of experience. There was no physical or mental torment that the poets were afraid to face, and none that daunted them for long. They were fighters of the same heroic race as the prophets and no more content than they with an easy victory. The psalms are happy poems because the fight was worth while and the victory certain, not because the poets averted their eyes from evil and lived in an unstable world of their own imaginings. Retreat has been the refuge of many men who have found the world too tragic to be borne, but retreat was not the way of the Hebrews.

Out of one hundred and fifty psalms, only four portray moods of unrelieved darkness: the thirty-eighth, a cry for deliverance; the seventy-fourth, a national hymn written in a time of persecution; the thirty-ninth, a plea strongly reminiscent of one of Job's; and the eighty-eighth, one of the saddest elegies on hopeless, terrified, tortured mortality ever written. But for one poem of this kind, where the poet sinks under the helpless conviction that his torment has been put on him by God, there are twenty in which the mood is met and wrestled with and God becomes instead the savior from it. Unrelieved despair was a quality that no poet of Israel could sustain for long.

The poems which record this struggle and deliverance are among the most frequent in the Psalter and among the greatest in the world. Sometimes the poet's foes are physical and sometimes mental—the distinction is not always clear and seldom of importance. What is important is the confident, almost cheerful spirit in which the odds are met and accepted, and the passing value that is put on everything except inward peace.

Sometimes, as in the third psalm, the conditions of the warfare are stated with such deceptive simplicity that they seem almost childlike.

> I lay me down and sleep;
> I awake, for the Lord sustains me.
> I am not afraid of the myriads of people
> That have set upon me round about. (*Ps.* iii. 5-6)

In complete contrast is the subtle and complex treatment of the thirty-first psalm, in which the poet has not only outside enemies to betray him but chiefly and insistently his own nature. He makes a statement he knows to be true, promptly doubts it, and then is obliged through much labor to work back to his original conviction. With similar lack of logic he pleads with God to be God, and yet knows all the time that he is wasting his breath.

The poet is in great trouble and he begins:

> Rescue me!
> Become for me a rock of refuge! (*Ps.* xxxi. 2)

As soon as he makes the prayer, however, he sees that he is asking for something he already has.

> For thou art my rock and my fortress;
> And for thy name's sake thou wilt lead me and guide me. (*Ps.* xxxi. 3)

For a moment this conviction is enough to bring peace, and the poem temporarily quiets into confidence. The poet is pleased to think how much more worthy he is than his foes, since he is upheld by his trust in God; and promptly he loses this trust of which he was so proud and falls into a catalog of all his misfortunes. Nothing has come of his confidence in God, for he is a grieviously stricken man encompassed by enemies, and he prays, and prays wildly, for the ability to attain his old confidence again. The rest of the poem is his struggle to get back his former conviction that there is a safe place "in the secret of thy presence" (*Ps.* xxxi. 20) where nothing evil can enter in. When the poet attains this conviction he attains, also, his own deliverance, and the poem ends with his counsel to those who may undergo the same struggle as he.

> Be strong, and let your heart be firm,
> All you who wait for the Lord. (*Ps.* xxxi. 24)

The forty-second psalm also takes for its subject the poet's warfare with himself. He has longed for God as a deer longs for the water-courses; he has spent his whole life looking for him, while men mock him and say, "Where is your God?" At this point comes the refrain, the poet's own answer to himself.

> Why art thou brought low, O my spirit?
> And why dost thou murmur within me?
> Wait thou for God; for I shall again praise him,
> The salvation of my countenance and my God.
> > (*Ps.* xlii. 5)

Again comes the cry of despair from a man oppressed by pain and surrounded by foes who ask him the unendurable question to which he can give no answer: "Where is your God?" Again comes the refrain in answer, carrying with it the cumulative force of repetition.

> Why art thou brought low, O my spirit?
> And why dost thou murmur within me?
> Wait thou for God; for I shall again praise him,
> The salvation of my countenance and my God.
>
> (*Ps.* xlii. 11)

The despair turns into a prayer that is nearly as despairing, that the light may be found which is now hidden and the supplicant be able to return to the holy hill that is God's dwelling-place. For the third time the refrain returns, unchanged and insistent, and the poem finally ends on its note of perfect confidence: "I shall again praise him, the salvation of my countenance and my God." (*Ps.* xliii. 5)

The psalms of struggle and deliverance are less intense on the whole when the dangers that threaten are only physical foes instead of a man's own inward enemies. The one hundred and eighth psalm is characteristic of the scorn that many Hebrews beside Isaiah felt for physical force, and the same idea finds stirring expression in the warrior's song in the eighteenth. But all terrors, mental as well as physical, are gathered together in the twenty-second psalm, which heaps up every conceivable symbol of agony into an overwhelming whole and then, at the moment of highest and almost unendurable tension, brings sudden deliverance in the middle of a sentence.

It is against this background of conquered pain and furious struggle that the lovely psalms of quietness stand out in a white radiance of peace, all the more beautiful because it has been won with such difficulty. In the twenty-third psalm, the peace which has been striven for so desperately and yet is so simple finds union with an art so perfect that it conceals itself and appears artless. The result is one of those occasional flowerings of lyric art that literally transcend criticism.

> The Lord is my shepherd;
> I shall not want.
> He makes me lie down in green pastures;
> He leads me beside the still waters.
> He gives me new life.
> He guides me in safe paths, for his name's sake.
>
> (*Ps.* xxiii. 1-3)

The ninety-first is another of these psalms of peace, an expansion of a line from the blessing of Moses in the *Book of Deuteronomy:* "Underneath are the everlasting arms." Since this lyric is more specific and less suggestive it is perhaps not as perfect a work of art as the shepherd psalm, but the mood is the same. It is a clear statement in poetry of the goal that Israel had set for herself, the "secret place of the Most High" (*Ps.* xci. 1) that would mean shelter and healing and peace; and the poem ends with a promise that the secret place will be found.

> Because he clings fast to me in love, I will deliver him;
> I will set him on high because he knows my name.
> When he calls upon me, I will answer him;
> I will be with him in trouble;
> I will set him free and honor him.
> With long life will I satisfy him,
> And show him my salvation. (*Ps.* xci. 14-16)

These are not the only psalms with the spirit of quietness upon them, although in the others it is an ultimate rather than a continuing illumination. But sometimes

the assurance both begins and ends the poem, as in the
twenty-seventh psalm.

> The Lord is my light and my salvation;
>> whom shall I fear?
> The Lord is the refuge of my life;
>> of whom shall I be afraid? (*Ps.* xxvii. 1)

The same idea is re-echoed in song after song, in as
many ways as there are images to declare it.

Although most of the psalms were either written for
public worship or adapted to it, only a few are really
public in mood and these are festal psalms written for
specific occasions. The majority are private and personal,
and belong not to the group but to the individual. The
struggle is a lonely one in the dark, and the triumph is
the secret one of a man's own spirit.

It is for this reason that so many of the psalms, even
though ultimately used for celebration on ritual occasions, have all Jeremiah's lack of respect for ritual. An
evening prayer offers no occasion for physical worship,
either public or private, and commands only :

> Commune with your own hearts upon your bed and be
> still. (*Ps.* iv. 4)

The fortieth psalm is technically liturgical in character,
and yet it maintains that the only possible worship of
God must be done inwardly and in silence.

> Sacrifice and offering thou dost not desire . . .
> Burnt-offering and sin-offering thou dost not de-
>> mand . . .
> I delight to do thy will, O my God;
> And thy law is in my very heart. (*Ps.* xl. 6-8)

The fifty-first psalm, one of the most personal of them
all, offers a beautiful elaboration of this same idea of
inward worship, but it is in the fiftieth psalm that it

finds its most forceful single expression. This psalm is not so much a song as a brief drama. God is the speaker, and he charges his worshippers with the crime of acting toward him as though he were like a man. "You thought that I was just like yourself." (*Ps.* l. 21) In a speech that is heavy with deliberate irony, the whole principle of sacrifice is treated as an absurdity.

> "For all the beasts of the forest are mine,
> The cattle upon a thousand hills.
> I know every bird of the mountains,
> And whatsoever moves in the field is mine.
> If I were hungry I would not tell you;
> For mine is the world and everything therein.
> Will I eat the flesh of oxen,
> And drink the blood of goats?"
> Offer to God the sacrifice of thanksgiving.
> (Ps. l. 10-14)

The search for God as recorded in these psalms has nothing to do with traditional ritual, and there is no substitute offered for individual effort and individual communion. "To God alone would I silently submit myself" (*Ps.* lxii. 1) is the spirit that animates them all. It is on this account that the makers of the psalms possess a sense of such intimate, loving friendliness with God. "In the shadow of thy wings I shout for joy." (*Ps.* lxiii. 7) He is the lord of the thunderstorm, but he is also a "dwelling-place in all generations," (*Ps.* xc. 1) and to possess that knowledge is the only thing of value in the whole world.

> Whom have I in the heavens but thee?
> And having thee, I wish naught else on earth.
> (Ps. lxxiii. 25)

The complete joy of this sense of communion is given with particular beauty in the eighty-fourth psalm, that famous song of a mental pilgrimage.

> How lovely is thy dwelling-place, O Lord of hosts!
> My spirit longs and pines
>   for the courts of the Lord.
> My heart and my flesh give a shout of joy
>   for the living God! (*Ps.* lxxxiv. 1-2)

At the end of this pilgrimage there is protection for the least of living things, and room for them all. Even the sparrow will be able to house herself on the altars of God, and the swallow will build a nest there where she may shelter her young. Very happy is the man who has reached this goal, but happy also is the man who is journeying towards it along the highways of his mind. If he passes through the Valley of Weeping he will find it a place of springs, blessed by the rain. He will go from strength unto strength until he at last appears before God, a day in whose courts is better than a thousand in the world outside.

This pilgrimage towards God is described in many different moods. In the one hundred and thirtieth psalm, one of the "Songs of Ascents," the spirit is of so excited an impatience that even the usual symbol of alertness is insufficient to express it.

> I wait for the Lord,
> More than watchmen for the dawn,
> Watchmen for the dawn. (*Ps.* cxxx. 6)

In the next song this longing has been trained into a difficult patience of which the poet himself is rather proud.

> I have certainly calmed and stilled my spirit,
> Like a weaned child with its mother;
> My spirit is with me like a weaned child. (*Ps.* cxxxi. 2)

Sometimes the mood has the profound humility of the fifty-first psalm, and sometimes the awed pride of the eighth.

What is man that thou shouldst think of him,
And the son of man that thou shouldst care for him?
Yet thou hast made him but little lower than God,
And dost crown him with honor and glory!

(*Ps.* viii. 4-5)

Occasionally there is sorrow, very often there is struggle, and always there is the abiding happiness that no combination of circumstances is able to dispel for long.

This mood of trust is echoed in the nationalistic psalms, where it becomes the trust of a nation instead of an individual. In these psalms, national prosperity and national justification tend to assume more importance than the desperate need of God that occupied the attention of the individual poets. Yet if the desire expressed in these nationalistic psalms is not of itself so magnificent, it is desire nevertheless and the trust in one power is as unshakable in public affairs as in private.

Some are strong through chariots and some through
    horses,
But we, through the name of the Lord, our God.

(*Ps.* xx. 7)

With the individual poet, the one great object of his love and desire was God and the knowledge of God; with the nationalistic poet, the center of love was Jerusalem, the holy city, the place of the Temple, God's decreed presence on earth. It was on the capital city, hallowed by a long series of literary and historical associations, that the love of the poets lingered; and they surrounded its name with all the splendor of which they were capable.

There is a river whose streams make glad the city of
    God,
The holiest habitation of the Most High;
God is in the midst of her; she shall not be moved.
God will help her at the dawn of the morning.

(*Ps.* xlvi. 4-5)

The psalms of the Babylonian Exile bear witness to
the real agony of its loss, mourning elegies of the ruined
city and the broken vine of Israel. The poet of the ninety-first psalm had a city of the spirit that no conqueror
could ever destroy; but the nationalistic poets had a
Jerusalem built of bricks and mortar, and when the walls
were pulled down they had lost their city. The pain of
the loss was the greater because of the bitter anger that
went with it. The writer of the one hundred and thirty-
seventh psalm describes the tragic singers of Zion hang-
ing their harps on the willow trees of Babylon because
they could not sing the songs of the Lord in a foreign
land. The poem ends on a note of such vicious hatred
that it is easy to see how such a conception of Jerusalem
could become an evil and why Jeremiah opposed it with
so much determination. It is easy to understand the intense love of their holy city that burned in the nationalistic poets, but it made them lesser men than the poets
who reserved their love for God, the great men of Israel
who knew that Jerusalem was only a symbol whose destruction could not affect the continued existence of the
"secret place of the Most High."

Among the most splendid of the nationalistic hymns
are those intimately associated with the Temple services.
These were usually songs of dedication or thanksgiving,
designed for the use of alternating choruses, and they
offered a magnificent opportunity for the Hebrew lyric
genius to find full expression. Yet even in these orna-
mental hymns of praise, where it would have been easy
to lapse into lavish rhetoric, the poets kept the steady
simplicity and honesty that characterized everything
they wrote. Their work was based not on poetic conven-
tions but personal conviction. They never wrote words
of praise unless they meant them, and it is in part this
unshakable artistic honesty that made them fine poets.

One of the loveliest of these Temple hymns is the twenty-fourth psalm. It was apparently sung in two parts by alternating choirs, the first part at the foot of the hill on which the Temple was built, and the second part in front of the gates. The first group of singers begins with a song of praise to God, and ends with the question:

> Who can ascend into the hill of the Lord?
> And who can stand in his holy place? (*Ps.* xxiv. 3)

The second choir brings back the answer: "He who has clean hands and a pure heart" (*Ps.* xxiv. 4) and as the company of singers mounts to the gates the members of the choir alternate question and answer with the full chorus.

> Lift up your heads, O gates,
> And lift up yourselves, O ancient doors,
> That the king of glory may come in. (*Ps.* xxiv. 7)

These hymns show a more musical and less complex happiness than those of the personal psalms, and over their easily won joy there is no shadow of conflict. In these festal songs not only do the people rejoice, but the fields exult, the waters clap their hands and all the trees of the wood shout for joy. Even in cold print the excitement is contagious, and when sung by a great gathering of trained voices to the accompaniment of musical instruments the psalms must have been marvellously effective.

> Praise him with the blast of the horn!
> Praise him with lyre and lute!
> Praise him with drum and dance!
> Praise him with strings and pipe!
> Praise him with clanging cymbals!
> Praise him with clashing cymbals!
> Let everything that breathes praise the Lord!
> Hallelujah! (*Ps.* cl. 3-6)

The occasional songs on nature are invariably linked
with this idea of praise. In the twenty-ninth psalm the
thunderstorm is pictured as God's word thundering over
the waters, breaking the cedars, whirling the sands of
the desert and stripping the forests, "While in his palace
everything says, 'Glory!' " (*Ps.* xxix. 9) More sober in
mood but similar in spirit is the one hundred and fourth
psalm, which is a wondering consideration of the power
of God. He decrees the hours of the sun, and he supplies
the stork with a cypress tree for her nest. This conception of the order and regularity of nature finds an obvious counterpart in a psalm like the nineteenth, in which
the ordered precision of the physical world is compared
with the same principle in the mental one, so that both
worlds, each in its own way, "are telling the glory of
God." (*Ps.* xix. 1)

The nationalistic spirit found its most complete expression in the psalms recounting the past history of the
nation. Especially was there an obvious parallel between
the procession that Moses led from Egypt to find God
and the procession of worshippers going up the hill to
the Temple. The sixty-eighth psalm is perhaps the most
beautiful of these processional anthems. The first part
is a masterpiece of implication in the way it traces the
original route through the wilderness; the second bal-
ances it with a picture of the procession going up to the
Temple, with the singers in front, the performers on
stringed instruments in the rear and between them
the girls playing on timbrels. In spite of the occasional
obscurity of its ideas, as a marching song the poem is
irresistible. Even in a translation it is impossible not to
hear the steady rhythm of the marching feet.

Many of the national anthems are of great beauty,
and none of them could well be spared. But they cannot
be compared in importance with the private songs of

Israel, the lonely, beautiful psalms of striving and rejoicing which the nation claimed as its own but which belonged first to individuals. If Israel were remembered now as a great nation, famous for the wealth of her kings and the might of her armies, her public history would have been important and the lyrics celebrating it correspondingly so. Instead, Israel founded a mental empire, one so powerful that it has outlasted most of the great nations of the world and is still, even if misunderstood, the most potent single force in the world today. Her physical history is insignificant in the face of this. It is not the kings and priests and warriors of Israel that are important. The men who entered into a lonely search for truth wrote the real history of Israel.

The value of the psalms, apart from their inherent beauty as poetry, is the fact that they show how important the search for God was to the men who undertook it. It was no bland philosophical abstraction with them, but a need for the truth so fundamental that it was a part of their very life. When one of their number wrote,

> My whole being thirsts for God, for the living God,
> (*Ps.* xlii. 2)

it was no exaggeration. It was a literal fact that the need for a reasonable mental peace was deeper than hunger or thirst, more holy than the Temple and more binding than the Law.

When the poet spoke of God as his "highest joy," (*Ps.* xliii. 4) that also was a literal fact. The search could never have been sustained for so long a period of time, and against such odds, if there had not been in it an abiding happiness.

CHAPTER XIV

> Not everyone who is descended from Israel
> really belongs to Israel.
>
> *Letter to the Romans* ix. 6

WHEN the men of Jerusalem left Babylon and were
allowed to return and rebuild their ruined city, they
were the heirs of the greatest legacy any nation ever
had. An extraordinary race of men had slowly created
it for them, and, as the great prophet of the Exile had
said, it was theirs to use and to carry to its glorious and
inevitable conclusion.

This gift to the nation from the prophets of Israel
was compounded of many things, but chiefly of an in-
domitable spiritual courage. There have been many attempts in the world's history to find an answer to the
riddle of existence, but the majority were still-born,
overwhelmed by the appalling magnitude of the task
almost before it was begun. It was only the men of
Israel who refused to accept the idea that there was any
limit to the reach of a man's intelligence, or that there
was anything that could not eventually be found out.
Faced with a mystery apparently too deep to fathom,
they set out to fathom it; and they never doubted but
that they would succeed.

The prophets were brave enough to refuse to accept a
false and easy consolation. The same quality that drove
Job into open rebellion against the religious platitudes
of his three friends animated all the great men of Israel.
It was this that made Amos defy the deceptive prosperity
of a whole nation, and that made Jeremiah willing to
be thought a traitor to his city and his God. To use the

vivid simile of the prophet of the Exile, these were not blind men cautiously feeling their way along a wall. They left the security of the wall of religious tradition and went on without it through the dark, trusting to the power of the truth itself that they would be able to walk safely.

Each prophet of Israel found himself placed in opposition to the religious ideas of his own day and time, and it was generations before the best in contemporary thought succeeded in catching up with the teachings of one of the "strivers with God." An excellent example of this is the matter of ritual worship. In Abraham's day, human sacrifice was the most honored of all religious offerings, and the patriarch's discovery that the murder of a son was not a gift pleasing to God was, to his contemporaries, a kind of blasphemy. The Hebrew people were still struggling with this innovation, and not entirely successfully, when the prophet Amos told them that the offering even of a bullock was not acceptable unless it were offered in righteousness.

The principle behind Amos' teaching was so advanced that even today it is accepted more often in theory than in practice. It had hardly begun to penetrate the popular mind even in theory when another prophet, Jeremiah, proclaimed in the Temple that outward worship was not important and that true worship demanded inward fellowship with God. The people as a whole never did accept this subversive theory, and they consequently failed to notice the great prophet of the Exile when he carried the idea to its logical conclusion and said that any outward offering to God, even the innocent gift of frankincense, was actual idolatry and no better than bowing before the statue of a heathen god.

The prophets were heretics to their contemporaries because they forsook the settled orthodoxy of their own

times, and their writings bear full witness to the way
they shocked and frightened the accredited religious
leaders of the people. There is nothing more terrifying
to the average mind than the unknown, and the blind
men clinging to the safety of the wall did not like to be
disturbed by the great iconoclasts who spoke in the name
of God.

Men like Isaiah and Jeremiah were not content with
a pleasing and comfortable theory. If they had wanted
no more than that, the deity portrayed in *Genesis* in the
story of Adam and Eve would have been acceptable to
them. He was one God, an idea that was still very advanced, the methods of his creation fully explained the
pain and struggle of mankind and the peculiar dual nature of each individual, and he was a ruler who would
be disposed to listen benignantly to his subjects if they
brought him gifts. He was a thoroughly acceptable and
obvious God, although it is true he also lacked all the
more admirable qualities of his own creation and showed
even less consistency in his dealings than the man he
made.

The prophets of Israel did not want an obvious God.
They wanted the truth.

The first step in the rejection of this obvious God, the
God of Adam and Eve, was made by Abraham when he
rejected the idea that God was pleased by the emotional
value of the sacrifice that was offered him. The next and
perhaps the greatest single step was made by Moses,
when he found a new name for God. This name took
the God of Israel forever out of the ranks of the gods
of the other nations, capricious and unstable overlords
that must be placated at any cost. The God of Israel was
no supernatural Eastern ruler, subject to sudden fits of
rage. He was Existence itself, I AM.

It was this conception of God that Elijah made his

own. When the prophet of the northern kingdom laid the dead child on his bed, he did not pray to God as to some omnipotent but irresolute ruler who might be persuaded to reverse temporarily one of his decrees if sufficient pressure were put upon him. Instead, Elijah found himself unable to believe that it was by a decree of God that the child had died; and as a result of that doubt, which to most people would have seemed blasphemy, he saw the child alive again before his eyes.

Since God was unchanging reality, not to be pleaded with or placated but to be discovered, any correct discovery that was made about God could be proven. When the prophet Isaiah wrote that faith in the power of God was stronger than the mightiest array of Assyrian military strength, he was not only prepared to prove it but he did prove it. He was offering the people what he knew to be a demonstrable fact, and if they accepted it as such it would be available to them. But it would not be available if they accepted it as a pious hope and then turned to furbishing their chariots against the enemy, expecting God to co-operate with the chariots only if the latter proved to be inadequate.

Because the prophets knew how great a gift lay before the people of Israel for the taking, they found themselves forced almost against their wills into the kind of writing that produced the dooms and the judgments. Like Moses, they were teachers, and they had to choose the methods of teaching that would be understood by the people. It is too often assumed that the prophets lived in a kind of vacuum, entirely unaffected by the state of mind of their audiences and writing the highest expression of truth of which they were capable. On the contrary, while the prophets never compromised with the truth, the manner in which they presented it was

almost invariably affected by the attitude of their
listeners.

Jeremiah, for instance, represents God as addressing
Judah with the fearful finality of :

> "You have kindled my wrath to a fire
>   Which shall burn forever." (*Jer.* xvii. 4)

A little later in Jeremiah's writings there is a complete
contradiction of this statement, given with exactly the
same force :

> "With an everlasting love have I loved you,
>   Therefore with kindness will I draw you to me."
>   (*Jer.* xxxi. 3)

Jeremiah had no wish to give the impression that God
had suddenly changed his mind. One of the earliest of
the prophets, Balaam, had long since dismissed such an
idea as impossible—"God is not a man that he should
break his work, nor a human being that he should
change his mind" (*Num.* xxiii. 19)—and Jeremiah
himself had already said of God that he has "spoken,
and will not retract." (*Jer.* iv. 28) Nor had Jeremiah's
own conception of God altered between the writing of
the two passages.

What had altered was Jeremiah's audience. When the
first passage was written, they were what the prophet
called "fat and sleek," sure that all was well with them
and that as God's chosen people they could come to no
harm. Even the sharp goad of fear, which Jeremiah
used deliberately, was hardly sufficient to pierce their fat
complacency, their bland conviction that God would protect Jerusalem forever. But Jeremiah's second passage
was written when the holy city was slowly crumbling
into ruins before the attack of the king of Babylon. Even
the strongest language could not prevent the catastrophe

that was now inevitable. What the people needed, and desperately, was comfort; and Jeremiah gave them then the consolation of a promise he had deliberately withheld from them before.

While the prophets of Israel spent their lives in an effort to teach the people the truths they themselves had found, at the same time they did not believe that reality had to be upheld by their lonely efforts. The truth was God's, and God himself would protect it.

It was this conviction that developed into the prophet's conception of the Day of the Lord. The phrase itself was an old one, and was popularly supposed to mean the time when the Chosen People would be exalted over their enemies and rewarded with good crops and safe pasture-land; but the great prophets, from Amos onward, rejected this complacent theory. To them, the Day of the Lord was the day when the search would be ended and God himself fully known.

When this day of understanding came, the prophets believed that it would bring with it a new world, a world from which death and injury and torment would somehow be absent, and each man would know God perfectly for himself. They expected, in other words, what is foreshadowed in the first account of creation in *Genesis*, that when they had found a perfect God they would find also a perfect world.

This was without doubt the most remarkable idea ever formulated by a group of men since the world began. Even if it had been only an intellectual abstraction it would have been a wonderful thing, and to the prophets of Israel it was no abstraction. Through centuries of labor they had given all their courage, their honesty, their intelligence and their profound love to the search for God, and they knew it could not fall short of success with the goal so near. It had only to continue as it had begun, not in bondage to traditional religious beliefs but free as the truth itself was free.

It was this legacy that was available to the men of Judah when they returned from exile in Babylon to rebuild their ruined city, and it was this legacy they unconsciously but specifically rejected.

The men of the Return did not want a universal truth. They wanted a secure ecclesiastical organization built along the lines of Josiah's earlier reformation. All the ecstasy and consecration that went into the rebuilding of the Temple under the leadership of Zerubbabel the governor and Joshua the high priest cannot hide the fact that the work was undertaken in exactly the same spirit that Jeremiah attacked with such determination before the city fell. It was the Temple and the Temple ritual they loved, and both had long since been outgrown. The prophets of Israel had not labored to establish a religious formula for Jews only; they had inaugurated a search for truth that could never be limited by racial lines.

It is true that the men of the Return had the writings of all these prophets before them and that they read them with careful reverence; but it is possible to read with blind eyes. If proof of this is needed, there is proof in the Bible itself. A Babylonian exile found himself reading what is now the fifty-first psalm, that beautiful plea for inward righteousness. "Create for me a clean heart, O God." (*Ps.* li. 10) Its last stanza, like so many of the psalms, is a specific rejection of the whole idea of outward worship.

> For thou desirest not sacrifice,
> And should I give burnt-offering thou wouldst not be pleased.
> The sacrifice of God is a broken spirit,
> A broken and a contrite heart. (*Ps.* li. 16-17)

The exile was much struck with this prayer. It had the undercurrent of sadness that suited the plight of his nation, but at the same time it seemed to lack the particularity that would make it wholly effective. Accordingly, he added another stanza of his own.

Do good in thy good will unto Zion;
Build thou the walls of Jerusalem.
Then shalt thou be pleased with right offerings,
Burnt-offering and whole burnt-offering;
Then shall bullocks come up upon thy altar.

(*Ps.* li. 18-19)

So sure was the exile that bullocks were "right offerings" to God that he failed to notice that the psalmist had a conception of worship exactly the reverse of his own, and that his own stanza was nonsense when considered in relation to the rest of the poem. The exile, however, was voicing a majority opinion, and his stanza remained, a permanent testimony to the unconscious blindness of a preconceived idea.

It was with the best of intentions that the unknown exile mutilated the fifty-first psalm, and it was with the best of intentions that the men of the Return betrayed the great trust that had been given them. They had no wish to reject the prophets' centuries of labor and all the discoveries the men of Israel had made. They wished only to preserve what they conceived these discoveries to be, and raised an ecclesiastical and religious barrier around them only to keep them safe. They did not realize that they might as well have boarded up a young oak to protect it from the sunlight and called the lifeless result a tree. To deprive the search for God of its freedom, and to offer it instead the safeguards of ritual and a jealous exclusiveness, was to lose it altogether.

If the men of the Return had been living at the time of Moses there might have been some justification for their attitude. Their ideal of racial exclusiveness might have been a necessity if the idea of one God were to be kept safe in a land of many gods like Canaan. But it was not Canaan they were returning to; it was Judah, and the men already living in the land believed as much in one God as they did. The natives of Judah even asked for permission to help in the work of rebuilding the Temple. "Let us build with you; for we seek your God, as you do." (*Ezra* iv. 2) But the governor and the high priest felt themselves justified in adopting a policy of exclusiveness much more rigid than the one Moses had instituted in Canaan, and they gave the natives of Judah a curt refusal. "You have nothing in common with us in building a house to God; but we ourselves will together build to the Lord, the God of Israel." (*Ezra* iv. 3)

Zerubbabel and Joshua were mistaken. It was not the God of Israel they were building a house for, but the God of Judah. Of the God of Israel it had already been said:

> My house shall be called a house of prayer for all the peoples. (*Isa.* lvi. 7)

and it was too late to turn him back into a tribal deity.

In spite of their undeniable zeal, the men of the Return were led astray by a fundamental disrespect for the truth. They were sure that the idea of one God could not endure unless they took it under their personal protection and refused to share it. The leaders of the community even felt justified in forcing the men to give up their foreign wives, since these women were somehow able to contaminate the religious purity of Judah.

The heads of the nation naturally encountered some difficulties in enforcing so arbitrary an ideal. When Ezra came up from Babylon to instruct his people in the Law, he succeeded in rousing them to such a pitch of excite-

ment that they all gathered together before the Temple
and swore to expel all foreigners from their midst,
"trembling on account of the occasion itself and also
because of the pouring rain." (*Ezra* x. 9) Yet when
Nehemiah arrived thirteen years later to finish the half-
built Temple, he found that the people's religious enthusiasm had weakened in the face of the love they bore
their foreign wives and that he was obliged to begin
all over again. According to Nehemiah's own statement,
he "contended with them and cursed them and beat some
of them and pulled out their hair" (*Neh.* xiii. 25) until
they were finally convinced by this gentle line of reasoning and agreed to abandon their wives and children.

Nehemiah undertook to purify the Temple ritual in
the same spirit, and dismissed the son of the high priest
from office because he was a relative by marriage of a
Horonite and therefore a great danger to the holiness of
the entire priesthood. As the last lines of his memoirs
show, Nehemiah took great pride in the way he had
saved the religious life of his people. "Thus I cleansed
them from all foreigners and established the duties for
the priests and the Levites, each for his own task, and
for the wood-offering at appointed times, and the first-
fruits. Remember it, O my God, to my credit." (*Neh.*
xiii. 30-31)

Nehemiah's memoirs show him to have been a brilliant executive, and in spite of his harshness he was a
just governor to the Jews; and his predecessor, Zerubbabel, was so outstandingly holy a man that a contemporary of his, the prophet Zechariah, believed him to be
the promised Messiah, the Lord's anointed one. Yet both
these governors of Judah devoted their very considerable
powers to a conception of religion that Israel had outgrown. When they rebuilt the city they thought they
were founding the new Jerusalem of which the poets

and prophets of their race had written, when in actual
fact their manner of doing it could not have been better
designed to keep the Jerusalem that the prophets looked
for off the earth indefinitely. It was too late to build in
worshipful piety a little house for God when it had already been written,

> "The heavens are my throne,
> And the earth is my footstool;
> What manner of house, then, would you build for
>   me?" (*Isa.* lxvi. 1)

The most characteristic piece of writing produced by
the narrow point of view of the men of the Return is the
ecclesiastical history known as the *Book of Chronicles*.
The book is not particularly valuable as history, since
the same ground is covered in the *Book of Samuel* and
the *Book of Kings*, and much more thoroughly. Its value
lies rather in its unconscious revelation of the principles
that animated the founders of Judaism.

The hero of the *Book of Chronicles* is the Temple, and
everything else in Israel's history is carefully subordinated to it. Elijah is not mentioned and neither is Isaiah,
but the list of doorkeepers to the Temple is given in the
most minute detail. The enormous passage of time between the beginning of the Hebrew race and the death
of its first king is covered only by genealogical tables in
which most of the attention is given to the sons of Levi,
because it was they who were the founders of the hereditary priesthood. The reigns of King David and King
Solomon are given in great detail, because it was David
who designed the first Temple and Solomon who built
it; but the Chronicler was unable to deal with the two
kings in the easy manner of the historian of *Kings*. He
did not dare mention David's sin with Bathsheba or the
apostasy of Solomon's old age, since to have done so

would have made the builders of the holy Temple somewhat less than holy themselves. For the same reason,
the Chronicler was obliged to ascribe a fictitious repentance to Manasseh, one of Judah's thoroughly evil kings,
to account for his long and prosperous reign; and he
was obliged to credit Asa with abolishing the "high
places" since it was inconceivable that Asa could have
been a good king and yet failed to do this. The honest
historian of *Kings* reports that "the high places were
not removed; nevertheless the heart of Asa was perfect
with the Lord all his days." (1 *Kings* xv. 14) But the
Chronicler was so burdened by a point of view that
anything like impartial history was impossible for him
to achieve.

Men like the Chronicler believed that the truth about
God was entirely contained in the Law and the Temple,
and as a result they naturally attempted to make both
institutions rigid enough to withstand any conceivable
onslaught. The Temple services became progressively
more elaborate and formalized, and the building itself
eventually became a glory of ivory and gold. Since the
God of Judah was a God of righteousness, the Law was
of almost equal importance and a class of men called
the Pharisees developed to formulate its application to
every aspect of daily living.

These Pharisees, the most influential of all the Jewish
sects, probably had their origin in the men who instituted the Maccabean revolt, the loyalist Jews who upheld the purity of the Jewish religion in the days when
the *Book of Daniel* was written and the Syrian king,
Antiochus Epiphanes, was trying to introduce the Greek
gods into the Jewish Temple. Antiochus actually
strengthened Jewish orthodoxy by the savage means he
took to destroy it, for Judaism stiffened instantly to
withstand the king and his blasphemies.

Some of the loyalist Jews carried obedience of the Law to almost impossible extremes. One group found themselves trapped by the Syrian troops on the Sabbath, and refused to fight even to save their wives and children from death, because the Law forbade warfare on the Sabbath; and it was Jews of the same fanaticism who forcibly circumcised every child they could lay their hands on as soon as they themselves triumphed. This state of mind reached its ultimate tragic expression some two centuries later in a class of men called the Zealots. In 70 A.D. they tried to hold Jerusalem in the face of a Roman attack, murdered all the Jews inside the walls who ventured to oppose them, and finally died in stoical endurance in the flames of the burning city, still waiting for the divine deliverance that the Jewish writings had promised would come.

The Zealots were an extreme expression of faith in the power of tradition, which was the basis of Judaism; and men like the Zealots inevitably came to the fore in Jewish history whenever that great symbol of ritual and tradition, the Temple at Jerusalem, was threatened with destruction. But in easier times the tight bonds of formalism slackened and loosened, and a variety of men worshipped the god of Judah in a variety of ways. They sacrificed in the same Temple, they observed the same Sabbath and they read the same Scripture; yet the variety of religious opinion that had developed under the name of Judaism by the first century B.C. is in striking contrast to the tight, anguished formalism that held the Jews together in days of persecution.

By the first century at least three major religious sects had emerged in Judea. These were the Pharisees, the Sadducees and the Essenes, and the differences between them were very marked.

The Essenes attempted to solve the ancient problem

of evil by avoiding it, like the monastic orders in Christianity. They were ascetics who banded together in small brotherhoods from which marriage and wealth were excluded and all men lived lives of contemplative morality and self-control. There was no buying and selling among the Essenes, no slavery and no politics.

The Sadducees, on the other hand, were thorough men of the world. The aristocrats and men of wealth in Judea were usually Sadducees, and the members of the group practiced the cool, formal, rather skeptical kind of worship that is often found among head men of a state religion.

The Sadducees had very little influence with the common people, and neither did the Essenes. It was the party of the Pharisees that really expressed the vital, living elements of Judaism as it was practiced in everyday life in the first century B.C.

It is especially important to understand the sect of the Pharisees since so large a part of the New Testament is the direct result of their teachings. Neither Paul nor any other Christian writer was the first to promulgate the doctrines of immortality of the soul, resurrection of the body, heaven and hell, angels, demons, eternal punishment of sinners, a Messiah who would judge the world on the Last Day, God as the Father of mankind, or the necessity for love and brotherhood among his sons. All these doctrines were specifically taught by the Pharisees, and lie recorded in the books that they wrote during the two centuries preceding the birth of Christ.

The doctrine of the immortality of the soul and the resurrection of the body was held by the Pharisees in direct contradiction to the theory of the Sadducees that soul and body perished together; and the most complete single exposition of this doctrine of a future life is the *Book of Enoch*. Written at some period between the second and first centuries B.C., the *Book of Enoch* was popularly supposed to contain the prophecies of the legendary Enoch who "walked with God" (*Gen.* v. 22) and it was treated with the utmost reverence.

The *Book of Enoch* was designed to tell the faithful exactly what would happen on the great Day of Judgment when all men would rise from the dead to stand accountable for their acts. The central figure of the book is a being called variously "the Son of Man," "the Elect One" and "my Son." His countenance has "the appearance of a man" but it is "full of graciousness, like one of the holy angels." (*Enoch* xlvi. 1) This being sits on a throne of glory and acts as a judge of the living and the dead on the Last Day, having been appointed to this high office as God's first act of creation.

> Yea, before the sun and the signs were created,
> Before the stars of the heaven were made,
> His name was named before the Lord of Spirits.
> (*Enoch* xlviii. 3)

This Son of Man is a terror to evil-doers, but he is the means of salvation to the righteous of whatever race.

> He shall be a light of the Gentiles,
> And the hope of those who are troubled of heart.
> All those who dwell on earth shall fall down and worship before him. (*Enoch* xlviii. 4-5)

The sinners will be swallowed up in Sheol, but the righteous will be given "the light of eternal life," (*Enoch* lviii. 3) for God and his Messiah will stay with them through all eternity.

> The Lord of Spirits shall abide with them,
> And with that Son of Man shall they eat
> And lie down and rise up for ever and ever.
> (*Enoch* lxii. 14)

In addition to its portrait of the kind of Messiah the
Jews were expecting, the *Book of Enoch* is interesting
for its expression of the complicated system of angels
and demons that had been worked out in the liberal fold
of Judaism. Nearly every religion is at some time irre-
sistibly attracted to the idea of good and evil spirits; and
the God of Judah had become so far-off and unapproachable under certain aspects of the legalistic regime that
he needed whole legions of angels to act as his inter-
mediaries. Most of these angels had their origin in the
Persian religion with its dualistic warfare between darkness and light, but the Jews adapted them freely and
made numerous additions of their own. Michael and
Gabriel and Raphael and the rest all had their specific
place in the hierarchy of the heavens. To balance this
angelology there was an equally complex demonology, and
the average Jew of the first century B.C. was haunted
by devils as thoroughly and consistently as any medieval
Christian.

This demonology was the childish side of the Jewish
religion, which possessed fundamentally an extremely
lofty and beautiful morality. The rabbinic schools, for
which the Pharisees were largely responsible, taught in
connection with the Law and the prophets a system of
ethics that produced some distinguished teachers. One
of the most honored of these was the great rabbi Hillel,
the first man to put into words what is now called the
Golden Rule: "Do not to others what thou wouldst not
have done to thyself."

The doctrine of the Golden Rule is implicit in much
of the teachings of the Pharisees, but it finds its clearest
expression in *The Testaments of the Twelve Patriarchs*,
a book which was written by a Pharisee about a hundred
years before the birth of Christ.

The Testaments of the Twelve Patriarchs was sup-

posed to contain the admonitions left to posterity by the
twelve sons of Jacob—Judah, Levi, Zebulun, Gad, and
so on; and within this framework the writer of the book
gives expression to an exceedingly high ethical concept.
Over and over again as he speaks in the names of the
patriarchs, he emphasizes the only kind of righteousness
that will find favor with the "holy Father."

The testament of Issachar gives the basic commandment, the one already given by Moses:

> Love the Lord and your neighbor. (*Iss.* v. 2)

Zebulun repeats and reinforces it:

> For in the degree in which a man hath compassion,
> upon his neighbors, in the same degree hath the Lord
> also upon him. (*Zeb.* viii. 3)

And in the testament of Gad, love of man is given us the
true basis of love of God.

> Beware, therefore, my children, of hatred; for it work-
> eth lawlessness. (*Gad* iv. 1) It will not hear the words
> of His commandments concerning the loving of one's
> neighbors, and it sinneth against God. (*Gad* iv. 2)
> For as love would quicken even the dead, and would
> call back them that are condemned to die, so hatred
> would slay the living. (*Gad* iv. 6) These things, there-
> fore, I say to you from experience, my children, that
> ye may drive forth hatred, which is of the devil, and
> cleave to the love of God. (*Gad* v. 2)

In the testament of Gad, true worship is not a matter
of acting and speaking in righteousness. It is a matter
of thinking righteously as well, for the true worshipper
of God "will not do wrong to any man even in thought."
(*Gad* v. 6) And in a man's love for his brothers, he must
not be content to love only his friends. He must love
his enemies.

Love ye one another from the heart; and if a man sin
against thee, speak peaceably to him, and in thy soul
hold not guile; and if he repent and confess, forgive
him. (*Gad* vi. 3) And though he deny it and yet have
a sense of shame when reproved, give over reproving
him. (*Gad* vi. 6) And if he be shameless and persist
in his wrong-doing, even so forgive him from the
heart. (*Gad* vi. 7)

In the book which contains this miniature Sermon
on the Mount there is another description of the Messiah
whose imminent coming figures so largely in all the
books of the Pharisees. In *The Testaments of the Twelve
Patriarchs*, the Messiah is priest rather than judge, "a
son, and a servant, and a minister of His presence."
(*Levi* iv. 2) He is an idealized personification of the
spirit of compassion and sinlessness in the book itself.
As the testament of Judah describes him,

A man shall arise from my seed, like the sun of right-
eousness,
Walking with the sons of men in meekness and right-
eousness;
And no sin shall be found in him. (*Judah* xxiv. 1)
And he shall pour out the spirit of grace upon you . . .
(*Judah* xxiv. 3)
To judge and to save all that call upon the Lord.
(*Judah* xxiv. 6)

Judaism was primarily an ethical religion, and the
Messiah of the Jews was an ethical figure. There were
a few men in Judea who expected the coming Messiah to
be a political savior who would free them from the yoke
of the Romans; but the majority believed in the books
of the Pharisees and expected a mighty and sinless judge,
a son of God who would give the righteous a permanent
reign of light and peace and who would terrify only
sinners.

The doctrine taught by the Pharisees in the first century B.C. was the expression of a lofty hope and a noble system of ethics. In spite of its accompanying superstitions, Judaism was a religion to which any man might be proud to belong, with its exalted monotheism and the high standard of inward righteousness it required. Nevertheless, it was the God of Judah that was taught in the synagogues and worshipped in the Temple. It was not the God of Israel.

The God of Israel was not a settled religious principle, to be honored with sacrifices in the Temple and studied in the schools and synagogues so that his ordinances might be fully obeyed. The God that Israel, the "striver with God," had set out to find was ultimate, provable reality, neither to be placated by sacrifices nor bound by a creed.

It was not by a reverence for tradition that a clearer conception of the God of Israel had been attained. It was by ignoring tradition. Each great prophet of Israel found himself directly antagonistic to the highest religious thought of his own day, and men like Amos and Jeremiah earned for themselves the names of madmen and blasphemers among their contemporaries, because they would not honor the God their contemporaries worshipped. As Amos said,

They loathe him who speaks the truth. (*Amos* v. 10)

The last prophet of Israel, and the greatest, had the same experience as the others. He also was called a madman and a blasphemer by the men of his day, who believed that they were worshipping correctly the only true God. The antagonism of the Pharisees to Jesus of Nazareth was abrupt, violent and conclusive, and they resorted almost at once to the desperate measures against him that the priests of Anathoth had tried to use against Jeremiah.

The Pharisees knew very well that it was not the God of Judaism that Jesus came to teach; and since they were convinced that the God of Judaism was the truth, they were equally convinced that the teachings of Jesus were inspired by the devil.

It was only men of the spiritual stature of Isaiah or Jeremiah who would have been capable of welcoming Jesus of Nazareth. They would have recognized him as one of themselves, born of the free line of Israel; and they would have honored him as greater than any of them, for with Jesus the search ended in victory.

The last prophet of Israel fulfilled in literal fact Isaiah's promise of the great Day of the Lord; for Jesus found God, and he conquered death.

THE FINDING

CHAPTER XV

So God created man in his own image; in the
image of God he created him.

The Book of Genesis i. 27

IN ATTEMPTING to understand the discovery that Jesus
made about God, the final discovery that ended the
search, it is important to remember that Jesus himself
left no written record of any kind. The four gospels were
written either by Jews or, in the case of Luke, by a man
who believed unquestioningly in the fundamental tenets
of Judaism.

The power by which Jesus conquered death would
seem clear enough to anyone who believed in Judaism;
and Matthew and Luke, Peter and Paul unite in giving
the same reason for what Jesus had done. "Death could
not control him" (*Acts* ii. 24) because he was the Messiah that the *Book of Enoch* and all the other Jewish
writings had promised, the great, conquering, righteous,
half-supernatural Son of Man who had been chosen before the world was made to be its judge and savior.

The faith of the early Christians was simple, straight-
forward, and quite orthodox from the Jewish point of
view. Jesus had conquered death. For that fact they had
the evidence of their own eyes. Therefore he must be the
Messiah, or, in the more familiar Greek translation of
the word, the Christ. The evidence of the resurrection
became the basis of the whole of their teaching, and they
were willing to have the validity of their message judged
by that one test alone. "If Christ was not raised, there is
nothing in our message; there is nothing in our faith
either." (1 *Cor.* xv. 14)

If the evidence of the resurrection had not seemed so conclusive to men like Paul and Peter, their conviction that Jesus was the Messiah of the Jews would otherwise have been very difficult to maintain. It was clearly stated in the Jewish apocalypses like *Enoch* that when the Messiah appeared heaven and earth would shake at his approach. He would make a supernatural appearance on the clouds, with all the angels in glory around him, and then he would sit on the throne of God to commit sinners to everlasting damnation and to usher in a reign of joy for the righteous in his holy name.

Jesus, however, had fulfilled none of these prophecies concerning the Messiah of the Jews. He had taught a "kingdom of God" in Judea, but it was a kingdom that had never become visible to his followers. He had done wonders in Judea that no man should have been able to do unless he were the Messiah, but he had never been surrounded by angels and a cloud of fire. He had conquered death, but no great Day of Judgment had followed after.

The easiest solution to this apparent mystery would have been to abandon the teachings of the Jewish apocalypses and to come to the conclusion that the "kingdom of God" that Jesus taught in Judea was not a physical kingdom. But men like Peter and Paul were good Jews, born and bred in the faith, and it did not occur to them to doubt their apocalypses.

They therefore took the only other way out of the difficulty, and taught the famous doctrine of the "second coming." This doctrine explained that the Day of Judgment had only been temporarily postponed so that more people might be saved, and that in a very short time the Messiah would return to the world in his true character of lord and judge. The whole Christian church kept itself in a state of sustained excitement throughout the first century, waiting for the day "when our Lord Jesus appears from heaven, with his mighty angels in a blaze of fire, and takes vengeance on the godless." (2 *Thess.* i. 7-8)

Inserted in each of the three gospels of Matthew, Mark and Luke is a "little apocalypse" which is a condensed version of the Day of Judgment described in the *Book of Enoch,* and a clear expression of the perfectly orthodox Judaism of the writers.

> Nation will rise in arms against nation, and kingdom against kingdom. There will be great earthquakes, and pestilence and famine here and there. There will be horrors and great signs in the sky. (*Luke* xxi. 10-11) There will be signs too in sun, moon, and stars, and on earth dismay among the heathen, bewildered at the roar of the sea and the waves. Men will swoon with fear and foreboding of what is to happen in the world, for the forces in the sky will shake. Then they will see the Son of Man coming in a cloud with great power and glory. (*Luke* xxi. 25-27) It will all happen before the present generation passes away. (*Luke* xxi. 32)

> The sun will be darkened and the moon will not shed its light and the stars will fall from the sky and the forces in the sky will shake. Then they will see the Son of Man coming on the clouds with great power and glory, and then he will send out the angels and gather his chosen people from the four winds, from one end of the earth to the other. (*Mark* xiii. 24-27) These things will all happen before the present age passes away. (*Mark.* xiii. 30)

> When the Son of Man comes in his splendor, with all his angels with him, he will take his seat on his glorious throne, and all the nations will be gathered before him, and he will separate them from one another . . . the sheep at his right hand and the goats at his left. Then the king will say to those at his right "Come, you whom my Father has blessed, take pos-

session of the kingdom." (*Matt.* xxv. 31-34) Then he
will say to those at his left, "Begone, you accursed
people, to the everlasting fire destined for the devil."
(*Matt.* xxv. 41) Then they will go away to everlasting punishment, and the upright to everlasting life.
(*Matt.* xxv. 46)

The three gospels of Matthew, Mark and Luke, called
the "synoptic gospels" because they resemble one another
so closely, are an expression of orthodox Judaism in their
attitude towards the Day of Judgment and the Messiah
who will usher it in. They are equally an expression of
orthodox Judaism in their attitude towards ethics, which
formed such a large part of the Jewish religion.

As far as his teachings are concerned, Jesus appears in
the three synoptic gospels as little more than an enlightened Jewish rabbi, one who believed that God was the
loving father of mankind, that he should be worshipped
righteously in thought as well as in deed, that all men
should love their brothers, and that of such was the kingdom of heaven.

Such teachings were orthodox and familiar to good
Jews. They had already been put into writing by the
Pharisee who wrote *The Testaments of the Twelve Patriarchs*, and every Jew knew the ethical basis upon
which he might expect to be judged worthy of the coming kingdom of the Messiah. There is nothing contrary
to the best in Judaism in the teachings of Jesus as recorded in the three synoptic gospels. On the contrary,
Jesus appears as a teacher of ethics whom the Pharisees
should have been eager to honor, in the same way that
they honored Hillel or any other great teacher of Jewish
morality.

It is at this point that the three synoptic gospels bear
witness against themselves. Written by men convinced
of the truth of the Jewish religion, they attempt at every

point to reconcile Jesus to Judaism and to prove that he was the Messiah of the Jewish apocalypses. Yet in recording the actual facts of Jesus' career, so that all men might be "reliably informed," (*Luke* i. 4) the gospels are also obliged to record that Jesus placed himself in irreconcilable opposition to Judaism and that his conflict with the Jewish authorities ended with crucifixion.

All three gospels emphasize that Jesus was executed for a crime that was not political, but religious. The Roman governor had no wish to see him die. It was the Pharisees who killed him, and they killed him for the specific crime of being a false prophet who was misleading the nation.

It was not as a teacher of morality that Jesus earned the desperate hatred of the Pharisees, any more than it could have been as a teacher of morality that he healed the sick and raised the dead. It was a much more revolutionary teaching than any recorded in *Matthew, Mark* and *Luke* that sent Jesus to the cross as a dangerous deceiver of the people.

If only the three synoptic gospels existed for testimony, the life of Jesus would have to remain an insoluble mystery. He appears in them as the Jewish Messiah, who nevertheless did nothing that the Messiah was supposed to do, and as a Jewish teacher of ethics who taught only what the Pharisees had been teaching and who was nevertheless murdered by them because they believed he constituted a deadly danger to the nation.

These gospels were written from the point of view of Judaism about a man whose career cannot be reconciled with Judaism; the contradictions are inevitable. But there is a fourth gospel which was not written primarily from the point of view of Judaism; and in this gospel no contradictions occur.

The Fourth Gospel does not attempt to present Jesus

as a Jewish Messiah who will shortly re-appear in the heavens with all his angels about him. Nor is there any attempt to present him as an enlightened teacher of Jewish ethics. More of the sayings of Jesus are recorded in the Fourth Gospel than in any other except Matthew's, yet none of them is on the subject of morality.

Jesus does not appear in the Fourth Gospel either as a Jewish rabbi or a Jewish Messiah. He appears, to use his own words, as "a man who has told you the truth," (*John* viii. 40) and this was not the truth about morality, but the truth about God.

The Fourth Gospel is a book so completely un-Jewish in spirit that a group of men who knew the author felt obliged to append a guarantee of authenticity at the end of it, to vouch for the fact that the John who wrote the book had been in actual fact a disciple of Jesus. Nevertheless, the only real guarantee of the book's authenticity does not lie in any external circumstance. It lies in the fact that John's gospel is the only reasonable explanation in existence of why Jesus' doctrine so terrified the Pharisees.

The structure of John's gospel is completely unlike that of the other three. It was written with one end in view, not to explain what Jesus did, but to explain how he did it. Everything else is subordinated to this single purpose. In the course of writing his gospel, John had occasion to correct errors in fact in the earlier books and to add biographical material from events of which he himself had been an eye-witness; but the primary purpose of his book was nevertheless not historical but explanatory. John was convinced that an account of what Jesus did could properly be based only on an account of what Jesus himself was.

The book is constructed with extreme care, so that no act of Jesus is given as an isolated phenomenon. The synoptic gospels are full of stories of how Jesus fed a multitude or healed the sick or raised the dead, but there is no attempt whatever to relate these actions to his teachings. In the Fourth Gospel they are related so closely that nothing can separate them. Jesus said, "I am the bread that gives life," (*John* vi. 35) and proved it by feeding a multitude without apparent supply. He said, "I am a light for the world," (*John* ix. 5) and healed a man who had been born blind. He said, "I myself am resurrection and life," (*John* xi. 25) and raised a man who had been four days dead.

Unlike the synoptic gospels, *John* does not present these actions as the inexplicable miracles of a Jewish Messiah. They are presented as "signs," not of a supernatural king and judge, but of "a man who has told you the truth."

It was this truth on which John concentrated his whole gospel. He presents the history of Jesus as the history of an idea which not only dominated Jesus' life, but which was his life and the whole purpose of his existence. "It was for this I was born and for this that I came to the world, to give testimony for truth." (*John* xviii. 37)

John was apparently the only disciple Jesus had who realized that his message could not be understood by the light of orthodox Judaism, and it was perhaps on this account that John was "the disciple who was very dear to Jesus." (*John* xxi. 20) It was only John who seems to have realized that the kingdom of God that Jesus taught was not a physical kingdom, and that the day of judgment he promised had nothing to do with the supernatural convulsions of the Jewish apocalypses. Jesus was a teacher who had come to the world to make known "the only true God"; (*John* xvii. 3) and the God he taught was not the God of Judaism.

John did not have the accurate, unassailable knowledge of God that Jesus himself possessed. But he was **suf-ficiently** in sympathy with Jesus' point of view to be able to remember and record what his master had said in a way that no other disciple was capable of doing; and John's gospel is sufficient to explain both the authority by which Jesus acted and the inescapable antagonism that sprang up between him and the Pharisees.

This conflict between the orthodox men of Judah and the great prophet of Israel had its roots in a single claim that Jesus made for himself, a claim that is repeated over and over again in the Fourth Gospel.

Jesus said, and was prepared to prove it, that he was the son of God.

There was nothing whatever in this claim, taken only at its face value, to antagonize the Pharisees or any other Jewish sect. The Jews had unanimously agreed for centuries to the proposition expressed by the prophet Malachi:

> Have we not all one father?
> Did not one God create us? (*Mal.* ii. 10)

The Jews always called God the "holy Father," and it was their proudest boast that they were all his sons if they followed his commandments.

But when Jesus used the term "son of God," he did not mean by it what the adherents of Judaism meant. There is one conversation in particular, recorded in the *Gospel of John*, which shows perfectly how wide was the chasm that separated the prophet of Israel from the theologians of Judah.

To understand the full force of this conversation, it is necessary to remember that Jesus was not speaking to enemies. John carefully states that Jesus was addressing himself to men who "believed in him." (*John* viii. 30) It was to these men that Jesus said:

> "If you abide by what I teach, you are really disciples
> of mine, and you will know the truth and the truth
> will set you free." (*John* viii. 31-32)

The men who were listening to him could not understand what Jesus meant by such a statement. No truth could set them "free." They were free men already. "We are descended from Abraham, and have never been anyone's slaves. How can you say to us, 'You will be set free'?" (*John* viii. 33)

Jesus told them they were not free; they were in bondage. And he added that they were obeying a father who was not God.

At this the Jews, not unnaturally, were furious. "We are not illegitimate children. We have one Father, God himself." (*John* viii. 41) Any good Jew would have said the same, and to any Jew what Jesus said next was sheer blasphemy.

> "Why is it that you do not understand what I say? It
> is because you cannot bear to listen to my message.
> The devil is the father you are sprung from, and you
> want to carry out your father's wishes. He was a
> murderer from the first, and he has nothing to do
> with the truth, for there is no truth in him. When
> he tells a lie, he speaks in his true character, for he
> is a liar and the father of them." (*John* viii. 43-44)

In other words, what the Jews had been calling "father," Jesus called the devil.

In order to understand what Jesus meant by such a statement, it is necessary to recall the exact nature of the deity in whom the Jews believed. The foundation of their religion was that all men were the sons of Adam. Adam had sinned and therefore died, and all his descendants were doomed likewise to sin and death. Continual worship at the Temple and strict obedience to the Law might take away the sin, but nothing could take away the certainty of death. God had created death, just as he had created life. He had made man of a body formed of the dust, and to the dust man was obliged to return. His only chance of salvation if he were not a Jew lay in being converted to Judaism. Only in this way could he assure for himself an ultimate life of eternal happiness beyond the grave, while the rest of the heathen, judged on the Last Day by God and his Messiah, were doomed to everlasting torment for their sins.

This was orthodox Judaism as it had developed in the intervening centuries since the last of Israel's prophets had fallen silent. It was this deity whom the Jews called "father," and it was this deity whom Jesus called "a murderer."

There is no doubt that Jesus' definition of the God of Judah is a just one, if all instinctive reverence for theology is laid aside. The God whom the Jews worshipped is the God by whom the coming of death into the world is explained in the *Book of Genesis*. He is the deity who first made Adam capable of evil, and then condemned him to death for the quality he himself had made. He is the author of death, the destroyer and torturer of his own creation. He is, as Jesus said, "a murderer from the first."

The history of the men of Israel, the "strivers with God," was the history of the slow, steady repudiation of the God of Adam and Eve, the kind of God whose nature might be deduced from the existence of an evil and dying world. He was the obvious God, but the men of Israel did not want the obvious God. Little by little and each according to the measure of his own understanding, they destroyed, one by one, the attributes of this creator. And the end of the search came when Jesus, the last of the prophets and the culmination of the line of Israel, was able to say of this obvious God: "He has nothing to do with the truth, for there is no truth in him."

To any Jew this statement was of course a blasphemy, and the group of Jews to whom Jesus was speaking cried out at once that he was "possessed"—a madman. (*John* viii. 48)

Jesus told them that, on the contrary, he was the only one who was giving true honor to God. "I have respect for my Father." (*John* viii. 49) The God to whom Jesus gave honor was not a murderer, and the sons of this Father were not subject to the bondage of Adam. "I tell you, if anyone observes my teaching, he will never experience death." (*John* viii. 51)

This final statement was all the Jews needed to convince them that they were dealing with a madman. Everyone was subject to death. Death was a fact, created by God, and not the best and holiest of God's sons could escape it. "Now we are sure that you are possessed! Abraham is dead and so are the prophets, and yet you say, 'If anyone observes my teaching, he will never know what death is'! Are you a greater man than our forefather Abraham? Yet he is dead and the prophets are dead. What do you claim to be?" (*John* viii. 52-53)

Jesus answered the Jews by telling them bluntly that they knew nothing whatever concerning the real nature of God. They had superimposed upon the name of God their own ignorance concerning him, and they were therefore liars when they called God their father. "You say he is your God, yet you have never come to know him." (*John* viii. 54-55) Jesus himself was entitled to call God his father because he really was his son. "I know him. If I say I do not know him, I will be a liar like yourselves. No! I do know him, and I am faithful to his message." (*John* viii. 55)

"And this is the message," wrote John as a summary,

"that we heard from him and announce to you: God is light; there is no darkness in him at all." (1 *John* i. 5)

It was to this message that Jesus remained faithful throughout the whole of his ministry: the conception of a perfect God in whom there is no darkness at all. He reversed the basic assumption of Judaism, which first accepted the evidence of the visible world and then deduced from it the existence of a God of both light and darkness, of both life and death. Jesus instead maintained the existence of a perfect God, a God of light only, and saw the world as made in his image.

Jesus maintained that he was the direct product of a living God, a son whose life could not be separated from that of the Father. In the face of all the apparent evidence to the contrary, he consistently refused to admit any other power as the source of his life. He meant it literally when he said to his followers: "You must not call anyone on earth your father, for you have only one father." (*Matt.* xxiii. 9)

Jesus refused to admit that Joseph was his father or Mary his mother. He refused to admit that he had been laboriously shaped in a womb and there implanted with the seeds of death, the product of the deity who said, "Dust you are, and to dust you must return." (*Gen.* iii. 19) Jesus denied this creator, and with it his creation. The only creator he acknowledged was a perfect and living God, and it was through this God that he possessed life. "I live because of the Father." (*John* vi. 57)

The principle of existence that Jesus called Father was the same principle of existence that was dimly perceived by Moses when he gave to God the name of I AM; and it is through Moses' name for God that the discovery of life which Jesus made can be most clearly expressed. "I and my Father are one." (*John* x. 30) I am. "The

Father is greater than I." (*John* xiv. 28) I am, but only
because my origin, my Father, is I AM itself. "For just
as the Father is self-existent, he has given self-existence
to the son." (*John* v. 26)

Of all the disciples, John was the only one who was
willing to give to Jesus the origin that Jesus claimed for
himself. Both Matthew and Luke tried to prove that Jesus
was born of the line of David, because that was the line
through which the Messiah was supposed to come, and
they copied out long genealogical tables to show how
Jesus could trace his ancestry back through his father
Joseph. Matthew and Luke then involved themselves in
another of their contradictions by stating that Jesus was
born of a virgin, thus invalidating their own tables. This
is not to say that Matthew and Luke were not as faithful
to the truth as they knew how to be. But they were
handicapped from the beginning because they did not
know what Jesus meant when he called himself "the son
of the living God." (*Matt.* xvi. 16)

Luke really believed that he could write an adequate
account of Jesus' life by gathering together the testimony
of "the original eye-witnesses" (*Luke* i. 2) and recording in order the events that they remembered. But John
knew that the outward events of Jesus' life had no importance except as they bore witness to the inward conviction of sonship upon which the whole of his life had
been based. In other words, he knew that a life of Jesus
could only be written from the standpoint of Jesus' discovery about life.

John was attempting to do an exceedingly difficult
thing in setting himself to write such a biography. He
could not invent a whole new vocabulary to express the
discovery Jesus had made concerning God. The new idea
had to be put into old language, like new wine into old

wineskins; and John knew that whatever he said of the "kingdom" or the "son" would be open to complete misunderstanding.

John seems to have chosen his words with great caution; and the same caution is necessary in the reader if he is not to be misled by the theological connotations possessed by the words John used in introducing his gospel. There is no evidence that John meant anything esoteric by his use of "the Word." He was using it in its ordinary and literal meaning, that of "communication."

> In the beginning the Word existed. The Word was with God, and the Word was divine. (*John* i. 1)

According to the discovery that Jesus had made, there was only one Word, one possible communication between God and man; and this was the fact, which had existed from the beginning, that man's existence was not separate from God's.

> It was he that was with God in the beginning. Everything came into existence through him, and apart from him nothing came to be. It was by him that life came into existence, and that life was the light of mankind. The light is still shining in the darkness, for the darkness has never put it out. (*John* i. 2-5)

Life, as Jesus taught it, meant union with the Father. The awareness of this union was the Word, the one communication between God and man. Without this communication, no real and undying existence was possible. The life that was lived in accordance with it was the only true life, and apart from it there was nothing else. No darkness could ever put it out, since it constituted perfect union with a God in whom there is no darkness at all.

> The Word became flesh and blood and lived for a
> while among us, abounding in blessing and truth, and
> we saw the honor God had given him, such honor as
> an only son receives from his father. (*John* i. 14)

The Word, the awareness of man's relationship to God,
appeared to the world in visible form as the life of a man
named Jesus. His was the true life, because it was lived
in perfect union with God, as his son. He was the "only
son" because he was the only man ever to understand
and live his true relationship to God.

> He came to his home, and his own family did not wel-
> come him. But to all who did receive him and believe
> in him he gave the right to become children of God,
> owing their birth not to nature nor to any human or
> physical impulse, but to God. (*John* i. 11-13)

Jesus came to his brothers, the sons of the one Father,
and they were unable to welcome him. But any man
capable of understanding the message he brought received the same life that Jesus himself possessed, the life
that did not owe itself "to nature nor to any human or
physical impulse, but to God."

The ability to live this life was to enter what Jesus
called the kingdom of heaven. This was not a physical
kingdom, of the kind prophesied by the Jewish apocalypses.

> The kingdom of God is not coming visibly, and people
> will not say, "Look! Here it is!" or "There it is!" for
> the kingdom of God is within you. (*Luke.* xvii. 21)

The kingdom of God consisted of a new and correct way
of looking at things, and the command that Jesus gave
as a necessary prelude to entering the kingdom was
"Change your minds." * (*Mark* i. 15)

* This is the literal meaning of the Greek word that is usually translated
"repent."

It was no physical change that enabled a man to be born into the kingdom of heaven. "Whatever owes its birth to the physical is physical, and whatever owes its birth to the Spirit is spiritual. Do not wonder at my telling you that you must be born over again from above." (*John* iii. 6-7) To be born again of the Spirit—"that Spirit of Truth that comes from the Father" (*John* xv. 26)—was to experience a mental rebirth into a kingdom that could never be destroyed because it had no physical origin.

To be born into this kingdom meant release from the old forms of physical bondage. It was a bondage caused by a lack of understanding of man's relationship to God, and as soon as the weight of this misunderstanding was lifted by a knowledge of the truth, the bondage could no longer exist. "You will know the truth and the truth will set you free." (*John* viii. 32)

Jesus himself walked as a free man. He did not need to be afraid that water would drown him or a lack of bread cause him to starve. As the son of God, owing his life to God only, he possessed an existence that nothing could alter or destroy.

This unassailable sense of existence, this knowledge of a living God from whom he could never be separated, was what Jesus meant in his use of the phrase "eternal life." The phrase itself was a familiar one to the Jews; it meant to them the glorified state that would be permitted to the righteous on the Last Day after they rose from their graves. But in John's gospel it is clear that Jesus was not referring to a future life, but to a present, continuing existence based securely on a correct knowledge of God.

Eternal life means knowing you as the only true God.
(*John* xvii. 3)

Once this knowledge was attained, life would be eternal because from that time forward it was lived in union with God.

Once a man found himself as the son of the living God he was no longer subject to death. "I tell you, whoever listens to my message and believes him who has sent me possesses eternal life, and will not come to judgment, but has already passed out of death into life." (*John* v. 24) "I tell you, if anyone observes my teaching, he will never experience death." (*John* viii. 51)

Jesus did not present a statement of this kind as a theoretical abstraction. He proved over and over again in the short period of his ministry that death had no power for the man who understood the "only true God." When Jairus mourned because he had received word that his only daughter had died, Jesus told him, "Do not be afraid." (*Luke* viii. 50) He said to those that wailed about the bedside of the child, "Stop wailing! For she is not dead." (*Luke* viii. 52) They laughed at him "for they knew that she was dead," (*Luke* viii. 53) but it was Jesus who proved to be right and not they. The mourners had the evidence of their own eyes to tell them that the girl was dead, but Jesus had a better evidence than theirs.

As Jesus said repeatedly, it was not by any innate authority of his own that he healed the sick and raised the dead. "I cannot do anything of my own accord." (*John* v. 30) It was by the authority of the truth that he acted. "The Father who is united with me is doing these things himself." (*John* xiv. 10) "I tell you, the son cannot do anything of his own accord, unless he sees the Father doing it." (*John* v. 19)

When Jesus gave the command, "Believe in me," he was careful to make clear what he meant by it. "Whoever believes in me, believes not in me but in him who has sent me." (*John* xii. 44) Jesus claimed nothing for himself; all power, all authority and all glory belonged only to God. Jesus would not even admit for himself personal righteousness. He once turned on a member of the Jewish council who had called him "Good master" and asked, "Why do you call me good? No one is good but God himself." (*Luke* xviii. 19)

Of himself, Jesus possessed nothing; but as the son of God, in perfect union with the Father, he possessed everything. "For whatever the Father does, the son also does." (*John* v. 19) The authority, always, was God's, so that any man who found his sonship with God would be able to do all that Jesus himself had done, and even more. "I tell you, whoever believes in me will do such things as I do, and things greater yet." (*John* xiv. 12) Jesus remained the "only son," as John called him, only because he never found another man willing to give God the authority that he himself gave him.

The kingdom that Jesus offered to the men of Judea was real sovereignty, and the eternal life he offered was real life. It was the truth itself he was offering them, and it could therefore be proven. Whenever Jesus was asked for his credentials, for some positive proof that the message he brought was the truth about God, the answer he gave was always the same: "The things I have been doing by my Father's authority are my credentials." (*John* x. 25) It was because the word of God was light itself that it could give eyes to a man born blind; because it was freedom that it could lift up a cripple whose back had been bent for eighteen years; because it was life that it could raise the dead son of the widow at Nain. It was because it was the truth that it could be proven.

It was by proofs such as these, and by no other gauge, that Jesus was willing to have the reality of his message judged. When John the Baptist, the most influential religious leader in Judea, called Jesus the son of God, Jesus

was not affected by John's sanction of his work. "I have higher testimony than John's, for the things that my Father has intrusted to me to accomplish, the very things that I am doing, are proof that my Father has sent me." (*John* v. 36) John the Baptist eventually began to wonder if he had been right in his indorsement of the new prophet, and he finally sent some of his disciples to Jesus to ask outright, "Are you the one who was to come, or should we look for someone else?" (*Matt.* xi. 3) Again Jesus answered by pointing to the one incontrovertible proof of the truth of his message. "Go and report to John what you hear and see. The blind are regaining their sight and the lame can walk, the lepers are being cured and the deaf can hear, the dead are being raised and good news is being preached to the poor." (*Matt.* xi. 4-5)

Jesus bewildered men like John the Baptist because they were looking for the wrong kind of Messiah. Jesus was not the Messiah of Judaism, and the "good news" he brought was not the kind that the men of Judah had been led to expect. It was only the prophets of Israel who would have rejoiced to see his coming.

The Day of the Lord that the men of Judah expected was a great physical cataclysm that would tear the sun and the moon out of their places. But the Day of the Lord that the men of Israel had foretold was the day of enlightenment upon which God would be fully known. The Messiah of the Lord that the men of Judah expected was a supernatural Son of Man who would destroy the wicked and give the righteous everlasting bliss. But the Messiah that the men of Israel had promised was

> a light to the nations—
> In opening blind eyes,
> In bringing prisoners out of the dungeon,
> Those who sit in darkness out of the prison.
>
> (*Isa.* xlii. 6-7)

The prophets of Israel believed that when the light of a perfect knowledge of God came into the world it would bring with it a life that was immortal and a freedom that was unassailable. All pain and destruction would cease forever on the holy mountain of the Lord; and death "the veil that veils all the people and the web that is woven over all the nations" (*Isa.* xxv. 7) would be destroyed forever.

It was this kingdom, the kingdom the prophets of Israel had seen afar off, that Jesus offered to the people of Judea. It was not a kingdom to be attained after death, and the prophets had never suggested that it would be. It was instead the kingdom that destroyed death with a knowledge of "the only true God."

Jesus was in every sense the climax and the culmination of Israel, the race that strove with God. He was the justification of Israel's conviction that a Day of the Lord would come upon which God would be fully known; and John was right when he said of Jesus that Isaiah "saw his glory; it was of him that he spoke." (*John* xii. 41)

CHAPTER XVI

Naught that this people call holy
Shall you call holy. *Book of Isaiah* viii. 12

FROM the beginning of his ministry in Judea, Jesus conducted himself as "one who had authority." (*Matt.* vii. 29) This authority was impregnable because, as Jesus said, it was not his own. "My teaching is not my own; it comes from him who has sent me." (*John* vii. 16) It was not in his own name that Jesus became a teacher in Judea. "I do nothing of my own accord, but speak as the Father has instructed me." (*John* viii. 28)

This conviction that he possessed nothing of his own, either as a teacher or as a healer, was no untried assumption with Jesus. At the beginning of his ministry he had been faced with the temptation that was obviously inherent in his discovery : the temptation to use the truth rather than to prove it, to honor himself and his own knowledge rather than God only. It was a very strong temptation, for it came to Jesus three times; and each time he rejected it and refused to give honor to any power apart from God.

Jesus called this temptation to exert personal authority "the devil." It came to him with a subtlety and an apparent innocence worthy of the serpent in *Genesis*, and to any other man but Jesus it would have seemed no devil at all but only a notable opportunity to prove the power of God. He was hungry, and the idea occurred to him that this would be a good opportunity to make a final test of his relationship to God; "if you are God's son, tell this stone to turn into bread." (*Luke* iv. 3)

Jesus turned on this suggestion at once as something wholly evil. The power he possessed was not the power to work personal miracles but the power to acknowledge God as the only life. His life was lived "because of the Father." (*John* vi. 57) Bread had no power to support that life, nor did lack of bread have the power to take it away. It was not by changing a stone into bread that he would prove he was God's son, but only by acknowledging no source of life except "the living Father." (*John* vi. 57) He answered the suggestion with a quotation from Moses. "The Scripture says, 'Not on bread alone is man to live'!" (*Luke* iv. 4)

Again the temptation to exert personal authority came to Jesus, and this time more openly. He realized what an enormous power lay inherent in his discovery, the power of getting and maintaining control over all physical things. It was as though the devil said to him, "I will give you all this power . . . I can give it to anyone I please. If you will do homage before me, it shall all be yours." (*Luke* iv. 6-7)

For a second time Jesus refused to acknowledge any power except the power of God. The devil possessed no "kingdoms of the world." (*Luke* iv. 5) The only kingdom was the kingdom of God, and Jesus unconditionally refused to accept any other. Again he answered with a quotation. "The Scripture says, 'You must do homage before the Lord your God, and worship him alone." (*Luke* iv. 8)

In this fact of God's power there was perfect safety, as Jesus knew. Perhaps, therefore, he would be willing to prove this fact once and for all? Perhaps he would be willing to throw himself down from some great height? In this way he could prove, finally and forever, that his life belonged to God, and that he was truly his son. For there is a beautiful passage in the Psalms testifying to the perfect safety of those who trust in God.

> For he will give his angels charge over you,
> To guard you in all your ways.
> They will bear you up upon their hands,
> Lest you strike your foot upon a stone. (*Ps.* xci. 11-12)

Again, and for the third time, Jesus did not permit himself to be deceived. For all the speciousness of the suggestion he knew it for what it was, an attempt to make him dishonor the truth, and he answered this quotation from the Psalms with one of his own: "You shall not try the Lord your God." (*Luke* iv. 12) The truth he had discovered and was going to teach in Judea was not a force that could be manipulated into arbitrary manifestations of power. The fact that God is Light could not be proven by first manufacturing a darkness for him to dispel. It could only be proven by showing that no darkness had ever existed.

It was "under the power of the Spirit" (*Luke* iv. 14) that Jesus returned to Galilee and began his ministry— "that Spirit of Truth that comes from the Father." (*John* xv. 26) From that time forward the great prophet of Israel was secure in the knowledge that he was not the master of the truth but its servant. "I am not seeking to do what I please, but what pleases him who has sent me." (*John* v. 30)

It was not in his own name that Jesus came as a teacher into Judea. "Whatever I say, I say only as the Father has told me." (*John* xii. 50) And it was not in his own name that he proved what he taught, giving light to the blind, healing the sick and raising the dead. "The Father who is united with me is doing these things himself." (*John* xiv. 10)

Since he knew that the authority by which he acted was impregnable, Jesus conducted himself throughout his ministry without caution and without compromise. The message he brought was the truth, and it could not be either modified or concealed. As he said himself, "Nobody lights a lamp and then covers it with a dish or puts it under a bed, but he puts it on its stand, so that those who come in may see the light." (*Luke* viii. 16) And this light was no flickering little doctrine of religious theory. It was the "light of life" (*John* viii. 12) and could be proven.

Jesus had come into Judea to teach radical, consecrated service to a God in whom there is no darkness at all. He had dedicated himself to this without qualification and without reservation. "My Father is still at work, and I work also." (*John* v. 17)

The completeness and wholeness of the honor that Jesus gave to God was what he expected all men to give. He was revolutionary in his demands, and he did not soften them to make them easy of popular acceptance. "The gate is narrow and the road is hard that leads to life." (*Matt.* vii. 14)

To follow this road meant the rejection of the whole of the visible world and the acceptance of an entirely new way of looking at things. No man could serve two masters. Either he abandoned his allegiance to everything in which he had formerly believed to find his life in God only; or else he did not. There was no third road possible.

Jesus emphasized repeatedly in his parables how completely the search for reality excluded everything but itself. "The kingdom of heaven is like a hoard of money, buried in a field, which a man found, and buried again. And he was overjoyed, and went and sold everything he had and bought the field. Again, the kingdom of heaven is like a dealer in search of fine pearls. He found one costly pearl, and went and sold everything he had, and bought it." (*Matt.* xiii. 44-46) Jesus told most of his parables to illustrate the consecration demanded of anyone who sought the kingdom. He illustrated it in the story of the servant who was punished because he had not multiplied the money placed in his care, in the story of the hopeful seedlings that let themselves be choked out by weeds, of the wedding guests who refused the bridegroom's invitation, of the bridesmaids who forgot to fill their lamps with oil.

If it were sought for with perfect consecration, the kingdom of heaven was available to any man. "Ask, and what you ask will be given you. Search, and you will find what you search for. Knock, and the door will open to you." (*Matt.* vii. 7) But no man could attain the kingdom of heaven unless he was willing to give up everything he had previously honored as reality, to honor only God. "Whoever wants to preserve his life will lose it, and whoever loses his life for me will preserve it. What good does it do a man to gain the whole world and lose or forfeit himself?" (*Luke* ix. 24-25)

The kingdom of heaven was not an easy theological doctrine that could be accepted emotionally and put to no practical use. It was instead a fact, to be accepted wholly and to be acted upon. "It is not everyone who says to me 'Lord! Lord!' who will get into the kingdom of heaven, but only those who do the will of my Father in heaven." (*Matt.* vii. 21) To do his will meant to honor his name, and to renounce literally, as Jesus himself had renounced it, any life, any power or any authority separate from God's.

It was this life that Jesus had accepted as his own, and any man who wanted to follow him had to accept it also. "Whoever lives on my flesh and drinks my blood possesses eternal life." (*John* vi. 54) After this statement many of his disciples drew back and refused to follow him any longer, not because of his use of symbols, for the Jews were accustomed to hearing their teachers speak in pictures, but because of the radical demands he made upon them. He would not let them continue with their old way of life.

The doctrine that Jesus taught in Judea demanded a complete mental re-birth, the rejection of everything unlike itself. It could not be accepted in part, or in theory. It had to be accepted wholly and practically, so that life was lived upon no other basis.

> "Everyone, therefore, who listens to this teaching of mine and acts upon it, will be like a sensible man who built his house on rock. And the rain fell, and the rivers rose, and the winds blew and beat about that house, and it did not go down, for its foundations were on rock. And anyone who listens to this teaching of mine and does not act upon it, will be like a foolish man who built his house on sand. And the rain fell, and the rivers rose, and the wind blew and beat about that house, and it went down, and its downfall was complete." (*Matt.* vii. 24-27)

Sand is an easier substance into which to dig a foundation, but it was rock that Jesus demanded.

Jesus taught a difficult and radical doctrine, one that demanded the utmost consecration and one, also, that had been branded as blasphemous by the religious authorities. Yet he was followed about Judea by such enormous crowds of people that there was often not enough room available for all of them. Wherever he taught—in the outer courts of the Temple, as a guest speaker in one of the synagogues, by the lake shore, in the village streets or in private houses—he was the center of an eager, jostling crowd of people, striving to touch his hand or the hem of his cloak. But they had not come to listen to his teaching. They had come to be healed.

There was one thing only that the people of Judea wanted of Jesus. "Word went all through Syria about him, and people brought to him all who were suffering with any kind of disease, or who were in great pain— demoniacs, epileptics, and paralytics—and he cured them all. Great crowds followed him about, from Galilee and the Ten Towns and Jerusalem and Judea and from the other side of the Jordan." (*Matt.* iv. 24-25) Jesus was brought madmen and cripples, lepers and dying children; and he healed them all and instantly.

So intense was the popular excitement over the great healer who had come into Judea and so dense the crowds, that some men who were bringing a paralytic to him were obliged to break a hole in the roof of the house where Jesus was staying and lower through it the man to be healed. Sometimes this excited faith itself wrought the cure, and nothing is more characteristic of Jesus than the way he distinguished these cases from the others. He told a woman who had fought her way to him through the crowds, convinced if she could only touch his clothes she would recover, that she had wrought the cure herself. "My daughter, it is your faith that has cured you." (*Mark* v. 34)

"All the people tried to touch him, because power went forth from him and cured them all." (*Luke* vi. 19) They also tried to worship him, crying aloud "Lord! Lord!" until he told them to stop, invoking blessings on his mother's head for producing such a son, and proclaiming for all to hear their admiration and wonder. "We never saw anything like this before." (*Mark* ii. 12) "A great prophet has appeared among us!" (*Luke* vii. 16)

The people of Judea were willing to do anything for Jesus, entertain him in their houses, follow him in ever-increasing throngs, and honor him as the greatest prophet who had ever appeared in Judea. "The news about him spread more and more, and great crowds gathered to hear him and to be cured of their diseases. But Jesus himself would retire into the desert and pray." (*Luke* v. 15-16)

"Why," Jesus asked them once, "do you call me 'Lord! Lord!' and not do what I tell you?" (*Luke* vi. 46) He had not come to the people of Judea to be worshipped for some private power of his own. He consistently refused to acknowledge any such power. He had come into Judea to teach the truth about God, and it was because of the truth itself that he was able to heal the sick and raise the dead. It was not because Jesus was an exceptionally powerful prophet that he had been able to give life to the daughter of Jairus and the son of the widow at Nain. It was because of the fact that his God was a living God and all creation was in his image.

The common people were hardly aware of Jesus' message in their excitement over his ability to cure them, but there was a group of men in Judea who were intensely aware of it: the Pharisees. They were educated, devout men and they knew from the first that the man who had so shaken the people was teaching a God who was not the God of Judaism.

From the point of view of the Pharisees, Jesus' doctrine of "the only true God" (*John* xvii. 3) was not only radical; it was blasphemous. He was misleading the people through an ability to heal that must have been given him by the devil since it did not come from the God that they themselves acknowledged.

Judaism had established itself in the minds of its adherents as the final, revealed, incontrovertible truth about the one true God and about the one way of salvation open to those who believed in him. Upon this settled conviction came the impact of a man who taught a different conception of God and a different kind of salvation, and who was able to prove what he said. A few of the

Pharisees and members of the Jewish council were so troubled by these proofs that they used to visit Jesus in secret and ask him questions; but the majority had no such doubts. They knew they were right, and, as their opponent said, it was this conviction of itself that condemned them. "If you were blind, you would be guilty of no sin, but as it is, you say, 'We can see'; so your sin continues." (*John* ix. 41)

Between Jesus and the Pharisees the issue was clear from the first: if the God that Jesus taught was the truth, then the God taught by the Pharisees was a lie with "no truth in him." (*John* viii. 44) The issue was inescapable, and Jesus himself made no effort to soften or modify it.

The language Jesus used with the Pharisees was not the gentle speech he used with the common people. The Pharisees were leaders and teachers, supposedly his equals, and Jesus did not hide his meaning when he spoke to them. To the common people he spoke in parables, using small, familiar things like farming and housework and weddings to give them his message. He described, for instance, the complete mental reversal his message required by giving them a little picture any housewife could understand. "No one tears a piece from a new coat and sews it on an old one, or if he does, he will both tear the new one and the piece from the new one will not match the old one." (*Luke* v. 36) But to the Pharisees Jesus said the same thing with an unsparing bluntness that shocked and terrified those righteous conservatives.

The unequivocal attack that Jesus made upon the Pharisees had nothing whatever to do with them as individuals. It was always the point of view Jesus attacked, never the man. He once turned on one of his own disciples and said, "Get out of my sight, you Satan!" (*Matt.*

xvi. 23) when he had said to the same man a few min-
utes earlier, "Your name is Peter, a rock, and on this
rock I will build my church, and the powers of death
shall not subdue it." (*Matt.* xvi. 18) Neither statement
had anything to do with Peter as a man. Both the rebuke
and the commendation were directed at the point of view
Peter happened to be expressing at the time.

Equally impersonal was Jesus' attack on the religious
authorities of Judea. Individuals like Nicodemus and
Joseph of Arimathea were close friends of his, but the
point of view represented by the sect of the Pharisees as
a whole was the point of view that Jesus had come to
destroy.

The whole of the Fourth Gospel is essentially the story
of this fundamental conflict between Jesus and the Jews.
John was not, of course, using the term 'Jew' in any
racial sense. He himself was a Jew, and so was Jesus. He
meant by it the unyielding Judaism that claimed a full
revelation of God and denied the possibility of any further revelation, the devout conservatism that knows itself
to be right and that will do murder, if necessary, to protect its conception of the truth.

It was this point of view that rejected Jesus as it had
rejected all the prophets before him. It was men with a
reverent regard for religious tradition who had tried
to silence Amos and kill Jeremiah for disagreeing with
the established order of things. The Pharisees were very
shocked when they read in their Scriptures that the men
of his own day had dared to call the great prophet Jeremiah a "madman who plays the prophet." (*Jer.* xxix.
26) But when a greater than Jeremiah appeared to the
men of Judah they cried at once, "He is possessed and
mad!" (*John* x. 20)

The Pharisees saw no contradiction in their attitude.
It was in perfect good faith that they marshalled Scrip-

tural quotations to prove that Jesus was in the wrong. To
the spirit of the Scriptures they attempted to oppose the
letter, quite unconscious that in denying Jesus they were
denying the whole line of Israel.

Jesus himself was well aware of his debt to the past.
As he told his disciples, "Other men have worked and
you have profited by their work." (*John* iv. 38) He
told the Pharisees outright that they were reading their
Scriptures with blind eyes. "You pore over the Scriptures, for you think that you will find eternal life in
them, and these very Scriptures testify to me, yet you refuse to come to me for life. (*John* v. 39-40) If you really
believed Moses, you would believe me, for it was about
me that he wrote. But if you refuse to believe what he
wrote, how are you ever to believe what I say?" (*John*
v. 46-47)

The men of Judah had never believed Moses. They
had accepted his name for God and revered it as a holy
thing, but they had never understood it. It was on this
account that they thought Jesus mad when he carried
Moses' name for God to its logical conclusion, and denied
the power of death. "Now we are sure that you are
possessed! Abraham is dead and so are the prophets, and
yet you say, 'If anyone observes my teaching, he will
never know what death is'! Are you a greater man than
our forefather Abraham? Yet he is dead and the prophets
are dead. What do you claim to be?" (*John* viii. 52-53)

"What do you claim to be?" That was the question the
Jews asked Jesus repeatedly, as though unable to believe
they could be hearing him correctly, and each time Jesus
gave them the same answer. He claimed to be what he
was, the son of God.

The oldest rite the Jews possessed was intended to
symbolize this fact of at-one-ment. Nevertheless, they
told Jesus that in claiming union with God he was setting

himself up as God's equal; and Jesus turned on them in deep anger.

> "Do you mean to say to me whom the Father has con-
> secrated and made his messenger to the world, 'You
> are blasphemous,' because I said, 'I am God's son'?
> If I am not doing the things my Father does, do not
> believe me. But if I am doing them, then even if you
> will not believe me, believe the things I do, in order
> that you may realize and learn that the Father is in
> union with me, and I am in union with the Father."
> *(John* x. 36-38)

There was no answer to this. For the God of Israel, the God of reality, there was stronger proof than arguments and Scriptural quotations. Jesus was able to live his doctrine, proving it hourly and daily, and against this fact the intricate reasoning of the Pharisees was useless.

The Pharisees found Jesus' power of proof especially terrifying because of its effect on the common people of Judea. They themselves were wise and learned men, sufficiently versed in the law and the prophets to be able to detect in Jesus an influence working to undermine Judaism "by the aid of the prince of demons." (*Matt.* ix. 34) But lesser folk were ignorant and therefore vulnerable. "These common people who do not know the Law are doomed." (*John* vii. 49)

The Pharisees argued for a long time with one man in an attempt to convince him that Jesus was an evil influence; but he could not follow their line of reasoning. "I do not know about his being a sinful man. All I know is that I was blind before and now I can see." (*John* ix. 25) They attempted to appeal to him in the name of Moses, but the man who had once been blind could not be convinced. "It was never heard of in this world that anyone made a man born blind able to see.

If this man were not from God, he could not do anything." (*John* ix. 32-33)

This one case could have been multiplied by the hundreds, as the Pharisees very well knew; and eventually an incident occurred that carried them beyond the limits of their endurance. This was the raising of Lazarus, which took place in the little village of Bethany. Bethany was only a mile or two outside Jerusalem, and the event aroused the people of the city to a high state of excitement.

The Pharisees found themselves placed in an impossible situation by the raising of Lazarus. They were obliged either to agree that Jesus was a true prophet or to prove that he was a false one; and they could do neither. Accordingly they called a full meeting of the Sanhedrin, the Jewish council, in order to debate the question that was growing daily more pressing: "What are we going to do about the fact that this man is showing so many signs? If we let him go on, everybody will believe in him." (*John* xi. 47-48)

The members of the Sanhedrin were upright men, kindly and law-abiding, and they apparently shrank from the one conclusive way out of their dilemma. It was the high priest for that year who finally succeeded in putting the matter before them in terms that succeeded in preserving their self-respect, so that they might appear to themselves as saviors rather than destroyers. It was better, he said, for one man to die than that the whole nation should be destroyed. This assurance that the end justified the means was all that the members of the Sanhedrin needed to support them in their self-imposed warfare against what they believed to be the powers of darkness. "So from that day they planned to kill Jesus." (*John* xi. 53)

The raising of Lazarus is important because it explains this final decision on the part of the Sanhedrin, but it is not on that account that John gave the event in Bethany so much space in his gospel. John was not writing his gospel to explain the darkness but to record the light. He was not writing about the Pharisees but about Jesus; and the account of the raising of Lazarus illustrates more perfectly than anything else in the Fourth Gospel the unwavering allegiance that Jesus gave to his discovery of eternal life.

When news came to Jesus that Lazarus had become ill, he said to his disciples, "This sickness is not to end in death." (*John* xi. 4) Nevertheless, Lazarus died. To any man but Jesus this would have been clear evidence of failure. He had said that his friend would recover, and his friend was dead.

If Jesus had been a teacher and healer acting on his own authority, he would have been obliged to acknowledge that he had failed. But Jesus never acted on his own authority. "I am not by myself, but the Father who sent me is with me." (*John* viii. 16) He had not built his house on sand but on rock, and he knew that the rock could never fail him.

He told his disciples that he was going back to Bethany. "Our friend Lazarus has fallen asleep, but I am going there to wake him." (*John* xi. 11) His disciples, not understanding what he meant, tried to tell him that if Lazarus had gone to sleep he would waken again without difficulty; and Jesus was obliged to tell them plainly, conforming to a phraseology which he otherwise refused to use, that Lazarus was dead.

When Jesus arrived in Bethany, Lazarus had already been buried for four days, and many of the Jews from Jerusalem had come out to the village to condole with his sisters. One of the two sisters, Martha, heard that Jesus had arrived and went out to meet him, saying, "Master, if you had been here, my brother would not have died!" (*John* xi. 21)

"Your brother will rise," Jesus said. (*John* xi. 23) Martha, like a good Jewess, thought he was referring to the familiar Jewish doctrine of the Day of Judgment, and assented. "I know that he will rise at the resurrection, on the Last Day." (*John* xi. 24)

That was not what Jesus had meant. He had not been referring to a future life beyond the grave, but to a present, continuing existence, permanently available to any man who understood his message. "I myself am resurrection and life. He who believes in me will live on, even if he dies, and no one who is alive and believes in me will ever die. Do you believe that?" (*John* xi. 25-26)

Martha said that she did. But she also believed, and much more firmly, that Lazarus had been dead for four days and that he was rotting. She went to get Mary, to tell her that Jesus had arrived, and Mary echoed her sister's heart-broken reproach. "Master, if you had been here, my brother would not have died!" (*John* xi. 32) She was weeping as she said it, and the friends of her brother who were with her were weeping too.

Jesus was deeply troubled. He had spent a long time teaching these people, and they had been very close to him. Yet they still believed in him rather than in the truth he brought. They still believed in some personal power he had as a healer, and this power obviously could have no control over a man four days dead. They did not yet understand that Jesus was acting in obedience to a principle that was wholly unaffected by the passage of days or the thickness of a tomb, and he grieved for them as he had once grieved over the blindness of Jerusalem.

They did not know his grief was for them. They thought it was for Lazarus, and some of the mourners said, "See how much he loved him!" (*John* xi. 36) Others, less reconciled to their own loss, shared the point of view of the dead man's two sisters. "Could not this man, who opened the eyes of that blind man, have kept Lazarus from dying?" (*John* xi. 37)

Jesus was not grieving for his dead friend. He had no dead friend. What he called "the glory of God" did not confine itself to certain localities and certain conditions. It was everywhere, and in its light there was no death.

Jesus ordered the stone that blocked the entrance of the tomb to be removed, and when Martha cried out in shocked protest he reassured her. "Have I not promised you that if you will believe in me you will see the glory of God?" (*John* xi. 40)

When the black entrance of the tomb was exposed, Jesus thanked God aloud for the glory he saw where everyone else saw death. "Father, I thank you for listening to me, though I knew that you always listen to me. But I have said this for the sake of the people that are standing around me that they may believe that you have made me your messenger." (*John* xi. 42) The message that Jesus brought was the truth. It never failed when it was trusted. And Lazarus came forth a living man.

In the raising of Lazarus at Bethany, Jesus had again fulfilled what he had defined earlier that winter as the fundamental purpose of his ministry. "I have come to let them have life, and to let them have it in abundance." (*John* x. 10) The doctrine that Jesus taught in Judea was not that of life after death—the orthodox theory of immortality already taught by the Jews—but of a continuing life based on a complete knowledge of God. In raising Lazarus, Jesus had again proved the statement that the Pharisees considered so blasphemous: "If any-

one observes my teaching, he will never experience
death." (*John* viii. 51)

Jesus had said from the beginning of his ministry that
it was his business to give proof of what he taught, since
in no other way could the reality of his doctrine be
tested. "If I am not doing the things my Father does,
do not believe me. But if I am doing them, then even
if you will not believe me, believe the things I do."
(*John* x. 37-38)

From the beginning of his ministry also, Jesus had
consistently repudiated the idea that he had some personal power of his own that made him a great teacher
and healer. "Whoever believes in me, believes not in
me but in him who has sent me; and whoever sees me,
sees him who has sent me. (*John* xii. 44) For I have not
spoken on my own account, but the Father who has sent
me has himself given me orders what to tell and what to
say. And I know his orders mean eternal life." (*John*
xii. 49-50)

Eternal life was the result of obedience to the Father,
of honoring him as the only true God. This life Jesus
had claimed as his own, and he was prepared to prove it.

Direct obedience to God was the one force that had
dominated the whole of Jesus' ministry in Judea. And it
was this force, rather than the helpless fury of the Pharisees, that led him to accept the crucifixion as the final
test of the reality of his message.

Jesus could not prove his doctrine of eternal life by
avoiding death. The house built on sand is quite as secure
as the house built on rock if no storm tests its foundations. Jesus was so certain of the rock upon which he had
built his life that he was willing to subject it to the full
fury of the storm to show that it was unassailable. He
was willing to submit to the worst that death could do
to him to show it could do nothing, to prove finally and

conclusively that murder itself was powerless to affect the man who understood his relationship to a living God.

Jesus was careful to make it perfectly clear that he was submitting deliberately to the test of the crucifixion. "I am giving my life, but giving it to take it back again. No one has taken it from me, but I am giving it of my own accord. I have power to give it, and I have power to take it back again. These are the orders I have received from my Father." (*John* x. 17-18)

In submitting to this final proof of his doctrine of eternal life Jesus was acting, as he had always acted, in direct obedience to God.

CHAPTER XVII

> And he will destroy on this mountain
> The veil that veils all the peoples,
> And the web that is woven over all the nations—
> He will destroy death forever.
>
> *Book of Isaiah* xxv. 7-8

IN SUBMITTING to the crucifixion, Jesus engaged in combat an enemy greater than the Pharisees and more powerful than the Roman empire. He placed himself in opposition to the power of death.

The whole world united to give testimony to the authority of death, but Jesus gave authority only to "the living Father." The origin of death's authority was a mistaken idea about life. It was this that had been "a murderer from the first," and it was the sons of this kind of father who died. Jesus opposed to this ancient dominion his discovery of a God "who is real, whom you do not know" (*John* vii. 28) and underwent the crucifixion to prove that no son of this Father could die.

The willingness to undergo such a test required a constancy and an unquestioning loyalty to the truth that make it clear why Jesus had full right to the title of Messiah, "the consecrated one." He was not only engaging in combat an enemy to whose power the whole of the visible world bore unceasing testimony, but he was also submitting to an apparent denial of the whole of his teaching. The man who had raised others from the dead was himself going to die.

Jesus had not entered upon his ministry to please himself, but to honor the true name of God. To do this, he was not permitted to take the easy way of teaching. He was obliged to take the hard way of proof. "My heart is troubled; what am I to say? Father, save me from this trial? And yet it was for this very purpose that I have come to this trial. Father, honor your own name." (*John* xii. 27-28)

Jesus made it clear that he was not submitting to death in letting "the evil genius of the world" come to him in the shape of an execution; he was conquering death. "He has nothing in common with me, but he is coming that the world may know that I love the Father." (*John* xiv. 30-31) It was only by accepting the full force of death and showing it to be powerless that Jesus could honor his Father as "the only true God"; and it was for this specific reason that he accepted the crucifixion.

Jesus called this test the day of judgment. "The judgment of this world is now in progress. Its evil genius is now to be expelled." (*John* xii. 31) It was the day that the prophets of Israel before him had called the Day of the Lord. The men of Judah were expecting another kind of Judgment Day, with a Messiah riding upon the clouds and ushering in a visible kingdom to the righteous. But the Messiah had already made the kingdom of God available to any man capable of understanding his message, and the test of the crucifixion was his final proof that the message he brought was the truth.

The last evening before his arrest, Jesus gathered together his disciples in private in an upstairs room. Only John remembered what he told them there. The others remembered only that Jesus had taken an ancient Jewish rite, symbolizing union, and applied it to himself. To unite his disciples into fellowship with him, he called the bread they ate that evening his body, using the act in the same sense that Paul applied it to the Temple services. "Do not those who eat what is sacrificed have divine fellowship at the sacrificial altar?" (1 *Cor.* x. 18) But John remembered more than that, and what he remembered is the highest point of the Fourth Gospel and the New Testament.

Jesus spoke that night "in figurative language," (*John* xvi. 25) and John must have carried the words a long time in his own memory before he wrote them down. Nevertheless, John's transcription has a light in it that is unmistakable, the shining authority that is inherent in everything Jesus said.

John's account lays no claim to literary ornament or decoration. It is written in white, in a manner so luminous in its simplicity that even the resplendent poetry of the Hebrew prophets grows dim beside it. There is no need to read into it grey complexities, or to paint it in the colors of a later theology that was directly derived from Judaism. Jesus did not speak as a Jew. He spoke as the light of the world; and it was something of that same quality of light that John, who did not listen as a Jew, was able to set down afterwards.

Jesus had gathered together his disciples that night to explain his coming execution to them, so that they would not be frightened when it occurred. "Your minds must not be troubled; you must believe in God, and believe in me. (*John* xiv. 1) I am going away to make ready a place for you. And if I go and make it ready, I will come back and take you with me, so that you may be where I am. You know the way to the place where I am going." (*John* xiv. 2-4)

His disciples should have known the way to the place where Jesus was going. He had taught it to them for at least a year. Yet Thomas was expressing a literal fact when he cried out, "Master, we do not know where you are going; how can we know the way?" (*John* xiv. 5)

Jesus answered that he was showing them the way through his own knowledge of God. "I am way and truth and life. No one can come to the Father except through

me. If you knew me, you would know my Father also."
(*John* xiv. 6-7)

This was the truth, but the disciples did not believe
it. They wanted a visible kingdom and a visible God, and
they had not understood Jesus when he said "God is
Spirit" (*John* iv. 24) and "The kingdom of God is
within you." (*Luke* xvii. 21) They wanted some outward and visible testimony to the truth, and Philip probably spoke for them all when he said, "Master, let us see
the Father, and it will satisfy us." (*John* xiv. 8)

Jesus might justly have said to his disciples what he
said once to the Pharisees: "You judge by material standards." (*John* viii. 15) They all judged by what they
could see, and were willing to trust nothing but the physical evidence of their own eyes.

It was this faith in material testimony that was forcing Jesus into his final, visible proof of the kingdom of
God, but it seemed strange to him that even his own
disciples should need it. "Have I been with you so long,
and yet you, Philip, have not recognized me? Whoever
has seen me has seen the Father. How can you say, 'Let
us see the Father'? Do you not believe that I am in union
with the Father and the Father is in union with me?"
(*John* xiv. 9-10)

The disciples had been agreeing for a long time that
Jesus was the son of God because he had told them so,
but none of them understood the discovery upon which
he based his assertion of sonship. Jesus himself, as John
says, was "fully aware that the Father had put everything into his hands, and that he had come from God"
(*John* xiii. 3) because he was also fully aware of the
nature of the God he called Father.

The disciples, however, had never understood his discovery. They worshipped Jesus for the great power and
authority he was able to show, but in spite of his repeated

explanations they persisted in believing that the power and authority were his rather than belonging only to God.

Jesus was well aware of this. Therefore he knew equally well what would happen to his disciples when he himself seemed to possess power and authority no longer. They had never believed in the God he called Father. They believed instead in the evidence of their own eyes; and when Jesus came to be arrested and this physical evidence seemed to contradict what Jesus himself had taught them, it was not the physical evidence they would disbelieve, but his teaching. Even the adoring Peter would be unable to believe that his master had ever been the son of God. "I tell you, before a cock crows, you will disown me thrice over!" (*John* xiii. 38)

Jesus knew that there were no words in existence effective enough to kindle in anyone else the light that he himself possessed. He could go out to a cross and give his disciples visible evidence that life was not a wind-blown candle liable at any moment to extinction, but the understanding of God upon which he based this proof of eternal life he could give to no man.

Neither by the clearness of his teaching nor by the authority of his proof could Jesus transmit his own knowledge of God. The men he had taught still remained children groping in the dark, looking anxiously to him for the only light they possessed. If Jesus had trusted to his own leadership and authority for their salvation, he would never have dared leave them.

But Jesus did not trust his own leadership and authority. He trusted only the authority of God. He knew that the message he had brought into the world was the truth and therefore did not need the protection either of his presence or of his teaching. It was the light, and it brought with it its own illumination.

It was this light, of the truth itself, that Jesus promised as permanently available. "I will ask the Father and he will give you another Helper to be with you always. It is the Spirit of Truth. The world cannot obtain that Spirit, because it does not see or recognize it; you recognize it because it stays with you and is within you. I am not going to leave you friendless." (*John* xiv. 16-18)

When Jesus left them, the spirit of the truth he had taught would remain as friend and helper, to give the illumination and security of perfect understanding. "The Helper, the holy Spirit which the Father will send in my place, will teach you everything and remind you of everything that I have told you. I leave you a blessing. I give you my own blessing. I do not give it to you as the world gives. Your minds must not be troubled or afraid." (*John* xiv. 26-27)

Nevertheless, the disciples of Jesus remained deeply troubled and deeply afraid. They wanted to continue as they had done in the past, worshipping a great prophet who could do many mighty works. They did not want to be separated from him to follow an impersonal truth, and Jesus was obliged to tell them that it was necessary they should be separated from him if they were ever to gain an understanding of God. "Your minds are full of sorrow because I have told you this. Yet it is only the truth when I tell you that it is better for you that I should go away. For if I do not go, the Helper will not come to you, but if I go I will send him to you." (*John* xvi. 6-7) It was only through the spirit of truth that the disciples could understand Jesus' message. "I have much more to tell you, but you cannot take it in now, but when the Spirit of Truth comes, he will guide you into the full truth." (*John* xvi. 12-13)

It was because Jesus trusted so completely "that Spirit of Truth that comes from the Father" (*John* xv. 26) that he spoke to his disciples that night as to equals. He did not treat them as the confused children they had shown themselves to be; he treated them as brothers, the sons of the one Father. "I call you friends, for I have made known to you everything that I have learned from my Father." (*John* xv. 15) His brothers possessed the same life that he possessed, and eventually they would find it out. "When that day comes you will know that I am in union with my Father and you are with me and I am with you." (*John* xiv. 20)

It was this awareness of union with the Father, this knowledge of a perfect relationship which Jesus called sonship, that Jesus was trying to give to the eleven men who loved him. He never made a more illuminating remark about himself than when he spoke to his disciples that night of "the happiness I have had." (*John* xv. 11) It was this same happiness he was offering to his frightened followers, a joy and security that nothing could darken or overthrow. "I have told you all this so that you may have the happiness I have had, and your happiness may be complete." (*John* xv. 11)

Whatever they might fear for him, Jesus was not leaving his disciples to go to his death. He never used the word in connection with his imminent crucifixion. He was leaving his disciples in order to prove again the glory of God, as he had proved it once before at a tomb. "I will see you again, and your hearts will be happy, and no one will rob you of your happiness." (*John* xvi. 22) Through his proof they would learn to accept the truth about God, so that Jesus would no longer be obliged to speak to them in pictures and symbols. "I have said all this to you in figurative language, but a time is coming when I shall not do so any longer, but will tell you plainly about the Father." (*John* xvi. 25) The truth itself would be their teacher and enlightener, and they would

need no other intermediary. "When that time comes
. . . I do not promise to intercede with the Father for
you, for the Father loves you himself." (*John* xvi.
26-27)

The disciples were listening closely to what Jesus was
saying, with a most earnest lack of understanding. They
had already confessed openly to each other, "We do not
know what he is talking about," (*John* xvi. 18) and they
unquestionably spoke the truth. But when Jesus gave
them this final promise, they suddenly decided that they
now understood him perfectly. "Why, now you are talking plainly and not speaking figuratively at all. Now
we know that you know everything and do not need to
have anyone ask you questions. This makes us believe
that you have really come from God." (*John* xvi. 29-30)

"Do you believe that now?" asked Jesus, with a gentleness that had no need to forgive them. "Why, a time is
coming—it has already come!—when you will all be
scattered to your homes and will leave me alone." Even
as he used the word, however, he corrected it. "And yet
I am not alone, for the Father is with me." (*John*
xvi. 31-32)

His disciples had not understood him, and they would
forsake him, but it did not matter. The truth was the
truth, and it would never forsake them. "I have told you
all this, so that through me you may find peace. In the
world you have trouble; but take courage. I have conquered the world." (*John* xvi. 33)

Jesus spoke no longer with his disciples. There was
nothing more he could say to them now. "Father, the
time has come. Do honor to your son, that your son may
do honor to you . . . so that he may give eternal life to
all whom you have given him. And eternal life means
knowing you as the only true God." (*John* xvii. 1-3)

"I have revealed your real self to the men you gave

me from the world. (*John* xvii. 6) I have given them the truths that you gave me. (*John* xvii. 8) Holy Father, keep them by your power which you gave me, so that they may be one just as we are. (*John* xvii. 11) I say this here in this world in order that they may have the happiness that I feel fully realized in their own hearts. I have given them your message. (*John* xvii. 13-14) Consecrate them by truth. Your message is truth." (*John* xvii. 17)

It was not only for his immediate disciples that Jesus prayed. "It is not for them only that I make this request. It is also for those who through their message come to believe in me. Let them all be one. Just as you, Father, are in union with me and I am with you, let them be in union with us. (*John* xvii. 20-21) I have given them the glory that you gave me, so that they may be one just as we are. (*John* xvii. 22) Father, I wish to have those whom you have given me with me where I am." (*John* xvii. 24)

It was for these men that Jesus was laying down his life. He himself did not need to submit to death to be aware of the reality of life. "Righteous Father, though the world did not know you, I knew you." (*John* xvii. 25) But the men he called his friends believed as the world believed, and it was for their sake that he fought his final battle to prove the glory of God. "It is for their sake that I consecrate myself, that they also may be consecrated by truth." (*John* xvii. 19)

In the final hour that remained to him before the arrival of the soldiers, Jesus asked three of his disciples to remain awake and pray. He himself withdrew a stone's throw away, and the three disciples fell asleep. It is not very likely, therefore, that the writers of the three synoptic gospels could have known the substance of Jesus' prayer. John, who was one of the three disciples, is characteristically silent upon this point, and all that can be known with certainty is that Jesus came back and wakened them with the gentle question, "Were you not able to watch for one hour?" (*Mark* xiv. 37) There was no reproach in the question, but there was full knowledge of how isolated he was even from the three men who loved him most. "And yet I am not alone, for the Father is with me." (*John* xvi. 32)

When the soldiers arrested Jesus, one of his disciples tried to defend him by force, and Jesus checked him at once. "Put your sword back where it belongs! For all who draw the sword will die by the sword." (*Matt.* xxvi. 52) The disciples were helpless, and appalled. If Jesus would not let them defend him, there was nothing they could do for him; and apparently he could do nothing for himself, when, if he were really the Messiah, now was the time for a legion of angels to come to his rescue and confound his enemies.

Jesus had foreseen accurately the effect his arrest would have on his disciples. They continued to judge, as they had always judged, by the physical evidence. Where they had once seen a mighty prophet doing many great works they now saw a discredited teacher seized by the authorities and committed for trial on a criminal charge. Their world fell in ruins about them, and they "left him and made their escape." (*Mark* xiv. 50) Only two of the disciples, Peter and John, followed him to the high priest's, and by morning Peter had denied him.

The ecclesiastical trial that was given Jesus was only a formality, since the verdict had already been decided upon in advance. The trial was not legal in any case. The witnesses contradicted each other, and the Sanhedrin had no right to try a man on a capital offense during any religious festival such as the Feast of the Passover. Nor was the charge of being a false prophet sufficient to have a man executed under Roman law, which had final jurisdiction in Judea.

The religious authorities in Jerusalem were obliged to amplify the charges against Jesus before they could send him to Pilate, governor of the province. "Here is a man whom we have found misleading our nation, and forbidding the payment of taxes to the emperor, and claiming to be an anointed king himself." (*Luke* xxiii. 2) The first charge was a full statement of the Jews' case against Jesus, but it was the political accusations that interested the Roman governor. The Romans had been having a difficult time with a series of wild-eyed Jews who saw themselves as the emancipators and rulers of their enslaved country. Pilate faced Jesus at once with the fundamental charge against him from the Roman point of view: "Are you the king of the Jews?"

According to the account of this interview given in the three synoptic gospels, Jesus assented and "made no further answer at all," (*Mark* xv. 5) whereupon Pilate took the very unlikely course of exerting himself to free a self-confessed political agitator. According to the Fourth Gospel, Jesus amplified his answer, and explained in what sense he called himself a king. "My kingdom is not a kingdom of this world. If my kingdom were a kingdom of this world, my men would have fought to keep me from being handed over to the Jews." (*John* xviii. 36)

This was a reasonable statement and Pilate was willing to let the prisoner go free, since a religious agitator was outside his province as governor. He was, however, sufficiently interested in Jesus to continue the conversation. "Then you are a king?" (*John* xviii. 37)

In whatever spirit Pilate asked the question, Jesus gave him a literal answer. "As you say, I am a king. It was for this that I was born and for this that I came to the world, to give testimony for truth." (*John* xviii. 37) In a kind of bitterness at such assurance, Pilate flung back, "What is truth!" (*John* xviii. 38) and went out to tell the waiting Jews that he could find nothing to charge him with.

Meanwhile the Jews had been skillfully manipulating the ancient forces of mob violence. The herd instinct that is willing to glorify a successful prophet is equally willing to murder an unsuccessful one, and the crowds began to shout, "Crucify him!" Pilate was not an essentially courageous man, although he did his best to withstand them. He tried to reason with the mob, but the mob was not to be reasoned with; and the Roman governors of all the provinces knew by unhappy experience the lengths to which Jews were capable of going if they thought their religion had been insulted. Pilate could see very clearly "that he was gaining nothing but that a riot was beginning instead" (*Matt.* xxvii. 24) and he gave in, apparently agreeing with the Sanhedrin's theory that it was better one innocent man should die than many perish.

According to Jewish law, Jesus was illegally tried; and according to Roman law, he was illegally condemned. With the consent of both, he died the usual death by torture of a condemned criminal. Crucifixion was an agonizingly slow method of execution, lasting sometimes for days, and it was customary to dull the pain by giving drugged wine to drink. This wine was offered to Jesus in the usual way, but he refused to take it.

Many men in the history of the world have died bravely for their conception of the truth. Jesus was doing something immeasurably more difficult: living for the truth.

To do it, he was obliged to face the inconceivable bitterness of letting the world believe that his Father had betrayed him and that his teaching was false. He was obliged to let it appear that the power that had been sufficient to save Lazarus and the daughter of Jairus and the son of the widow at Nain was incapable of saving his own life. He had to listen in silence while the people shouted. "He has saved others, let him save himself if he is really God's Christ, his chosen one!" (*Luke* xxiii. 35)

The warfare upon which Jesus had entered for love of his friends, to show them the glory of God, was one of violence and great loneliness. It was natural that his thoughts should turn to the great book of struggle and victory, the Hebrew Psalter, and especially to one psalm that recorded in miniature a struggle almost exactly like his own.

The twenty-second psalm records details so exactly similar to those of the crucifixion that the resemblance is almost incredible. The poet is compassed about by enemies who jeer at him for having trusted God.

> All who see me make sport of me;
> They make mouths at me and toss their heads:
> "Let him rejoice in the Lord; let him deliver him;
> Let him rescue him." (*Ps.* xxii. 7-8)
>
> They have bound my hands and my feet.
> I can count all my bones;
> They look, they stare at me.
> They distribute my garments among them
> And over my robe they cast lots. (*Ps.* xxii. 16-18)

But the twenty-second psalm is not a psalm of darkness and despair; it is one of the greatest psalms of victory. This is the psalm that reaches a moment of deepest terror and then suddenly rises up into a shout of joy.

> Deliver my life from the sword,
> My only one from the power of the dog.
> Save me from the lion's mouth—

YEA, FROM THE HORNS OF THE WILD OX
THOU HAST ANSWERED ME!
(*Ps.* xxii. 20-21)

The poem continues to its end rejoicing, praising the glory and the power and the sovereignty of God. "For the kingdom belongs to the Lord." (*Ps.* xxii. 28)

It was this psalm of which Jesus quoted aloud the opening line, the famous, "My God, my God, why hast thou forsaken me?" (*Ps.* xxii. 1) (*Matt.* xxvii. 46) The people listening to him misunderstood his meaning as thoroughly as it has been misunderstood ever since but in a different way. They heard the "Eli, Eli" of the Hebrew psalm and thought, "The man is calling for Elijah!" (*Matt.* xxvii. 47) This seemed natural enough to them, for it was recorded in their Scriptures that Elijah was the one prophet who had never undergone death, and the man now on the cross had consistently denied the power of death in all his teachings. "Let us see whether Elijah will come to save him." (*Matt.* xxvii. 49) Half fearfully, half hopefully, they waited for some supernatural aid to come down from heaven; but none came.

Again Jesus quoted from the Hebrew Psalter: "Father, into thy hands I commit my spirit." (*Luke* xxiii. 46) This is a line from the thirty-first psalm, and one of complete, undisturbed confidence.

> For thou art my refuge.
> Into thy hand I commit my spirit.
> Thou wilt redeem me, O Lord God of truth.
> (*Ps.* xxxi. 4-5)

Then he said, "It is finished," (*John* xix. 30) and died.

Jesus was buried by two members of the Sanhedrin who loved him, and who had received permission from Pilate to take his body down from the cross. The tomb in which they put him was then sealed over by order of the

Jewish authorities. Jesus had claimed so openly that death could not conquer him that it was feared his disciples would steal his body and pretend that he had risen.

The precaution was a natural one for the authorities to take, since they believed that Jesus had been a false prophet and that his disciples were equally capable of fraud. But it would have been small comfort to the disciples to stage an elaborate deception when they themselves were in despair.

The crucifixion had finally convinced the disciples that nothing Jesus told them could have been true. He had said he was a king, and they had seen common soldiers jeer at him. He had said he was the son of God, and God had let him hang helpless on a cross. He had said he possessed eternal life, and they had seen him die. They had dreamed a brief dream in which they thought they had discovered in a carpenter's son the Messiah of the Jews, but their dream had vanished in the brutal reality of the crucifixion.

Again the disciples trusted to the evidence of their own eyes, and again they were wrong.

There are two versions extant of the way in which they discovered that Jesus had spoken the truth, but the version given in the Fourth Gospel is inherently the more probable of the two.

The synoptic gospels say that three of the women discovered that the seal was broken and the tomb empty, and concluded at once, "He has risen from the dead." (*Matt.* xxviii. 7) This was not a very probable explanation to occur to grief-stricken women, since either friends or enemies might have taken the body away; and the synoptic gospels justify it by saying this information was given the women by an angel.

John's account does not depend on angels. He says that Mary of Magdala discovered, early in the morning the day after the Sabbath, that the stone at the entrance of the tomb had been taken away. Mary hurried back to Jerusalem to get Peter and him, telling them that someone had taken away the body of Jesus. With the vividness of detail John was able to give incidents in which he himself had figured, he describes how he ran out and reached the tomb first, stopping short when he saw it was empty. Peter entered the tomb and saw the bandages on the ground and the handkerchief that had covered the face lying folded by itself. John followed him, and then both men went unhappily back to the city. "For they did not yet understand." (*John* xx. 9)

Mary stayed by the tomb, in tears, and as she turned she saw a man standing beside her. She thought he was the gardener, and that it might be he who was responsible for the rifled tomb. "If it was you, sir, that carried him away, tell me where you have put him." (*John* xx. 15)

"Mary!" said Jesus.

She turned then and recognized him, and cried out "Master!" She apparently made no move to touch him, but all the personal adoration that had been lavished on Jesus during the period of his ministry was in her reverent cry, and once again Jesus was obliged to ask a follower of his not to hold him so closely. "You must not cling to me." (*John* xx. 17)

Jesus did not want worship for himself. He wanted worship for the truth, and recognition of the fact that he and all men belonged to the same brotherhood. He emphasized the fact of this relationship to Mary. "Go to my brothers and say to them that I am going up to my Father and your Father, to my God and your God." (*John* xx. 17)

The disciples found it hard to believe Mary's story. They found it hard to believe some of their number who told of seeing Jesus on the road to Emmaus. Even when Jesus himself stood before them, they found it difficult to believe the truth. They had confused his promise of eternal life with the Jewish doctrine of a future immortality, and it had never occurred to them that Jesus had been teaching a literal and provable fact. When they were faced with the proof of it, they reverted at once to another Jewish belief, that of spirits. "They were startled and panic stricken, and thought they saw a ghost." (*Luke* xxiv. 37)

Jesus knew what they were thinking, and almost laughed at them. "Why are you so disturbed, and why do doubts arise in your minds? Look at my hands and feet, for it is I myself! Feel of me and see, for a ghost has not flesh and bones, as you see I have." (*Luke* xxiv. 38-39) But still they could not believe him "for sheer joy," (*Luke* xxiv. 41) and Jesus was obliged to eat with them before they could be convinced it was the same Jesus, and that executioner's nails and a soldier's spear had made no difference to his life.

One of the disciples was not there at the time, and not all the excited joy of the others could make him believe what had happened until he saw it with his own eyes. Like all the rest, Thomas demanded physical proof; and Jesus gave it to him. Although he added that it was better to believe the truth because it was the truth than because visible proofs had been offered. "Is it because you have seen me that you believe? Blessed be those who believe without having seen me!" (*John* xx. 29)

Jesus had always been capable of giving full proof of his teaching. He said the word of God was bread, and proved it by feeding a multitude. He said it was light, and proved it by healing a man born blind. He said it was freedom, and raised a cripple upright. He said it was life, and by it he conquered death. But he did not want his followers to trust these proofs in themselves. He wanted them to trust God. He wanted them to share in the understanding of God that made the proofs possible, and to become in actual fact his brothers.

The disciples were unable to do this. Only Peter and John seem to have possessed any understanding of Jesus' message, and Peter was handicapped by an impassioned love of his master that made him more anxious to adore Jesus than to follow him. If at one moment he was capable of acknowledging that Jesus was the son of God, he earned a stern rebuke immediately by contradicting himself and trying to protect the man who needed no protecting. It was this same blind, emotional love that made him beg Jesus before his arrest to be allowed to die for him; and one of the last things Jesus did was to ask this most passionate of his disciples if he loved him. Three times he asked Peter that question, and each time Peter answered with a pathetic protestation of his devotion, only to be met with the steady rejoinder, "Then feed my sheep." (*John* xxi. 17) If Peter loved Jesus he could prove it in one way only, by doing what Jesus himself had done.

John, as his gospel shows, came a little nearer to being the kind of disciple that Jesus wanted. To John, Jesus was always the understanding of God incarnate, the word of God made flesh, and he loved the understanding even more than he loved the man. John understood better than any of the others how truly Jesus was the Messiah that had been promised, the light-bringer of whose coming all the prophets of Israel had dreamed; yet it is characteristic of John that while the other Christian writers of the first century wrote chiefly of the Messiah, John wrote chiefly of God. "God is Spirit." (*John* iv. 24) "God is Light." (1 *John* i. 5) "God is Love." (1 *John* iv. 16) These are the only three definitions of God in the whole of the Bible, and all three come from the writings of John.

John was well aware that he did not possess the understanding of God that Jesus himself possessed. But he did know that Jesus was the revelation of the truth about God in its complete and final form; and in that knowledge he gave Jesus much greater honor than Thomas did when he abased himself before the man who had called them his brothers and cried, "My Master and my God!" (*John* xx. 28)

The men who established the early Christian church were more like Thomas than like John. They were bound together by an exalted faith in Jesus as the risen Lord which nothing could shake. Even the members of his immediate family, who had thought him subject to religious delusions during the period of his ministry, believed in Jesus firmly and unshakably when they saw him again after the crucifixion. But for all their honest fervor and eagerness, his followers missed the essential point of Jesus' teaching. They preached him instead of his discovery, a risen Messiah instead of eternal life.

Jesus knew that he had not been understood, and yet he was content to leave them. He was content to leave the truth he had discovered without safeguards of any kind, not even of one written word.

There existed only one testimony to Jesus in the world, the power he called the "spirit of truth that comes from the Father." (*John* xv. 26) It was this power that Jesus trusted, as all the great prophets of Israel before him had trusted it, and he knew that it was sufficient. The truth was the truth. It did not need to be sheltered in temples and creeds, or protected by the efforts of well-meaning men. It needed no protection. It was itself protection. The light was the light and illumined itself.

It was to this spirit of truth, the spirit of reality that

comes from the Father, that the greatest of Jesus' disciples bore witness when he said, "The light is still shining in the darkness, for the darkness has never put it out." (*John* i. 5) No darkness could ever put it out. The whole of the Bible is testimony to that fact, and the testimony still remains.

THE END